Heal For Life

First published in 2019 by
Heal For Life Foundation
72, Belford Street
Broadmeadow
NSW 2292

Heal for Life Foundation
https://healforlife.com.au

All proceeds from the sale of this book will go to help survivors of child abuse to heal.

Mullinar, Liz
Second Edition, 2020
Heal For Life: How To Heal Yourself from the Pain of Childhood Trauma ISBN: 978-0-6485365-2-9
Mental health. Childhood trauma. Cognitive psychology. Self help. Non-fiction.

A catalogue record for this book is available from the National Library of Australia

Cover artwork by Ekaterina Dashkova
Cover design by Gary Walmsey (Made North)
Book production by Grammar Factory.

Heal For Life

How to Heal Yourself from the Pain of Childhood Trauma

By Liz Mullinar AM.

Referenced by M. Grant
Edited by Tristan Rosko
Assisted by Jessica Frisina M.Ed.Psych
and Taijah Lush M.Couns
Illustrated by Samantha Perham (patchwork-d)

"If you are looking for a comprehensive presentation on the subject of trauma, look no further than pioneer healer Liz Mullinar's Heal for Life. In this compilation, Liz shares the wealth of her life's journey of healing, and helping others to heal, interrupting the myth of being 'never whole again'. This 'by survivors for survivors' model shares the faith, hope, and love of what can be. With thousands of testimonies to support her work, Liz has committed her life to the healing of yours. Let your journey begin."

Dr. Ivy Bonk, Ed. D. MBA
IMAGINAL Education Group. Author, *The Day Trauma Came to Class*

"I met Liz Mullinar over twenty five years ago as she and her husband were beginning to agitate for services for complex trauma survivors. Out of her dedication and hard work was born a wonderful healing centre in NSW which has been providing a safe place for trauma survivors ever since. I am thrilled to endorse Heal For Life where you will find information, empowerment and healing."

Dr Rebecca Braid, PhD, MSW, GradDipC&FT, BSW
Founder, Eden Therapy Services

"Essential reading for professionals who work in the area of trauma and mental health. Unless we learn more about trauma and its consequences, trauma and associated mental health issues will continue to destroy and take lives in increasing numbers."

Jenny Chapman, BA (Psych) (Hons)
Director of Interactions Psychological Services

"A wonderful book by an amazing person. A very helpful guide for healing from the trauma of child sexual abuse."

Christabel Chamarette, MPsych.(UWA), MAPS, ANZAPPL, ISPCAN
Clinical Psychologist (former Director of SafeCare Inc)

"As an author, survivor of child sexual abuse and avid consumer of self help books, I have found this work one of the most comprehensive, scientifically based and useful I have read. It not only explains how and why trauma affects the brain, and therefore behaviour, it gives practical, easy to understand advice and a compassionate road out of the tortured maze of post traumatic stress. Everybody will have a better understanding of behavioural patterns about themselves, loved ones or clients, by reading it, and then have tools to effect, or help effect, real change. I highly recommend this book to professionals as well as survivors of childhood trauma and their families."

Barbara Biggs
Journalist and Author, *Moral Danger*

"By picking up this book you have taken the first step to taking responsibility for your healing through embarking on a journey of selfdiscovery. Keep reading and your life will change in ways you never dared to dream."

Dr Peri O'Shea, B.Soc.Sc., Psych.Hons., M.Soc.Pol., PhD
Lived Experience Academic and Consultant

"Liz invited me to attend Heal For Life before the court case against the star of Hey Dad, to make sure I was ready for the battle. I'm so grateful for my week at Heal For Life. I'm not sure I would have made it through the court case without it, and I've enjoyed a mental calm since then... one can heal so much more effectively with her methods than years spent in traditional therapy.

The world has a lot to learn from Liz, and hopefully this book can impart some of those wisdoms that she's trying to share. I'm forever grateful for the lessons she shared with me."

Sarah Monaghan
Actress and Activist for survivors

"I wish I'd had access to its wealth of knowledge when my teenage granddaughter was suffering PTSD throughout her teenage years. It would have helped me understand so much more about her condition and enabled me to help her more effectively. It is essential reading for anyone raising children who have suffered trauma – whether from mental physical or sexual abuse, drug addiction, neglect, accident or crime. If worrying signs of behaviour are emerging they will find extremely well-researched and helpful information. This book should be compulsory reading for anyone working in child welfare – Liz Mullinar's compassion shines through."

Judy Turner
Author, *A Different Kind of Courage – a Story of Teenage PTSD*

"Reading Heal For Life for me has elicited extremes of emotions. I feel anger and sadness, joy and hope. I feel angry that I was not taught about the significance of childhood trauma in the development of chronic disease, then saddened that I have missed so many opportunities to ask about what really in society is seen as a taboo subject. Heal For Life is a book that benefits not only survivors of childhood trauma, it is critical for health professionals to broaden their empathy and influence their treatment strategies, it helps any reflective reader to learn about psychological models underpinning fundamental human emotions and interactions."

Dr Jenny Draper, MB BS, DCH, FRACGP, ACAAM. **GP**
Team Leader, Wingham Wellbeing

"Liz's Heal For Life book conveys everything you need to know about healing from childhood trauma. The enormity and excitement of reading a book on healing of this calibre left me with a huge feeling of hope. Survivors need to find tools, knowledge and a way to heal to go forward in life, this book provides this.

I know what Liz has written, works. Through my own lived experience of bringing everything which Liz has endeavoured to write into my life. I feel incredibly happy and hopeful of a way forward for survivors of childhood traumas, after reading Heal For Life by Liz Mullinar."

Lorraine Hall
Author, *Our Little Secret*

LIZ MULLINAR AM. B.Th. M.Couns.

Post grad diploma in Past. Couns.

Liz Mullinar is a survivor of childhood trauma and the founder of Heal For Life Foundation. She developed the HFL Model in the early nineties when she felt along with other survivors of trauma that there had to be a permanent way of healing from the impact of childhood memories.

She is an internationally renowned speaker and has delivered many papers at international conferences on the Heal For Life Model of healing. She is the author of two books published by Hodder Headline: Breaking The Silence and The Liz Mullinar Story.

Liz concentrates most of her time on the training and supervision of therapists in the Heal For life treatment model and training teams in other countries to run the program.

She is a member of the order of Australia for services to the Arts and survivors of childhood trauma. In 2000 she was awarded the inaugural Australian Humanitarian of the Year award.

I feel happiness, I feel joy,
I now have tools that I can employ,
I've found calm and discovered peace,
I can actually feel my endorphins increase,
I've learnt to laugh, I love to sing,
I want to experience everything,
I now can run, inside I fly,
I'm ready to wave depression good-bye,
In my mind my dreams can soar,
Others can't scare me anymore,
Something's changed inside of me,
Something only I can see,
New colours gleam, my world has grown,
It's a new way of being that I've been shown,
My body feels so free and light,
I have contentment within my sight,
I am no longer running scared,
I'm open to things I wouldn't have dared,
But best of all I've found real love,
Love from inside, outside and above,
I don't have to live in shame,
I feel brand new but look the same,
I love most people and they love me,
I'm now happy just to be,
My eyes are open and I'm so glad,
'cos I've learnt that I'm not all bad,
I was born complete and whole,
A beautiful being, a pure soul,
But that got lost so early for me,
I had no idea that I could be free,
No-one told me that I could,
Look within and find some good,
I've felt tainted for so long,

The world has always felt so wrong,
But I've taken my power back,
By giving myself all that I lack,
I've made a decision to learn to trust,
That inside I know what's right and just,
I have so much yet to give,
So much life I've yet to live,
With love and faith and courage too,
That's now something I can do,
I love myself, I've made that choice,
I've found my truth, my inner voice,
I've discovered what I had all along,
Who ever thought I could be so strong,
I can feel free to wash and be clean,
I'm uncontaminated despite where I've been,
I deserve to be here, I don't want to die,
I'm allowed to laugh as well as to cry,
I'm allowed to eat a healthy range,
Though nurturing does still feel strange,
I'm allowed to be weary and rest my head,
On a nice soft pillow in a warm safe bed,
I can close my eyes and go to sleep,
because my worries 'til morning will keep,
In the new day, I can jump out of bed,
And welcome the challenge of the day ahead.
I can't forget so I shall embrace,
The sadness I carry with acceptance and grace,
I'm here now so I'll approach each day,
With flourish, and hope, that I'll be okay.
I will never forget my past,
But now in the present I'm alive at last.

Written by a wonderful Heal For Life guest after a healing week.

CHAPTER ONE

Me

I am writing this book to encourage you to heal from the often devastating impact of childhood trauma. I have been healing and supporting thousands of others to heal for over twenty years, and I hope to encourage you to really know that your life can change, that you can permanently heal from childhood trauma and enjoy life to the full.

My world changed in 1993 when I started my own long healing journey. At the time, I was at the peak of my career as a casting director for film and television – my company, Liz Mullinar Casting Consultants, had offices in Sydney and Melbourne and a staff of twelve. I considered myself a very lucky woman. I had achieved a position of considerable importance in the film, television and theatre industries: I was a director of the Smith Family, an Australian Film Commissioner; on the board of studies at the National Institute of Dramatic Art (NIDA); Chair of the Belvoir Street Theatre; and a member of the board of the Griffin Theatre Company.

My world changed suddenly and dramatically, as did my view of it. My journey from successful businesswoman to supporting people to heal from child abuse was quite swift. I was unknowingly reminded of the truth of my childhood by visiting my newborn niece in hospital – a visit that prevented me from sleeping and led to many weeks of illness, until, with the help of a professional, I recognised that the trip to the hospital had triggered my brain to remember a night time trip to a hospital many years ago when, as a five year old child, I had been rushed to a hospital after breaking my arm. Back then, on that fateful stay at the hospital, there was no space for me in the relevant children's ward and I was placed in an eye ward where most of the recovering patients were unable to see. I was there for a week, and I was sadistically, sexually abused each night by a doctor. I was able to see (having broken only a bone in my arm), but most of the children in that ward could not, so the doctor was free at night to abuse at will when the nurses were on their evening break.

The uncovering of this formerly, completely suppressed, abuse was a great shock to me, as I had always considered myself as someone who had enjoyed a happy childhood. More shocking to me was the way I changed with the uncovering of this childhood trauma. I felt that I was no longer in control. I was no longer in charge of my emotions. I would cry unexpectedly, and was no longer the person I thought I was. Although, at the same time, this revelation made a lot of sense of behaviour I had displayed both in my childhood and adult life.

I looked around to find people to help me while reliving this trauma, and was very disappointed to find that the professionals did not seem to understand the issues I was experiencing. I also could not find a single organisation to turn to for validation and support. I seemed to be alone. At the same time that I was going through this, I noticed that there were appalling untruths being played out in the media about 'false memories', and I felt totally dismayed – I knew that the nightmare I was going through could not be 'false memories' because it was such hell. One particular day I read an article by Richard Guilliatt in The Australian newspaper that incensed me, so I wrote to the paper and told them, quite simply, that even the best actress in the world could not be confused with a person genuinely suffering from recovering memories. The paper's response was immediate, likely due to my media profile, and I wound up with a lot of public coverage. At that time, there was no one in the public eye that was admitting to recovering memories of childhood trauma, and I was certainly the first person in Australia with a high profile revealing sexual abuse. No one could say I was doing it for attention (my business was 20 years strong, very well-established, and I did not rely on press or public attention for success), so it was much harder to discredit me as they had tried to do with previous survivors who had spoken out.

The response to the various articles in newspapers was a deluge of letters from people 'recovering memories', as it was referred to then, and their telling of the hell it was, and how there was nowhere they could turn to for help. I attended a public meeting with four psychologists who were there to discuss the effects of trauma, and I felt that they did not appear to understand the complexity of the issue, nor did they seem to be suggesting helpful ways of healing. So, I made the decision there and then to start an organisation for survivors, run by survivors. I knew that the only way was to learn how to help ourselves, and then we could set about teaching the health professionals what it is that we need help with, in order to heal. I always knew that I, and everyone else, *could* heal.

Research on peer support has proved that I was right in my intuition that a program run by survivors would indeed be the key to our successful program. There is no question in my mind that appropriately trained health professionals who are survivors of childhood trauma provide the right, safe, non-hierarchical environment for healing.

Due to being so ahead of the curve in relation to understanding the critical importance of peer support, we discovered that we would have to develop our own intensive training programs to support and develop our peer workers. From day one, we have been committed to really finding the best possible and most effective way of healing. We measure outcomes and we have continuously adapted and improved our peer support training over the years. I am really proud of our achievements in this area. Even now, very little is taught in colleges about trauma and effective ways to heal, let alone how to take that knowledge and use it to support others on their healing journey.

A small group contacted me after that meeting, and together we formed an organisation: Advocates for Survivors of Child Abuse (ASCA), now called the Blue Knot Foundation. We set up an office in the basement of my family home in Paddington, Sydney, and we started to reach out to other survivors. Within two years we had 55 groups all over Australia; we were small but keen, with a sense of connectivity and purpose. The need was so great, as it still is.

I was kept very busy between my day job and growing the organisation, and early on I recognised that although so many people were willing to pitch in, the impact of their trauma often made it very hard for them to contribute what was needed. I began to see, irrespective of a person's ability and intelligence, just how devastating the impact of trauma is on the way we can organise and use our brains for effective living. From the very beginning I knew that trauma is not a gender issue – that boys as well as girls are abused – and I saw just how wrong it was that, although there were a very limited number of services for women, there was absolutely nothing that I could find to support men. On checking statistics, I discovered that just as many boys as girls were being removed from families because of abuse. This didn't make sense. What happened to all those abused boys when they grew up? Wonderfully, Chris Thompson, the film director, signed on as one of the founding members of ASCA, and he worked tirelessly to help men until his untimely death.

I continued to receive so many letters from people who were in so much pain with so little support desperate to find help. Yet, interestingly, the letters revealed that all of us seemed to know what we needed in order to heal: a place where we could feel safe to heal and be understood. A place where we could release our feelings, a place where we could stay and feel safe enough to connect with our inner pain, and a place where we could validate each other. Group meetings once a week were being helpful and validating (as already mentioned we had established 55 groups all over Australia) but group meetings did not actually heal the deep hurt and damage that child abuse inflicts. I felt the only solution was to find the funds and build a place for survivors where survivors who were health professionals could design a program by survivors for survivors – a place where our needs could be met, where real healing could and would take place.

Early on in my healing I had an extraordinary encounter with Jesus while recovering memories of being raped while I was with my psychologist. I knew that

Jesus was with me and in that moment realised that love was stronger than fear and that there was no childhood pain I could not overcome. This realisation that love will always be stronger than fear, that love can always overcome fear, re-ignited my Christian faith, (My father, besides sexually abusing me, was a vicar in the Anglican Church) so I decided to attend a conference on spirituality and sexual abuse. I was stunned to discover the depth of the faith of the people gathered there – I remember one woman spoke of an angel catching her when she threw herself from a balcony – however, all but two of the forty something people in attendance felt rejected, ignored, and unsupported by the Church they were attending. This seemed so sad to me that this group of people whose faith was so strong should not feel loved or be contributing to their Church community. After the conference, I felt strongly that God wanted me to create a place where people could go to heal.

This feeling was so strong in me that it overcame everything else in my life. The film industry no longer mattered. It was clear that the time had come to leave my career, so I sold my company, and with my husband Rod, I set about the search for a property big enough to be subdivided. We knew we wanted to dedicate 100 acres to build a healing centre, and also have enough land to live on for ourselves. We knew we needed a place where we could live and be on-hand to take care of the day-to-day functioning of the centre. Finally, we found the perfect place: 200 acres of virgin land that had never been built on, and had only ever been used as grazing land for cattle. It meant we could divide the property into two; 100 acres for our own home, and we could gift 100 acres to our charity.

I thought the next step would be for me to be ordained as a priest in the Anglican Church. My hope was that the Anglican Church would then allow me to run a special ministry for survivors of abuse from the centre. I felt very strongly that I was called to build a bridge between the Church and the suffering of survivors. However, I discovered that was not meant to be.

I attended theological college near Newcastle, and loved it. While I was studying, I wrote two books that had been commissioned by Hodder Headline (this commission enabled ASCA to continue while I was studying.) One was my autobiography, the other 'Breaking The Silence' so survivors would feel less alone.

The Newcastle diocese was a challenge for me, and I was rejected for ordination (later, in the Royal Commission, the reason became clear: the diocese was controlled by a ring of paedophiles who, it seemed to me, were determined for me not to be a part of the Church.) In the end, it was apparent to me that the Newcastle Diocese was not ready to be part of my vision of the Church supporting survivors to heal from trauma and abuse by creating a loving, healing centre. I realised that I would need to leave college and build the centre on my own.

I still hope that one day the Church will recognise the evil of child abuse, and that the Church (of all denominations, such as Anglican, Catholic, Presbyterian, and Pentecostal) will recognise that the Church has a huge role it can play to help us heal – after all, there is a great destruction of spirit in being abused. Sadly the churches, collectively, still do not seem to realise the importance of recognising that challenge or recognising how much survivors would enrich the spiritual strength of the Church, maybe one day…

When I left Theological College, rather than moving back to Sydney, I headed for the land we had purchased and camped there while we started to create the healing centre. We sold our beautiful home in the city, as well as our muchloved, shared country house, to fund the building of the centre and our new home. What to build was the challenge – I knew we needed water, a big expanse of water, and I felt separate buildings would give a sense of privacy. I felt that we needed a workshop area, and I wanted to build a Chapel or sacred space, as I wanted the spirituality of our guests to be encouraged – not necessarily Christian faith, but whatever spirituality or religion felt right for each person, as it always felt clear to me that nobody should try to impose any set of beliefs on our guests.

One day a woman phoned me and said, 'my husband went into a book shop and your eyes on the cover followed him round the shop – he bought your book but he cannot see the reason for this feeling he had'. I asked her, 'is your husband an architect?' she replied, 'yes'. I asked her if he lived in Newcastle, and she answered again, 'yes'. I told her I was looking for an architect, and consequently her husband Randell Boydell designed the Centre for us. This was one of many extraordinary things that happened during the construction of Mayumarri.

My husband had researched and found the name 'Mayumarri', which, in one of the many Aboriginal languages from the Port Hedland area, translates to place of peace.

We brought together so many volunteers, state prisoners on weekend community work, survivors who wanted to be part of creating Mayumarri, as well as people from churches in Cessnock – there was an amazing number of people who contributed to building our peaceful place. Within a year we had our buildings. All of the support we received from people who were not survivors of trauma was very validating and reassuring – the resounding message was felt: we do matter.

Once built, the big question for Mayumarri was the program; what was it we really needed? As I pondered this question, I received a phone call from a woman named Margaret Williams in Queensland. Margaret was a survivor and very experienced counsellor. She felt very strongly that she was supposed to join us, which was perfect because at that time I had not yet started any relevant training, and did not have experience in counselling. My only vision was to create a safe place where a person could feel and release emotions without comment or judgment, however I had not thought about the actual process of healing, or how we would go about it. Margaret came on board.

A few weeks after Margaret had started with us, I picked up Luciano Capaccione's book, 'Recovery of Your Inner Child,' and, although by now I had been healing for nearly three years, processing lots of memories from childhood, I had never encountered the concept of working with the inner child. It was revelatory to me, so exciting, and I couldn't wait to share the idea with Margaret. The next morning I suggested we devise a program to encourage our guests (from the beginning we deliberately called our guests by that title rather than clients or patients, as it is our honour to help them) to meet and work with their inner child. Margaret was not surprised, and told me that she had been waiting for me to recognise the importance of the inner child, and that she had designed the perfect program for us to run. We trialled Margaret's concept, and it was immediately successful. The program has developed and grown over the last 20 years, but it is in essence the same now as it was then – you can read about it in the last chapter of this book. During the last 20 years, over 8,500 people have attended our five day program with phenomenal results. Over the years an average of 96% have reported finding it very positive or life changing, which has been extremely rewarding and I know the success is because the program was devised by, and is always run by, survivors. As we set up and put in place psychologists, carers, and support people for the day-to-day running of the centre, I realised that for it to be a success I was going to need to train as a therapist, so I undertook a Post Graduate Diploma in Counselling (I had already completed my degree in

Theology) and later I also completed a Masters in

Counselling. The first thing that struck me during my course work was how inspiring I found the process of studying the brain and human behaviour, especially in light of my experiences as a survivor of trauma combined with my role of working with survivors of child abuse at the centre and with ASCA. I was, however, immensely saddened by the complete lack of course content on trauma.

Over the years, as I have continued to study and learn about the brain, it has been really exciting to see that each new discovery about the brain validates our program's structure, and explaining the neurology of the brain is very empowering to our guests. For survivors to understand that they are not inadequate, but rather are suffering from an illness (just like cancer, liver, or heart disease), has been transformational to many people. To know that healing is possible, that we can actually heal the brain just as we can heal any other organ (through processes specific to the brain), that we need not accept mere management of the problem with medication, and finally, that we have the right to heal just like everyone else who is suffering from any illness. This information offers real hope to survivors.

Over the years I have learned so much about what is effective for us in healing, as well as what isn't, and I believe that part of our healing is to understand what happened to our brain because of the trauma, and know what actions we can take to change the way our brain responds.

This book offers all I have learned over the years in the hope that it might support your healing too.

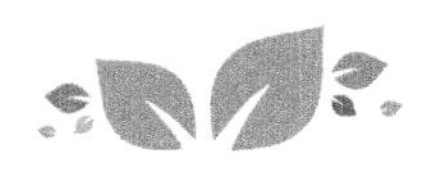

CHAPTER TWO
Defining Trauma and Self-Healing

I want to start by defining the model which forms the basis of the healing program at Heal For Life – the Heal For Life model – then define trauma and its impact as referred to in this book, before I discuss suggested paths to healing.

Healing Program at Heal For Life

The healing program at Heal For Life is based on assisting those affected by trauma to become aware of the unconscious processes in the brain that were formed as a result of traumatic event/s, and empowering them to heal. Trauma is having your power taken away, so any healing from trauma has to encompass re-empowerment and autonomy in all aspects of healing.

Trauma-Informed Self Healing

Health professionals have developed a model throughout the Western World called Trauma Informed Practice. This practice is to improve outcomes for staff when working with people who have been affected by trauma (mostly in the social welfare field) by teaching them how to recognise the impact of trauma on the developing brain and utilising the latest neuroscience, and knowledge gained from survivors. As the most effective and helpful approach. I am choosing to use the same terminology, 'trauma-informed', to describe our model of healing

– The Heal For Life model – for permanent healing from childhood trauma and abuse which also utilises the latest neuroscience combined with survivors knowledge.

The Heal For Life model (HFL), based on Trauma Informed Self Healing describes best practice for our healing which honours our own intuitive knowledge and incorporates the latest evidence about the impact of trauma on the brain so that we can all heal ***permanently*** from the devastating impact of childhood trauma. It is an approach that empowers survivors to take control of their own healing. My hope is that you may use this same approach to optimise your own healing journey, with or, without a therapist.

As a survivor, I was anxious to heal myself as quickly as possible, and I tried many different modalities in search of the most effective way to overcome my trauma. It was on this journey, and through watching and working with other survivors, that I realised that in order to heal the first essential step (after knowing the feeling of being safe) is to take control of, and responsibility for, my own journey. To do that, I needed to be informed, interested, and self-aware. Even though we may not know it yet, each of us does know our own mind better than anyone else. If we trust ourselves enough, we do know what we need to do in order to heal. This book recommends active participation, for you to *lead* your own healing process. It recognises that you, and you alone, are responsible for your own wellbeing. That may be difficult to accept because our trauma has led to so much *disempowerment*, but I have found it to be absolutely true.

We are the experts for our own healing.

The Heal For Life approach does not reject the need for good, therapeutic care. Many studies have found that a strong, trusting relationship between a therapist and their client is what leads to positive outcomes for a range of clients and referral problems[1]. There is no doubt that to have a knowledgeable trauma-informed therapist walk alongside us is of primary importance, particularly as a trauma-informed therapist will invite us to lead the way and encourage empowerment. However, it can be very tough to access the therapeutic support we deserve, either because of financial constraints or physical location. It is also hard to find someone who really understands trauma. Healing is *your right*, regardless of location or financial means. It is my hope that one day it will be recognised that mental health services must be as freely available as services for physical health. Until then, I hope that this book will act as a support for those struggling to access suitable and appropriate mental health care.

Historically it was believed that the role of therapists was to tell us what we had to do in order to heal, it was their job to heal us, and we needed a therapist if we were to heal. I would like to suggest that it is important that we recognise our own ability to know what we need to do in order to heal.

So, although therapists are critically important to our healing, in my opinion many of us have looked to therapists to tell us what to do, to heal us, because we have been so disempowered by our trauma. We have handed our power over to others and we have all too often let them dictate our journey towards healing instead of recognising that we have that ability within ourselves. How many of you have been to your first counselling session and been asked all sorts of questions about yourself, been asked to share your trauma history, without being asked if that is what you wanted to do? How much better if they asked the question, 'What do you want to achieve in this session?' or 'What do you need?' or 'What do you want from me?' However, the Heal For Life approach empowers us to take responsibility for our own healing. It reminds us that we are not empowered if we are led, advised, or directly instructed by others. It helps us understand that we are the expert on ourselves rather than the counsellor, despite their years of training. This recognition of the innate knowledge of our own abilities is one of the principal keys to successful healing and our model. Of course, good therapists do know all this but sadly others feel it is their job and personal responsibility to work out what we need to do in each session prior to our arrival.

The Heal For Life model is about instilling hope and a knowledge that healing is achievable. It is also about each one of us gaining the education regarding the effects of trauma on our brain, so we can understand why we behave the way we do. Neuroscience has provided the platform on which we can understand the impact of trauma on the developing brain and the behavioural issues that result. Heal for Life has discovered which neuroscience now validates, and what we as survivors have intuitively known, are one and the same. Let me repeat it. Each one of us *can heal.*

Knowledge gives us power as well as understanding, and allows us to stop the self-blame and self-doubt inherited from our childhood experiences.

Without understanding the impact of trauma on the developing brain, we can often consider ourselves to be hopeless, useless, pathetic, and inadequate. We can blame ourselves for our behaviour and can be open to be labeled as manipulative, controlling, resistant, and uncooperative. These labels are judgmental and unfair to ourselves, and the more we believe them and hear them, the more our brain believes them to be truths. The Heal for Life model encourages us to put aside this negative narrative, and invites us to change our own self-beliefs. *Our trauma was not our fault*. The way we reacted and continue to react to reminders of our trauma is not our fault – it is the way our brain coped with abnormal circumstances.

We may have received diagnoses from health professionals such as Bipolar Disorder, Post-Traumatic Stress Disorder

(PTSD), Adult Attention Deficit Disorder, Major Depressive Disorder, or Borderline Personality Disorder. These diagnoses and their symptoms are defined by an American manual called the Diagnostic Statistical Manual (DSM). It was started to help the insurance industry in the States know what payment the diagnosis warranted; if you fit the symptoms listed in the DSM, you are given the diagnosis and the cost of the treatment recommended is covered by the Health Insurance companies in the States. However, it is not recognised that those symptoms are usually also the sign of having suffered from trauma (except for PTSD), particularly in childhood. It can become a label through which many health professionals determine your identity, rather than regarding it as an illness that can be healed by addressing the trauma. The word 'disorder' in many diagnoses implies that we suffer from a permanent personality problem. In Australia, many of these diagnoses can lead to receiving permanent sickness benefit as if it is always a life-long condition and unchangeable. However, what we suffer from, is not a disorder, it is the way our brains have developed in order to cope. The word disorder tends to make our disease less important than, say, cancer or heart disease, whereas in fact a disease of the brain – which, as you will read – is what we have, is just as severe and certainly as life threatening. The great news, however, is that in most cases it is totally curable. Our brain needs healing in just the same way as any other disease or physical injury. Brain injury is caused by trauma, and while other illnesses of the brain will have different methods of healing, this book focuses on healing the brain caused by the impact from trauma suffered in our childhood.

Heal for Life has been researching and implementing Trauma Informed Self Healing principles and practices since 1999. Independent research has shown that our model has a profound, long-term improvement on the lives of many survivors suffering from the debilitating effects of childhood trauma and abuse[2]. I have experienced and witnessed the effectiveness of the Heal for Life approach, and that is why I want to share all that I have learned with you, so that you too can change your life through self-directed healing. This book is an invitation to be responsible for your own healing, and I hope you will find all the tools and information you need in the following chapters.

Here are some quotes:

'Traditional treatment approaches for survivors of trauma have tended to focus on their defects, illness or disorders (pathology), giving an impression of something wrong with the person or their personality.' (Kezelman, 2011)

'Labelling people with personality disorders (pathologising) is like saying there is something wrong with your soul'. (Epstein, 2011)

'Development of more integrated approaches will likely contribute to more meaningful diagnoses, improved treatment of affected persons, and better integration of research priorities, preventative and social services, and legal avenues.' (Anda, 2007)

What is Trauma?

As this book is all about how to heal from trauma, perhaps we first need to define what I mean by trauma. There is often confusion between the words trauma and abuse. At Heal For Life we have always preferred to use the word trauma as abuse has a blaming element. Abuse is something that is done to us, while trauma can happen from a variety of different circumstances, some of which are completely random. Trauma can be an intentional act from one person against another, or completely accidental.

If we research the definition of trauma, it is described as a 'deeply distressing or disturbing experience[3]. This is a very broad definition, and arguably one that implies that trauma could be an everyday experience with no long-term impact.

For the purpose of this book, however, I prefer to use a tighter, more specific definition agreed on by most therapists specialising in this area that recognises the impact profound trauma has on the developing brain. So, at Heal For Life and for the purpose of this book, we define trauma as:

- More emotion than a person can handle; one that is perceived as life-threatening at the age it is experienced and overwhelms the ability to adapt.
- It can be a singular or continuing event that has a lifechanging impact.

Here some other quotes:

'A potentially traumatising event is any event that overwhelms an individual's capacity to cope. This can be a one-off event or ongoing in nature.' (Heim & Buhler, 2006)

Psychological trauma may be understood as a life-threatening event that triggers a strong emotional shock. This emotion preserves the experience of the trauma. Emotional shock is a strong reaction that always reoccurs in the same way and is chronic. In this respect, chronic, unprocessed emotions are the cause of psychological trauma (Heim & Buhler, 2006)

Thus, a traumatic event or situation creates psychological trauma when it overwhelms the individual's ability to cope, and leaves that person fearing death, annihilation, mutilation, or psychosis. The individual may feel emotionally, cognitively, and physically overwhelmed. The circumstances of the event commonly include abuse of power, betrayal of trust, entrapment, helplessness, pain, confusion, and/or loss. (Giller, 1999)

Using our definition, as written above, 'trauma' is **never remembered (not consciously accessible)** and why this is the case is explained more fully in the next chapter.

Examples of Trauma

Let me give you some examples of trauma. They may not cover what happened to you, but I want to help you realise that trauma is varied and wide-ranging. What happened shouldn't have happened, and it was not our fault.

Interpersonal trauma:

- Abandonment: caused by separation from parents or a significant other person. This can be from adoption, divorce, death or suicidal loss (all perceived as abandonment by a young child).
- Neglect: not having your emotional and/or physical needs met.
- Abuse: physical, emotional, sexual, psychological, verbal, bullying, spiritual, cultural, financial.
- Bullying
- Personal attack by another person, group, or by an animal.
- Torture, forcible confinement, and imprisonment.
- Being the victim of a crime or an attempted crime e.g.
- murder, rape, mugging, kidnapping.
- Witnessing violence, including homicide, violence in the neighbourhood or in a school setting, domestic violence, drive-by shootings, law enforcement or military actions, terrorism.

External trauma:

- Severe natural disaster including flood, earthquake, tornado, hurricane, etc.
- War, holocaust or other military actions.
- Famine, living in extreme poverty.
- Hospitalisation, medical procedures, surgery, accident, injury or serious illness. This includes premature births.
- Historical trauma: colonialisation, institutionalisation, forcible removal from family and home: destruction of culture, language, and heritage.
- Societal trauma: when a dominant society imposes its beliefs on a non-dominant one, causing shame and dissociation from the individual's culture. Dr Joy De Gruy has named the trauma specificity of these events as 'Post Traumatic Slave Syndrome[4].

The above examples are not exclusive; it is very important to remember that trauma is any moment in time when the situation overwhelms the individual's ability to cope, and when that event is perceived as life threatening. While all trauma, as defined above, has a devastating impact, ***all trauma can be healed***.

Trauma impacts the way the brain develops, and it defines how we view the world, how we feel, behave and react to events in our lives. In children, the impact of trauma often first shows itself with behavioural problems. However, it is common for people of any age who have suffered from trauma to experience feelings of fear, terror, horror, anxiety, anger, grief, loss, guilt (sometimes about surviving), helplessness and, very often, depression[5]. Depression takes over when the need to suppress these emotions becomes overwhelming.

The traumatic event is life-threatening in an age-appropriate way. What is traumatic for a child may seem of no real significance to an adult, and may even appear to be 'harmless'. What is life-threatening to a baby is not an issue for an older child. Abandonment is felt more deeply by a young child as they do not have a concept of time and need to depend on their parents for survival. For example, when a primary caregiver leaves their baby, this is perceived as lifethreatening to a child in their formative years as they cannot understand a logical explanation. When a baby is removed at birth from their mother this is very traumatising as the baby has learned to recognise its mother's voice in the womb, and nature has ensured a strong attachment to the birth-mother, including the release of special bonding hormones during the birth process (Oxytocin).

No one has the right to judge how bad another's trauma is, or how badly affected they will be from a trauma, as there are so many different aspects to a traumatic event such as our age (typically, the younger the child when the trauma occurs, the greater the impact), our relationship with our parents, and the support we receive when the trauma occurs. Our survival is dependent on our caregiver so their reaction at the time of trauma is of key importance. If we suffer with more than one trauma it can increase the impact on the rest of our lives. There is a questionnaire called 'Adverse Childhood Experiences' – you can easily find it online – and those ten questions may help you understand that there can be a variety of seemingly small incidents that combine to have a profound impact on our adult lives.

Sexual abuse is only one of the many traumas that can deeply impact a child's mental, emotional and physical development, and inform their resulting adult world-view. Our experience at Heal For Life is that all forms of trauma – from abandonment, emotional abuse, to neglect – all have the same potential to have a huge impact on the developing brain. Some feel that their trauma isn't 'bad enough' to warrant healing, but I want to stress here that if you are still suffering from the events of something that occurred in your childhood, *it is* bad enough, and *you can* benefit from healing. It's also helpful to note that the approach of downplaying the effects of the trauma is often used as a coping strategy by many of us. If we pretend to ourselves that the effects of the trauma are less than they really are, it means we don't have to face up to the truth which may have implications for our relationship with someone we care about due to their actions towards us when we were little. If we recognise what they did was the opposite of loving, then we may feel they did not love us and that is too big to consider, so it is easier to believe it was our fault or to minimise their behaviour. *Most of us minimise our trauma.*

I think the self-denial is a way of surviving.

Sadly 'betrayal trauma', that is trauma from someone we love, creates special difficulties and usually a greater denial and ability to remember as we do not want to believe the trauma was caused by someone we love and we would want to believe loves us. Indeed, perhaps the hardest form of trauma from which to heal are those traumas perpetrated by the mother – regardless of whether the trauma was emotional, physical, sexual, or abandonment-related. Our guests often find that it was the mothers' lack of support after a child has revealed sexual abuse that has a far greater impact on the child than the sexual abuse.

I have found the best way to ascertain the level of trauma is to look at the impact on the development of the survivor's resilience and coping strategies as that usually provides the answer.

If a child is securely attached to his or her primary carer in the first two years of life, and feels loved and nurtured when the brain is developing, that person will be less impacted by the powerlessness of trauma[6]. You will learn more about Attachment in Chapter Six. Understanding out attachment style is also a key to understanding the way we have responded to trauma.

Trauma affects everyone differently. Let me remind you that if a person receives loving support from significant people in their lives immediately after the trauma, then the impact can be greatly decreased. A loving response to the trauma is critical in terms of minimising the long-term impact.

What are the Impacts of Trauma?

It is probably easiest if I give you some statistics to show how huge the impact is and how many social problems are caused by trauma. Survivors are judged because of the impact of trauma on their behaviour – for example, some may be considered weak because they are addicted to drugs or alcohol, whereas, in fact, their addictions may be the only way their brain can cope with the pain of trauma. Australian statistics show the overwhelming majority of people addicted to drugs have, by their own admission, suffered from trauma. 92% of heroin addicts admitted to suffering from some form of trauma. 94% of amphetamine users admitted to suffering some form of trauma[7].

A vast majority of people suffering with mental health problems have experienced trauma, *so why don't health professionals ask if we have suffered from childhood trauma as a first step towards healing and our own recognition that childhood trauma could be the cause of our problem?*

It is interesting to note that 80% of guests at Heal For Life Foundation have been diagnosed with a serious mental illness[8].

Here are some other statistics:

79.9% of people diagnosed with depression had suffered some form of trauma, the most common being emotional and physical abuse[9].

68.8% of psychiatric in-patients have suffered from child sexual or physical abuse, at least half of whom were diagnosed as psychotic[10].

82% to 86% of people with bipolar disorder (BPD) have reported severe child sexual abuse[11].

91% Border Personality Disorder (BPD) patients report childhood abuse, 92% of them from neglect[12]. *Referring to BPD: 'Abuse is a nearly ubiquitous experience in the early lives of these patients'* [13].

Up to 85% of those suffering from eating disorders had been sexually abused[14].

54% of alcoholics in treatment centres have experienced trauma of some kind with consequent mental illness diagnoses[15].

Child sexual abuse has been found to be a key factor in the cause and continuation of youth homelessness with between 50-70% of young people within Supported Accommodation Assistance Programs having experienced childhood sexual assault[16].

These statistics are horrifying. I consider it a tragedy that, if we are not helped when first we suffer from trauma, *it is the symptoms of our trauma that will become the focal point of the social welfare system, rather than the trauma, the core problem.*

What are the Possible Symptoms of Trauma?

All of you will have different symptoms, however, there are some common effects which I have listed, in order to encourage you to realise that what you may have thought as a personal character deficit may actually be because of what was done to you, and over which you had no control.

Sometimes these effects can be delayed for months or even years. Often people do not even initially associate their symptoms with the childhood trauma. One way to determine whether an emotional or psychological trauma has occurred (which can be early in life before language or conscious awareness were in place) is to look at the kinds of recurring problems you might be experiencing. These can serve as clues to an earlier situation that caused a *dysregulation* in the structure or function of your brain.

The following are symptoms that may result from unresolved trauma, particularly if there have been multiple traumas, as the effect is cumulative.

Physical:

- Eating disturbances (eating more or less than usual)
- Sleep disturbances (sleeping more or less than usual)
- Sexual dysfunction
- Low energy
- Chronic, unexplained pain including Chronic Fatigue Syndrome
- Migraines, constant head aches
- Poor body temperature control (especially cold hands and feet)
- Somatic illnesses (no known physical cause)

Emotional:

- *Depression*, spontaneous crying, despair and hopelessness
- *Anxiety*
- Excessive fears
- Self-destructive and impulsive behaviour
- Uncontrollable reactive thoughts
- Compulsive and obsessive behaviours
- Feeling out of control
- Irritability, anger, and resentment
- Emotional numbness, not feeling any emotions.
- Amnesia
- Avoidance of situations that resemble the initial event
- Detachment

- Guilt
- Grief reactions
- Altered sense of time, usually for people with severe dissociation
- Withdrawal from normal routine and relationships
- Dissociative symptoms ('splitting off' parts of the self)
- Feelings of ineffectiveness, shame, despair, or hopelessness
- Feeling permanently damaged

Re-experiencing the Trauma:

- Intrusive thoughts
- Flashbacks or nightmares
- Sudden floods of emotions or images related to the traumatic event

Increased Arousal:

- Hyper-vigilance, jumpiness, an extreme sense of being 'on guard'
- Over-reactions, including sudden unprovoked anger
- General anxiety
- Insomnia
- Obsessions with death

Cognitive:

- Memory lapses, especially about the trauma

- Difficulty making decisions
- Decreased ability to concentrate
- Feeling distracted
- Procrastinating

Common Behavioural Effects of Trauma:

- Substance abuse
- Compulsive behaviour patterns
- Inability to make healthy professional or lifestyle choices
- Isolation/ agoraphobia
- Obsessive compulsive behaviour
- Controlling behavior

Common Effects of Trauma on Interpersonal Relationships:

- Inability to maintain close relationships or choose appropriate friends and/ or intimate partners
- Sexual dysfunction
- Hostility
- Arguments with family members, employers or coworkers

- Social withdrawal
- Feeling constantly threatened[17].

When these symptoms are dominating our lives, we tend to get blamed for our subsequent behaviours by others and we put ourselves down, however I want to remind you right now that the ***trauma was not your fault***. Once you realise that some behaviours and emotional reactions are because of trauma then you can start to take responsibility for them and change your behaviours as you heal.

I aim to effectively explain how trauma impacts the brain, and then illustrate how this impact affects our behaviour and emotional wellbeing in more detail. I will also discuss understanding boundaries (where I stop and you start), attachment style (so as to understand how your childhood affects the way you relate to others), how Transactional Analysis helps us understand our inner voices and, most importantly, how to actually heal ourselves by connecting with our inner child or inner self. All of this information is to inspire you to know that you have the ability to heal yourself – ***healing takes all that you've got, but you've got all that it takes. (J. Fell)***

CHAPTER THREE

Impact of Trauma on the Brain: A Basic Scientific Explanation

I think it is very empowering to recognise that the effects of childhood trauma are *not so much psychological as they are physical* – trauma physically affects the way the brain develops, which means that trauma impacts our behaviour, as well as our way of thinking and processing information. In the same way that lungs affect our ability to breathe, our brain affects our ability to process information, and that impacts on our behaviour and our emotional wellbeing.

So to understand how to heal from trauma we first need to understand some very simplified information about the brain, how the brain functions, and how trauma is stored in the brain. In understanding this you will hopefully be able to understand the scientific reasons behind everything I am going to suggest in relation to healing. You will also find this information in far greater detail at the end of the book.

All the knowledge about the brain that has been learned in recent years, is due to the development of imaging technology that has transformed scientific knowledge about the way the brain works. Imaging means scientists can now see what is happening in the brain in a living person while they are actually experiencing any thought or mental process. This was obviously previously impossible. This ability to see inside the brain while a person is alive has eliminated the need to rely on philosophy or secondguessing when trying to ascertain how the brain works under different circumstances.

Now that the brain can be examined in the living person, perhaps the most important discovery is that the brain is not static – *it grows and changes throughout our lives depending on our experiences*[18]. This is huge – it is incredibly important because previously all mental illness (which I would call a physical illness that has affected the brain) was considered to be permanent, and any diagnosis was a life sentence. It is now understood that the brain *can* change. Therefore, the effects of trauma on our lives (resulting in mental illness) can no longer be regarded as permanent. *We definitely can heal from the devastating impact of trauma on our developing brain.* It also means that it can no longer be stated that childhood, or indeed adult, trauma is a life sentence that will affect you forever[19]. Through brain scanning it is likely that, in the future, scientists will be able to tell exactly at what critical stages we suffered. They will be able to pinpoint what sort of trauma, and even at what age it occurred. Already brain scans can inform us by showing the damage our trauma has created, and how our brain changes once we heal.

Here is a brain scan done by Dr. Daniel Amen one of 80,000 such scans that he has taken. It is worth looking at them all and his TED talks. You can easily see the difference between the healthy brain on the left and the traumatised brain on the right. You can see the brain damage.

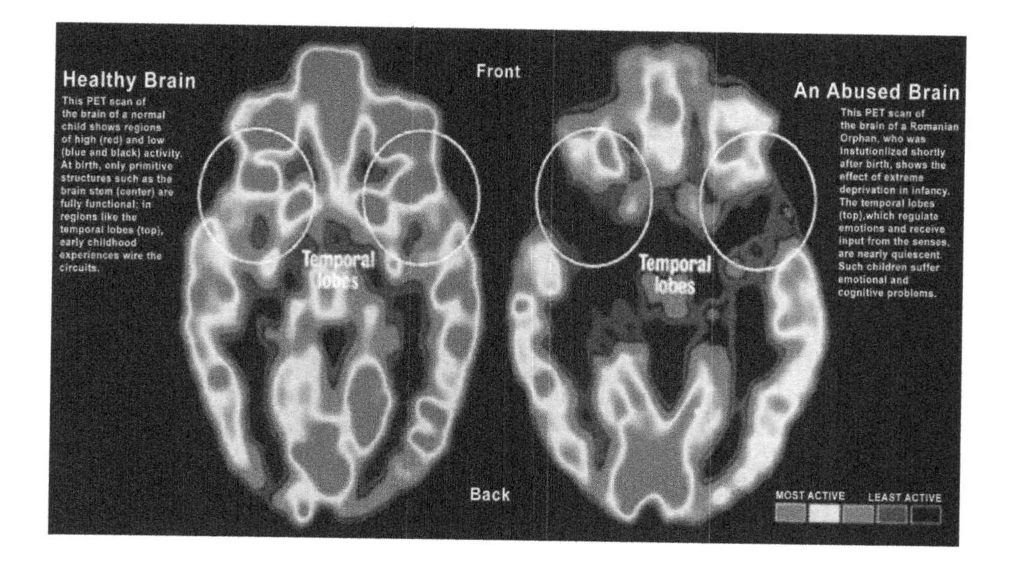

Brain damage is known to affect behaviour. Scientists know that there is no such thing as an evil child: there may be a child with severe brain damage, or a child who has suffered terribly in their first years which has impacted on their brain and so is affecting the way they behave[20].

The plasticity of the brain means our brain, besides being incredibly complex for each one of us, is totally unique. The brain develops dependent on what we learn from others in this world. If a child discovers the best way to keep safe when their parents yell is to hide under the bed then as soon as the child hears yelling, without stopping to think, they will run and hide under the bed because the brain has become used to that response and has neurons (the means by which messages are carried throughout the body) which are connected to enable that reaction to happen quickly. Our brain has 80 billion neurons that are uniquely connected.

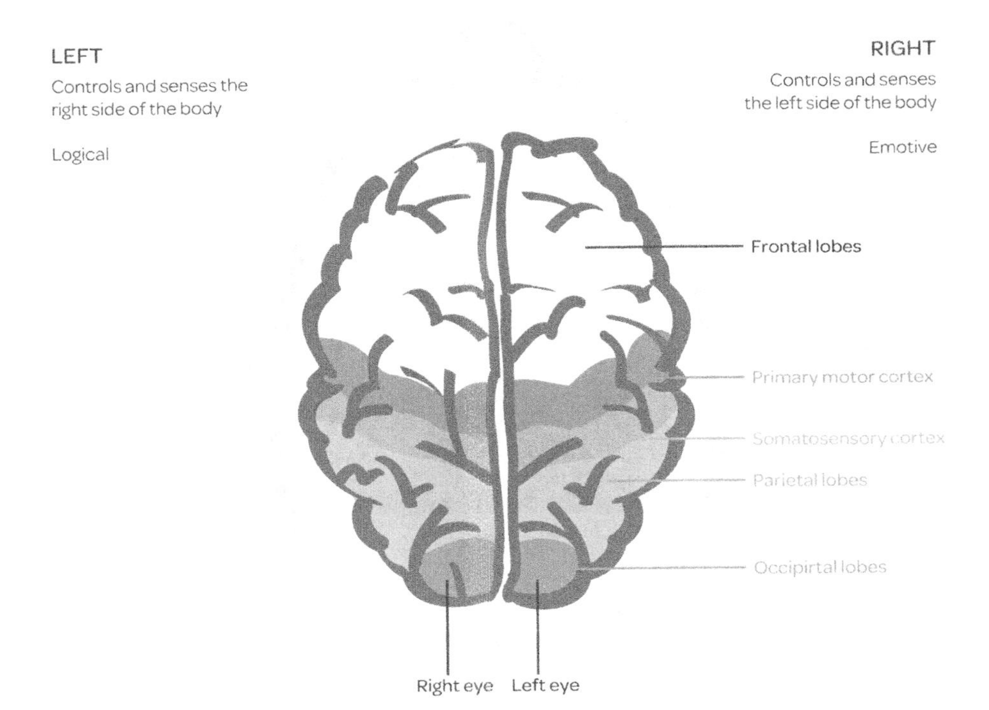

Right and Left brain

Our brain has two halves or hemispheres; the right and left hemisphere, each has a different function. The right brain is *unconscious, non-verbal, creative,* and relates to *emotions*, the left brain is *conscious, verbal, logical,* and *unemotional.*

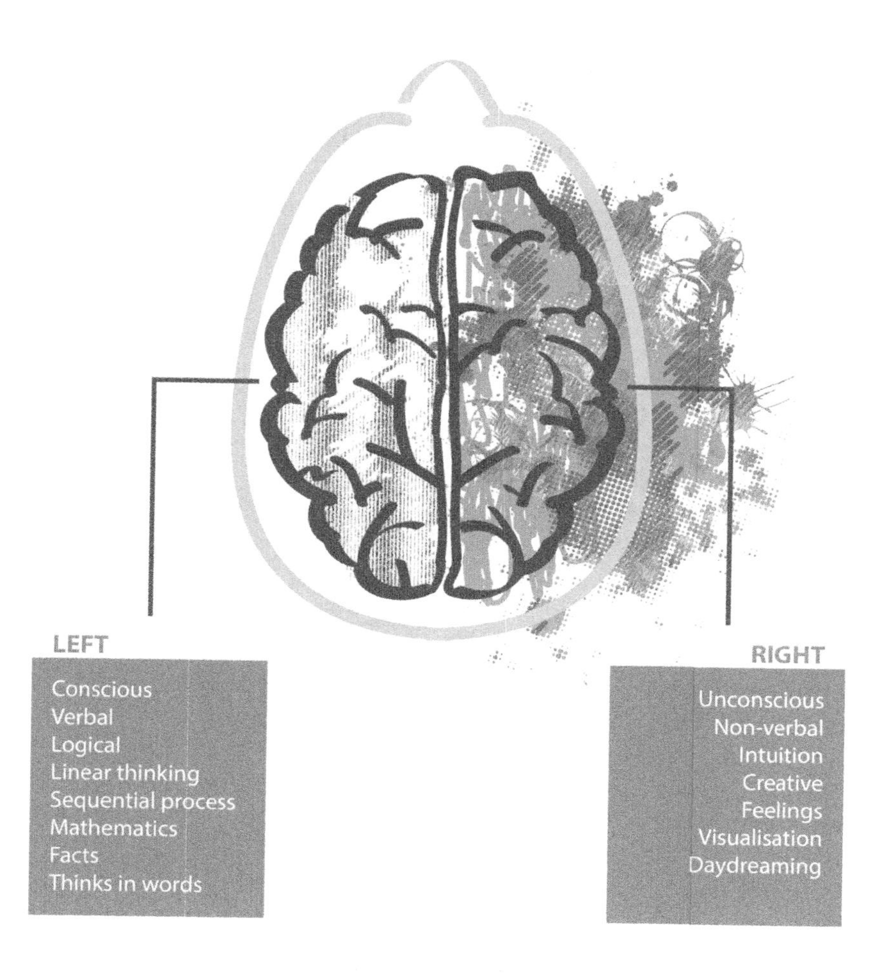

The Corpus Callosum

The two halves of the brain are connected by a bridge joining them known as the corpus callosum; this bridge ensures that we use both parts of our brains to make decisions in our lives. We use our thinking logical left brain with our emotional right brain which results in appropriate responses. However, for many survivors the bridge is much smaller, in fact the more dissociative you are, the smaller the link between the two sides. The consequence is that most of us either think too much or feel too much. The aim of healing is to build the bridge so we use both halves of our brain more effectively and so can make wiser and happier decisions in our lives. As you will discover we need to access our right brain for healing.

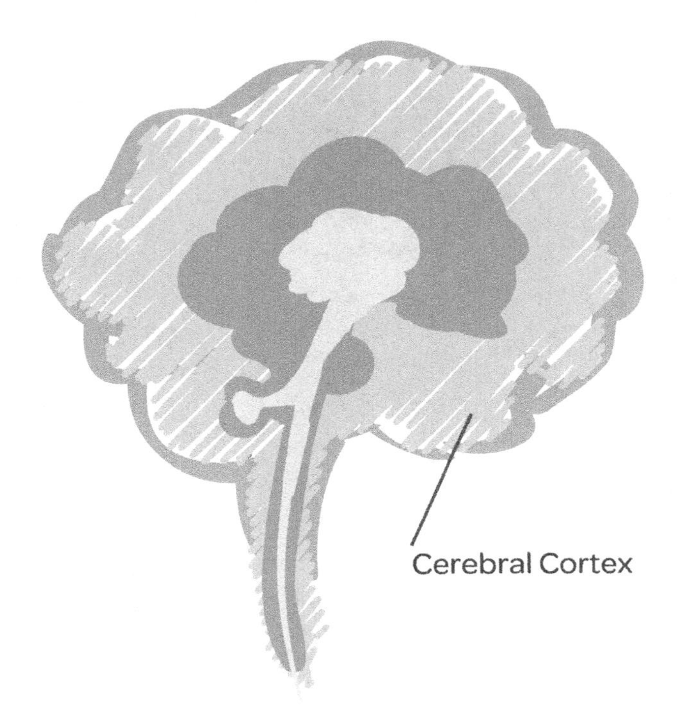

There are three main areas of the brain.

The Cerebral Cortex

Our brain has an outer layer that is our *thinking brain*, called the cerebral cortex which includes the prefrontal cortex.

The Brain Stem

At the base of the brain is the brain stem that controls all our basic actions like breathing, heartbeat, and body temperature.

The Limbic System

Closely connected to the brain stem so it can influence the basic functions of the brain stem such as breathing and heartbeat, is our limbic system which is responsible for caring, bonding, empathy, and most importantly in relation to trauma, it contains the amygdala[21].

Predominantly from the right brain the amygdala has an incredibly important function, to warn us of fear. At Heal For Life we call it – *the fear centre*. The amygdala contains the memory of anything that has frightened us, this *includes trauma memories*. The 'fear centre' has to remember anything very scary that has happened to us, in order to warn us if it might be going to happen again. *The fear centre is dominant* as it is essential to preserve life, to keep us safe from danger. For this reason, it previews all sensations, everything we receive through our senses, everything we smell, touch, taste, hear, and see, is reviewed by the amygdala before it goes to our thinking brain, to check if we have experienced this sensation before when something frightened us in the past. It takes about a fifth of a second for any sensation to travel from the fear centre(amygdala) to the rest of the brain[22]. For instance, if I saw a piece of wood in the shape of a snake I would react from my amygdala, as the shape reminds me of a snake which is scary, however when the visual message reaches my thinking brain I would recognise that it is just a piece of wood, and no cause for alarm. I might think how stupid I was to react to a piece of wood!

This is the amygdala at work ensuring my safety. *I react before I think when my fear centre thinks something scary or dangerous is happening.*

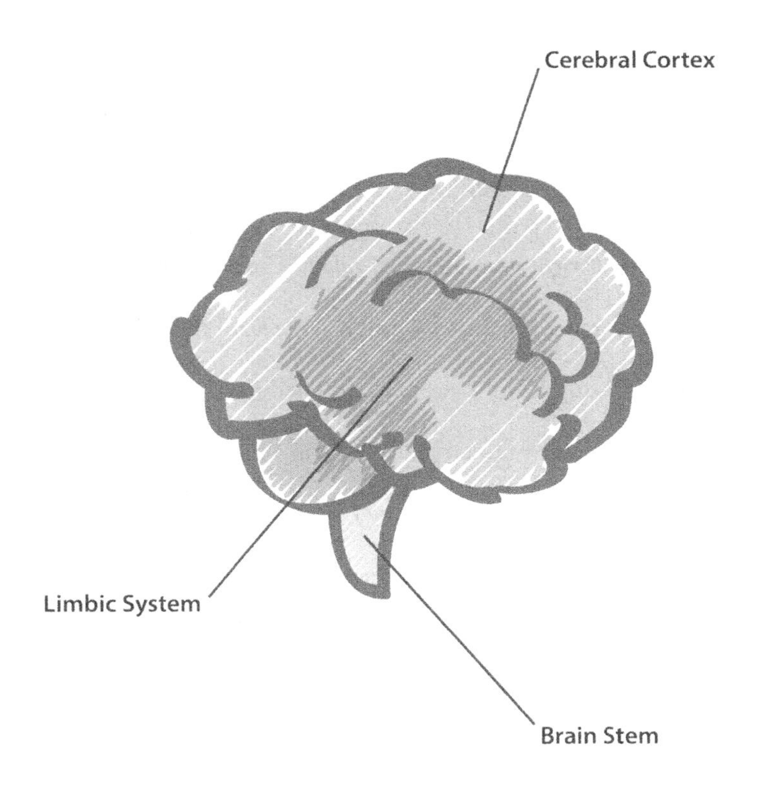

Interestingly, the fear centre is also the first part of the brain to form while in the womb. So, trauma may be experienced 'in utero'[23]. Many guests have remembered something scary that happened before they were born. Some of these memories have been easily corroborated such as when my sister remembered losing a twin in the womb, my older sister knew this to be true although her younger sister had never been told. The fear centre has to develop first, because it needs to learn before birth what is dangerous in the outside world. Trauma recollection prior to birth usually has has a deep lasting impact on the person.

The Fear centre has *no* ability to remember chronologically, so all our trauma memories when we experience them again feel as if they are happening right now, such as when we have a flashback or panic attack[24].

The amygdala has to remember our moments of trauma and be ready to react, because these were – as I discussed in the last chapter – life-threatening experiences. The amygdala records critical elements of that event so that whenever we are reminded of something that happened in moments of trauma, we will react. This reaction is called triggering. The fear centre is in the unconscious right brain which is why we cannot remember trauma.

The Hippocampus

Back to the limbic system: another important part of the limbic system is the hippocampus (this time in the conscious left brain) that holds all our conscious memories. It's like a filing cabinet that stores everything we want to remember or directs the information to other parts of the brain for storage. *Trauma is not stored in the hippocampus, so it is not consciously remembered. Healing involves the process of getting the unconscious memory in the more right-brained dominant amyg-*

dala (that we are always reacting to), into the more left-brained dominant hippocampus where it will be stored as a conscious memory of a past event[25].

The Action in the Brain When We Experience Trauma

When the fear centre (amygdala) is activated by receiving, through the senses, something that is scary and dangerous, it sends a message to the hypothalamicpituitary-adrenal axis (HPA).

The HPA releases hormones to the Autonomic Nervous System(ANS) to prepare the body to respond to the danger. This is called the fight, flight or freeze response. The HPA also releases cortisol (a collective word for the stress hormones) to the brain, and this impacts on three critical areas of the brain. These are the *Broca's area*, responsible for speech, *the prefrontal cortex* (part of the cerebral cortex, the thinking brain), and the aforementioned *hippocampus in the left brain*.

The impact is that as we become more and more frightened by an event and more and more cortisol (stress hormones)is released we are less able to:

- *Speak*, because of disconnecting from the Broca's area (speechless terror)
- *Think clearly* or be aware of what others are thinking or feeling (disconnection from the prefrontal cortex)
- *Remember* the incident (disconnection from the hippocampus)[26]

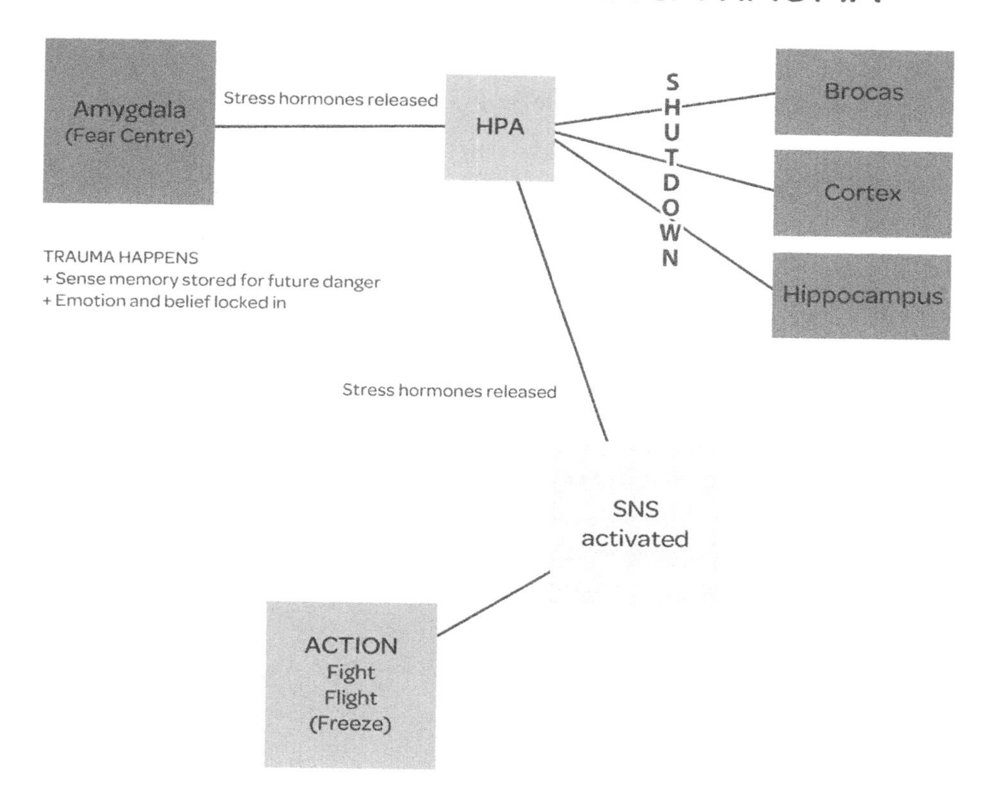

Let me illustrate this with a story:

There is a little girl and she is very excited because it is her birthday, and she and her friends start to play hide and seek. She hides herself in a cupboard that smells of mothballs. She waits and waits and then she starts to get a bit anxious (*a message goes from her amygdala to the HPA releasing cortisol which means she starts to feel frightened, her brain starts to stop her ability to think and it also starts to activate her body through the sympathetic nervous system and so she begins to tense her muscles, her mouth goes dry, her breathing becomes faster, and so does her heart, preparing the body for possible action to escape from the danger).* She tries the door but it won't open (*now more cortisol is released as she becomes more frightened, more in danger in her mind, all of her body is on high alert, she is breathing faster, her heart is beating quickly, her digestive system ceases to function, her hands feel clammy*).

After a further period of time she becomes terrified; she thinks she will die in the cupboard (*now her brain does a full trauma response – Cortisol and other stress hormones cut off her ability to speak as it has disconnected her from the Broca's area in her left brain, she no longer has any connection to her left-brain dominant hippocampus, so she will not remember anything from this moment on, the stress hormones have disconnected her from her prefrontal cortex so she can no longer think. Her senses are on high alert, her amygdala now retains information for future signs of danger. Her amygdala takes in the smell of mothballs, the dark of the cupboard, and she can hear outside the sound of church bells, so that sound is also stored in her amygdala as warning signs of danger, her body which was totally tense now begins to be disconnected from her brain, and she dissociates.*

Finally, her mother opens the cupboard door (*the flow of cortisol and other stress hormones start to slow, she can start to speak and feels less tense*).

There can be two conclusions to this story, either her mother can hug her and hold her and comfort her, in which case the child will relax, come out of her sympathetic nervous system and return to a relaxed state; she may tremble as she releases all sense of danger from her body. By comforting her, her mother has removed the fear of the danger, and the little girl will likely experience very few traumatic reactions to the event. The amygdala will not store the memory of this event; it will be stored via the hippocampus.

However, if her mother scolds the child for being so stupid as to lock herself in the cupboard, the child may think it is all her fault and there will be no release of the trauma. So, in the future whenever the child smells mothballs, hears church bells, or is in the dark she will release cortisol and other stress associated hormones and have a flight or fight reaction identical to when she first experienced the trauma. This is called *being triggered.* She will not know why she is triggered as she will have little memory of hiding in the cupboard. Unless she is supported, to release the trauma and heal from this event, for the rest of her life she will be 'triggered' by the dark, church bells and the smell of mothballs.

Do you know of any triggers you may suffer from? Triggers are an enormous problem for most of us as we can have so many. When we are triggered we go into a flight, fight or freeze response – *and how to heal from our triggers is the purpose of this book.*

Dan Siegel (2012) suggested this idea. To remember the shape of the brain: fold your fingers over your thumb, the wrist represents the brain stem the part of the brain containing basic functions, the thumb represents the amygdala and the whole limbic system, the four fingers represent the four parts of the cerebral cortex. When we suffer a trauma, or are triggered through our senses we flip our lid – we can see this by opening our hand up. When this happens, we are not in control of our thinking brain and we just react to keep ourselves safe by fighting, running away, or freezing in some form[27].

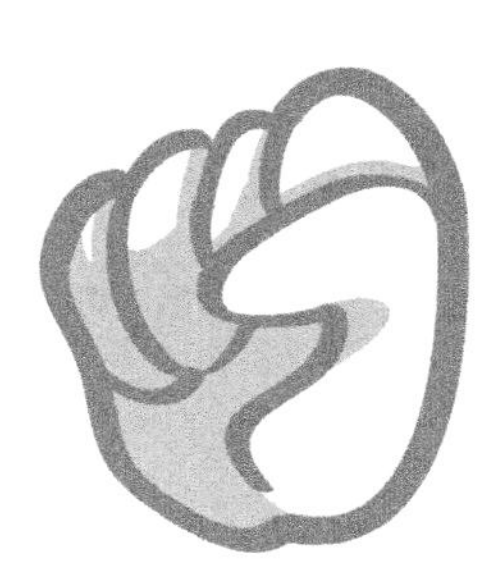
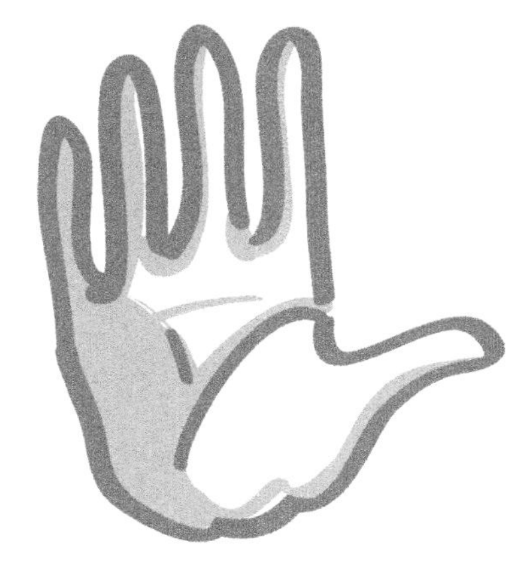

You will find extra information about the brain and trauma at the end of this book.

The brain is altered by human experience[28].

Every part of the brain is affected by trauma[29].

The brain is impacted by adverse childhood experiences. Different parts of the brain are impacted depending on the type of trauma. The time of the trauma also determines which part of the brain is most affected[30].

The level of impact on the brain is not necessarily a determinant of level of mental illness[31].

CHAPTER FOUR

Impact on Nervous System and Hormones; What Happens To Us When We Experience Trauma

Now to discuss what actually happens when we experience trauma in more detail.

Trauma being an event that has more emotion than the person can tolerate and which is perceived as life threatening. I also want to explain what happens when we are reminded of that original trauma in our lives today. To start with, I think it is important to recognise and understand the role of the autonomic nervous system.

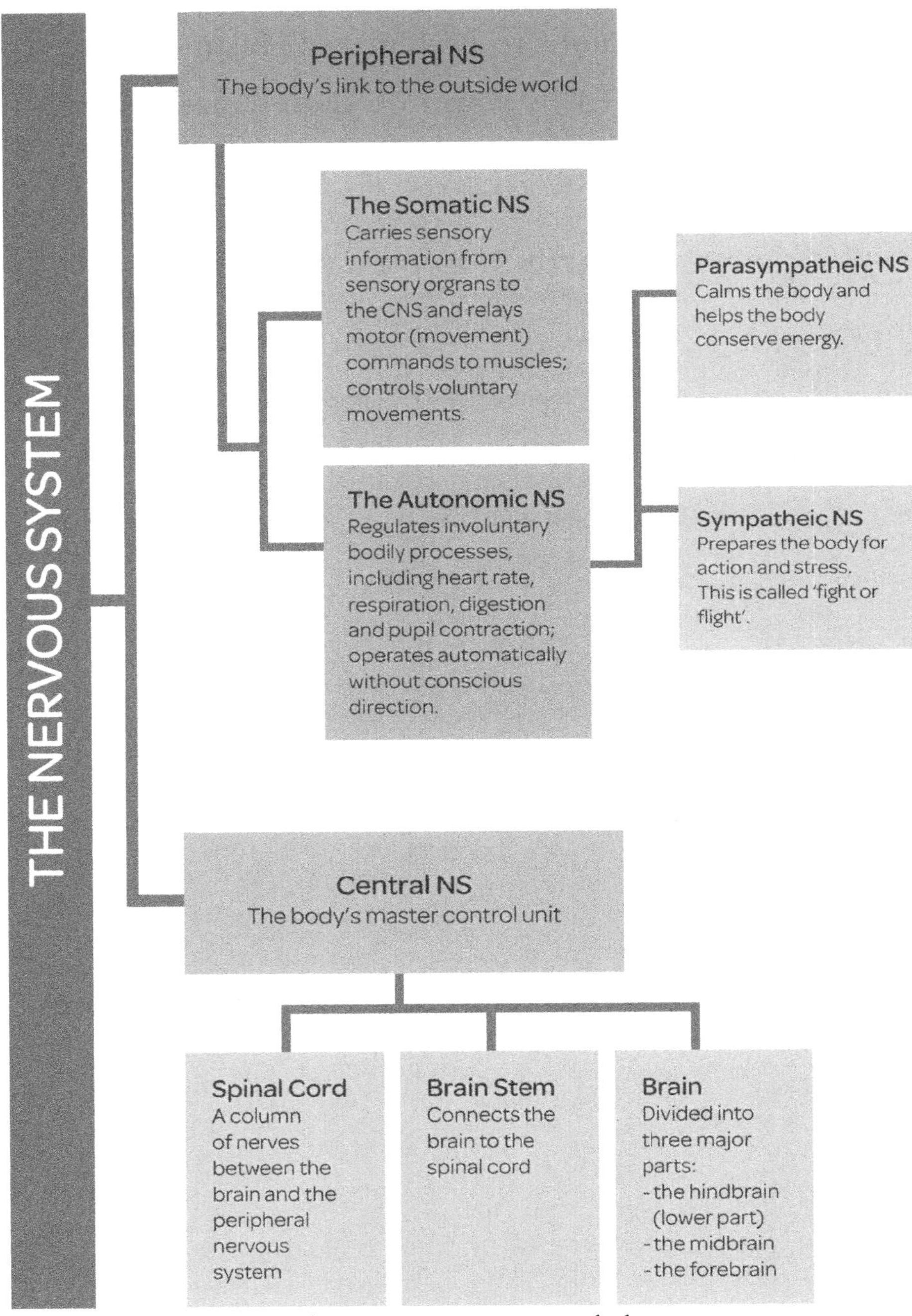

To do that, let us look at the nervous system as a whole.

The brain and spinal cord make up the central nervous system (CNS). All the other nerves distributed throughout our bodies belong to the peripheral nervous system that includes the autonomic nervous system (ANS). *The ANS tells the body how to physically respond to trauma or reminders of trauma.* The ANS helps to control the body's state of arousal dependent on how safe the person is feeling. It does this through the parasympathetic nervous system and the sympathetic nervous system[32].

The ANS is involved in controlling many relatively automatic bodily functions. It monitors internal conditions such as digestion, body temperature, and reflexes and keeps the brain and spinal cord informed of changes in the body. Most of the functions of the ANS occur without us necessarily being aware of them.

The ANS is primarily activated by right brain (emotion-based) mechanisms[33]. *It connects to all of our organs through hormones* (hormones are special chemicals your body makes to help it do certain things, carried through the blood and other tissue fluids) The possible response from all of our organs can be seen in the diagram dependent on whether we are relaxed (para sympathetic system) or anxious (sympathetic nervous system).

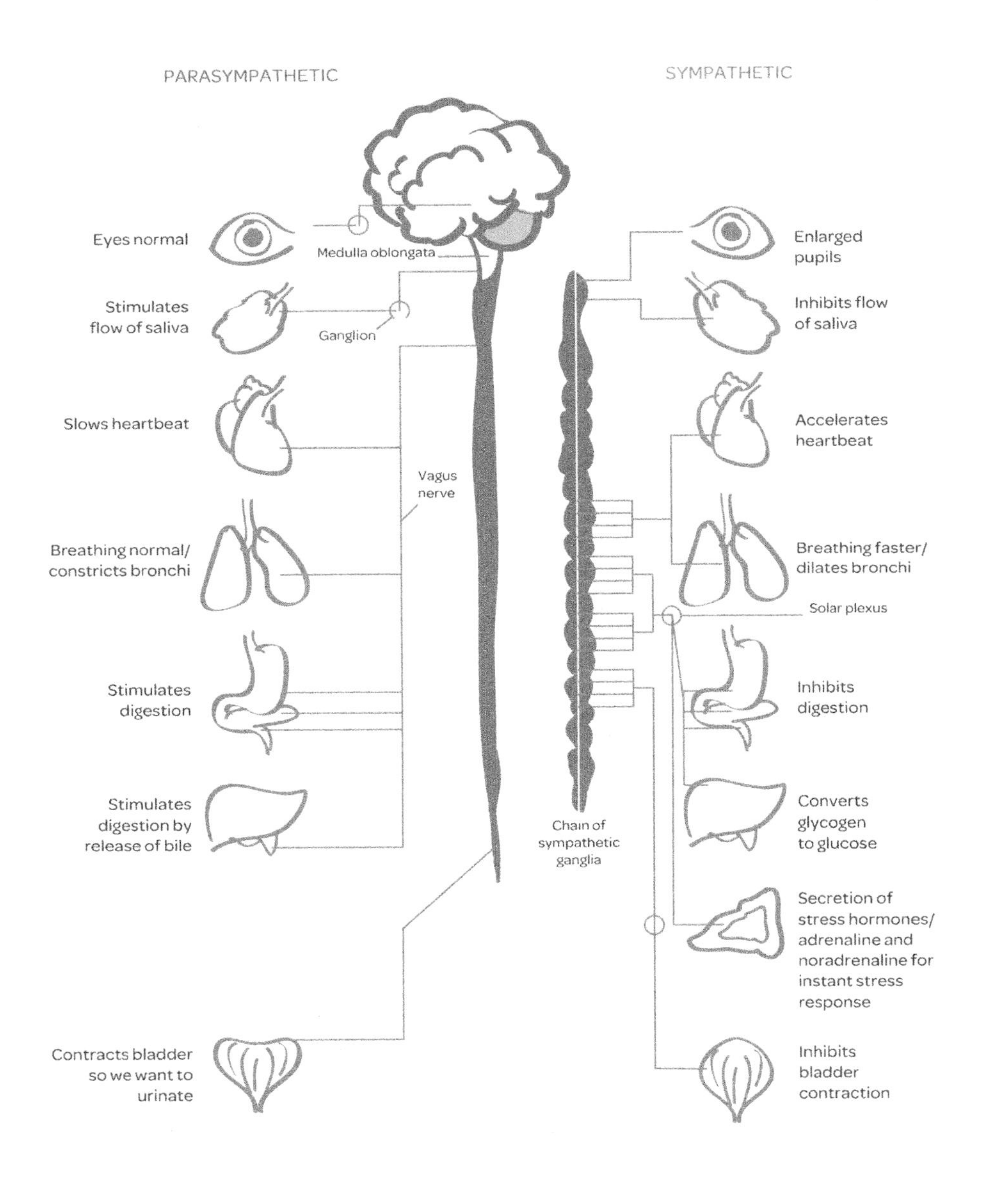
PARASYMPATHETIC
SYMPATHETIC
Eyes normal
Medulla oblongata
Stimulates flow of saliva
Ganglion
Slows heartbeat
Vagus nerve
Breathing normal/ constricts bronchi
Stimulates digestion
Stimulates digestion by release of bile
Contracts bladder so we want to urinate
Chain of sympathetic ganglia
Enlarged pupils
Inhibits flow of saliva
Accelerates heartbeat
Breathing faster/ dilates bronchi
Solar plexus
Inhibits digestion
Converts glycogen to glucose
Secretion of stress hormones/ adrenaline and noradrenaline for instant stress response
Inhibits bladder contraction

The Sympathetic Nervous System

The sympathetic nervous system arouses and prepares the body to meet perceived danger. These reactions to danger can be either fight, flight, or freeze. The body's response to the perceived danger will depend on the possibility of either fight or flight from the danger. When it is completely impossible to escape from the danger, freeze is the reaction. Freeze is what happened when the trauma was originally experienced[34].

Let's go through each of these responses.

Fight

The fight reaction occurs when the person perceives that fight is necessary and possible for survival. In survivors, fight can be expressed as anger and can be displayed physically, verbally, or emotionally. We tend to use this fight reaction on anyone close by who is safe (like our partner), as, when they are present our brain feels safe enough to activate the fight response. If you become angry for no apparent reason and are unable to control it, it is likely you have been triggered. This is the triggered reaction so often experienced by children in school which gets them into terrible trouble when in reality they are just kids who are giving a fear reaction to some reminder of their trauma.

Flight

This reaction is activated when flight is the best option for survival and in humans it is often expressed simply by running away. For example, a survivor of trauma smells alcohol on the breath of a stranger at a party, and suddenly has to leave the gathering. Many survivors are constantly moving home, using the flight reaction to danger.

Flight can occur as a learned response to fear, when feeling unsafe. Have you spent your life constantly on the move? Having to leave somewhere, or someone, without really understanding why? Sadly, often blaming and separating from someone important in your life, who may have been the source of the trigger but nothing to do with the original trauma.

Freeze

If neither fight nor flight is an option for a person who is triggered, immobility (freezing) is the instinctive reaction. It covers many different reactions.

Freeze involves dissociation from reality; it is as though the person is no longer present. The person psychologically splits their consciousness off from the reality of the environment. Some people describe this as being above their body and looking down on it, while others take their mind to an imaginary place, and yet others simply unconsciously block out the sounds, sights and feelings of what is happening around them. The freeze reaction occurs when the parasympathetic system and sympathetic nervous system are activated at the same time. A good example happens in nature when a mouse 'acts' as if they are dead until the cat has become bored and walked away. The mouse then revives and runs away[35].

People with several inner children (often called Dissociative Identity Disorder) can freeze by switching to another part or child in their brain[36].

Freeze can also be experienced as a body reaction such as a severe headache or a pain at the source of the original trauma. This is the hardest trauma reaction to recognise as people can try to treat the physical pain unaware of the real cause. This physical response to a trigger can also show as a physical symptom such as losing the voice (usually means the memory will be about not being heard), or not sleeping (usually when the trauma happened at night) or stomach or bowel problems. I had constant constipation until I remembered I had experienced anal abuse.

Physical reactions to triggers are quite common. A physical trigger reaction can include some people who develop chronic fatigue, fibromyalgia and migraines. I believe that in some cases these health issues can start when a person is triggered, the person does not recognise the cause and cannot understand why their body has suddenly closed down and why they no longer have any energy. Other people suffer with migraines for which they can find no cause (and think only medicine can relieve). So far, I have not seen any official scientific research as to how this physical reaction occurs, but from my experience I can estimate that about 20% of survivors I have met have a physical reaction to triggers. So, if you suffer from migraines, chronic fatigue syndrome or fibromyalgia, next time the symptoms come on strongly you can try the exercise to detrigger (which as you read on you will learn how to do) – I have seen detriggering work so many times, to the amazement of the sufferer[37].

There are a number of reasons why the brain may use the 'freeze' response.

- In nature freezing can deceive a predator into believing the prey is dead or spoiled. Many predatory animals will not prey on an immobile animal unless they are very hungry.
- Some animals can only detect moving prey so will not be able to locate a still prey.
- In a herd, if one member of the herd suddenly drops, immobile, it can distract the predator and allow the rest of the herd time to escape.
- The body's preservation mode – if you don't exist you can't be in danger.
- Freezing can't make the danger worse.

More recent research acknowledges a fourth reaction which occurs when the first three have failed known as either flop, fold, or drop – this is when the person actually becomes unconscious. This reaction can be the cause, in some people, of epileptic fits or similar symptoms. This reaction I have found is much less common and only from severely dissociated people[38]. For many of us who suffered trauma in childhood, the sympathetic nervous system is on high alert all the time because we do not know how to 'turn it off'. This means we react more than other people to perceived danger such as loud noises or anything which we perceive threatens our power, safety, or ability to be in control. We release stress hormones very easily and go into a fight, flight or freeze response whenever we feel even slightly unsafe. As a heightened state of our nervous system is familiar, our brain often feels safest in a slightly anxious state, however, this stops us from enjoying and fully living life.

We experience the sympathetic nervous system activation (fight flight, freeze) whenever we feel anxious, and the more anxious we feel the greater the symptoms;

Increased sweating, sweaty palms – body temperature regulation is compromised as the body is using its resources to meet the danger. *Quickened heart beat* – to pump more blood through the body to meet the danger

Increased blood pressure – as the blood circulates more quickly

Taste buds less effective – there is a theory that this could lead to weight problems as we may eat more salt or sugar than necessary[40].

Our digestive system is not functioning, as all of our energy is diverted to address perceived danger[39]. *Our immune system does not function*, as it is not needed for immediate survival, leaving us susceptible to all manner of illnesses as well as those relating to the immune system. This can lead to auto-immune diseases, and whole of body illnesses.

Growth is limited when the sympathetic nervous system is overly active[41]. Children who suffer a high degree of neglect and a complete lack of touch and connection with others in their first years often suffer from physically stunted growth because of too much early stress.

Very cold extremities – for me, one of the first signs of healing was no longer having freezing cold hands and feet – such a welcome relief!

- Fidgety, restless, and unable to concentrate or listen effectively. In this state, we cannot do any healing or learning and our bodies are not functioning in the way they were created to.
- Less ability to digest – as digestion is not essential for immediate survival.

The reasons for all these body changes are because all our energy is needed to escape from the danger. An engaged sympathetic nervous system is an energy-consuming state and so any unnecessary bodily functions are disabled. When we are constantly stressed or frightened as a child it can result in critical areas being so compromised that they no longer function efficiently when we are not in danger. Do you suffer from irritable bowel syndrome, nausea, or digestive problems?

Sympathetic dominance with an avoidant attachment style, is expressed as a low level of emotional expression, avoidance of eye contact, or a withdrawal from the world and others. It blocks exploration of the environment and the need to seek emotional support[42].

The sympathetic nervous system dominates in the first year of life. The para sympathetic nervous system, (the relaxed soothing state) which I am going to describe in detail shortly, develops in the second year of life[43]. Children are an emotional extension of their mother in the first year of life, therefore they are dependent on their mother to regulate and emotionally hold them[44]. *The baby has no ability to calm itself.* This means if they receive unregulated and intense doses of emotion from parents (usually parents who have unresolved trauma or loss), they will have no ability to self soothe and so will grow up considerably more anxious than a child with a mother who was responding appropriately to their emotional needs.

Such children may also display irritable, rebellious behaviour and an ongoing decreased ability to recover from stress. This will, in turn, lessen the ability of the hippocampus to function, so memory will be compromised[45].

For most of us it is really important that we develop more activation of our parasympathetic nervous system(relaxed sooting state) so that we can be healthier, more aware and feel less stressed. This will be a particularly hard state to enjoy if we did not receive enough nurturing in those first vital years before the parasympathetic nervous system was formed. I will describe the parasympathetic nervous system now – it is the state people are trying to help you reach when they suggest you try deep breathing to calm yourself. They are trying to encourage you, by physical means, to calm yourself by reducing the activation of the sympathetic nervous system and increasing the activation of the parasympathetic nervous system.

Parasympathetic State

The parasympathetic nervous system is largely responsible for calming the body and bringing it back to a state of relaxation once the danger has passed. The parasympathetic state is dominant during rest and relaxation, sexual arousal, happiness, *after* the release of anger, grief, and/or sadness. It balances the actions of the sympathetic nervous system by fostering conservation of bodily energy and repair of damaged systems, necessary for healthy bodies and minds.

Physical Signs of Parasympathetic System:

- Slower heart beat; the blood does not need to circulate quickly
- Slower, deeper breathing; our bodies can be fully oxygenated
- Decreased blood pressure; everything can slow down
- Constricted pupils; we do not need to see as clearly
- Warm, dry skin; body temperature well regulated
- Increased digestion; digestive system can use spare energy.

The parasympathetic system begins to regulate at around four months of age. Usually, by the second year of life the infant has sufficient capacity to have a sound self-regulatory capacity, however will still require soothing from the mother or primary caregiver[46]. The parasympathetic state regulates the interest, excitement, and joy of the child. When the sympathetic nervous system is constantly on high alert it can become over stimulated and then the parasympathetic state has more work to do to try and stabilize the body's automatic functioning[47].

We cannot heal when one state is dominant – achieving a balance between the parasympathetic and the sympathetic systems is the goal.

From all of this you will realise that it is important to our healing that we counteract the dominance of the sympathetic nervous system caused from our childhood trauma by working on ways to calm our over active sympathetic nervous system. Here are some ways you can do this:

Calming the Sympathetic Nervous System

Quiet Activities:

- Be aware, practice mindfulness, be grounded in your own body, and be aware of the present
- Meditate (very hard for some of us to do)
- Breathe (awareness and concentration on breath)
- Be still and connect with nature
- Practice yoga, or listen to calm music
- Cry
- Relax in a bubble bath
- Walk with bare feet
- Gargle
- Hum/Chant
- Pray
- Try to actively love all the things that are required of you in daily life, like cooking, cleaning, shopping, or talking to people so as to lower your stress
- Hug, hold and love a doll to represent your inner child
- Watch a movie and see if you can remember what happened in it at the end!

- Wrap yourself in blanket or hammock.

Further Activities that Involve the Parasympathetic System and Prefrontal Cortex to Support Integration:

- Create and maintain lists; train the mind to concentrate on bringing down anxiety levels
- Self-reflection and journaling
- Be creative – paint, draw, play, or learn to play, an instrument
- Focus on rhythms by drumming, tapping, or moving to a beat
- Laugh
- Sex (safe and loving)
- Make 'I feel' statements
- Talk to someone, communicate openly – fight the desire to be in isolation, as healing cannot occur in isolation
- Exercise (increases serotonin, a feel good hormone)
- Eye contact with others or yourself in a mirror • Walk – read about the cerebellum in the appendix
- Make repetitive movements or sounds.

The more we can become aware of being in our sympathetic nervous system and the more we work on staying longer in our parasympathetic state, the easier and more relaxed life becomes.

Here are a few other details about the way the brain functions that you may find helpful to selfunderstanding.

The Impact of Communication on the Brain The brain develops from communication and interaction with others; without communication, the brain cannot grow and develop[48]. This means that it is hard to heal in isolation, and we really need to connect with other survivors, helpful organisations, and in particular, if possible, a trauma-informed therapist. It means that we have *to fight* the wish to isolate ourselves, as isolation is ultimately very destructive to brain development. As the brain develops from communication, one of the most difficult traumas to heal from is neglect[49].

Interacting in relationship with others stimulates brain structures to activate and mature, a child's brain will develop more from an angry mother than a completely disconnected mother (such as a mother on drugs). Brain activation is mirrored by the person with whom we interact[50].

The brain learns from communication with others so it can predict and control outcomes based on past experiences[52]. The learning is particularly strong if these were negative experiences, because we are wired for survival. Our brain organises and controls our current way of thinking dependent on our past experiences[53].

The brain can only respond to what it knows. If a child never received a loving hug, then as an adult they have no sense of warmth and safety, therefore they are not able to give it to themselves or feel it when giving it to others. Healing may need to involve receiving a caring hug from a trusted person, so the feeling from this hug can create a blueprint in the brain of what it feels like to be hugged. Do you get a warm reaction inside yourself when you share a hug with someone? If you don't it will most likely be because you did not receive loving hugs when you were a child, so your brain has no learned response, and therefore no internal blueprint of what warmth feels like.

Our brain is biased towards early learning, it is more influenced by early experiences than later ones[51]. In these early years our brain learns what to be frightened of, and gains a sense of our own self-worth.

The very foundation of our self-belief and understanding of the world is developed in our earliest years.

The brain encourages us to repeat patterns (it can be said that the brain prefers the devil it knows). We learn how to survive from the experience of early relationships and so if we have a violent father we may feel subconsciously safer being in a relationship with a violent partner even though we hated the experience because our brain knows how to cope with violence.

Although we are unsafe, we may choose that option. This can be very confusing, as we cannot understand why we return to unsafe relationships or keep being attracted to unsafe people[54].

The vast majority of the brain's processing occurs below the level of consciousness, in hidden layers of neural processing. This is reflexive and automatic. We cannot control what is unconscious to us. The majority of what we experience is unconsciously stored and we behave from this unconscious memory. Unconscious memories are called 'implicit memories'. Our right brain (unconscious) dominates our first two years of life before the left brain (conscious) is fully developed and functioning. This means we are often unaware how much our adult behaviour is being influenced by our early childhood[55].

Let us now summarise what happens during trauma, so you can begin to understand why our method of healing is so effective.

Remember What Happens During Trauma?

When a child feels frightened, overwhelmed and scared for their life, the amygdala (Fear centre) is activated. Information about this external danger is received via the senses, (sight, sound, taste, touch, smell and intuition) and the amygdala activates the fear response through the hypothalamic-pituitaryadrenal (HPA) axis. The HPA releases stress hormones into the blood stream and the sympathetic nervous system is activated to prepare the body for action to preserve life. The resulting reaction may be one of either fight, flight, or freeze in reaction to the perceived danger[56]. Remember: *the amygdala reacts faster than other parts of the brain and before we can 'think' about the situation through our neo-cortex*[56].

As previously described, the stress hormones released during trauma cause a number of areas of the brain to shut down. The ***Broca's area***, shuts down, which results that victims of trauma are ultimately unable to speak, sometimes known as 'speechless terror'[57]. ***The cerebral cortex*** shuts down, rendering victims unable to think clearly while the trauma is occurring. This may contribute to the interference with short and long- term learning. ***Predominantly the left brain hippocampus*** shuts down during trauma – this means that we often cannot remember moments of lifethreatening trauma. It also means we can suffer from a less conscious awareness of time, place and sequence of events, when we recall the traumatic moments, which has profound implications for legal processes that may follow, as well as reduced conscious memory[58].

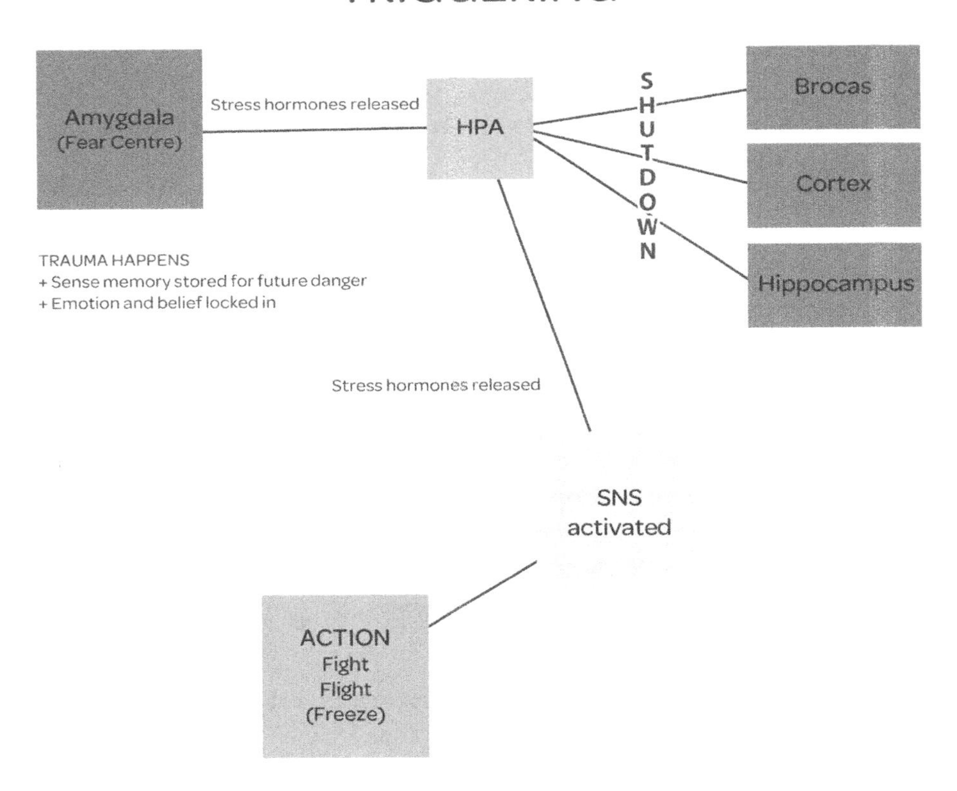

Triggering

Triggering is the reminder of a trauma or an unsafe event that occurs when a person experiences, through the senses, a reminder of a similar sensual experience at the time of the original trauma. Trauma memory involves overwhelming fear. *Trauma memory is from our unconscious and so we often have no idea for the reason for the triggering.* Triggering is, I believe, the greatest problem for us as we grow into adults, as it causes consistent reactive behaviour that we are unable to control or understand[59].

Triggering creates the same mental and physical reaction as the original trauma, the same action occurs which you can see in a very simplified version in the diagram above. It is the same action as during the original trauma. The body prepares to respond to the danger via the sympathetic nervous system, and in the brain, the same areas become disconnected: Broca's area for speech, the Prefrontal Cortex for thinking and awareness of others, and the hippocampus for storing memory.

Importantly, because the thinking brain is cut off, it is not possible to control such reactions.

When a survivor of childhood trauma is reminded of the original, painful and psychologically overwhelming event in the now, the person is said to be 'triggered', and they may feel like they are back in the original experience at the age they were when the original trauma occurred. This is because the fear is remembered through the same sense that originally experienced the trauma, such as the alcoholic breath of a father that was a warning of bad things about to happen.

So, when you are an adult, even though the person who smells of alcohol may be unknown to you and quite harmless, your brain will respond in the same way it did with your father – it will activate stress hormones and the same flight or freeze response as if the unknown person is your father. You will also feel as though the fear is happening right now, in the present, because the amygdala has no sense of chronology.

The fear reaction will be the same as when the original trauma occurred[60].

Another example, if we grew up in a violent household we may be triggered by the *sound* of raised voices or smashing china. If we were *touched* in a certain way then we may react when we are touched in the same way. If we *see* someone who looks like our perpetrator or is wearing similar clothes then we may react. Triggers come in many guises. It can be something as ordinary as seeing someone eating an apple, because the perpetrator used to eat apples after abuse. Anything that you react strongly to, or are frightened of, is likely to be a trigger. A reminder of a trauma you have experienced.

One of my triggers was the word 'Jesus', so I would find myself dissociating in Church and at theological college. I didn't realise I was doing this, I just wondered why I found it so difficult to remember what had happened there. One day when the word was being used excessively by some guests on a healing week, I was very triggered and I turned to flight rather than freeze. I had to leave the room. I de-triggered myself (you will learn how to do this in the next few pages). Later, it all came flooding back to me just how this word was used in my abuse. Triggers can be a great opportunity to grow and heal; they can also be very difficult to navigate or understand in daily life.

Our brain 'remembers' anything it considers important on each life threatening occasion. It holds onto trauma memory predominantly in the right hemisphere's amygdala as an unconscious implicit, sense memory. This is how a mouse 'remembers' a cat is dangerous and how a deer 'remembers' a lion is dangerous. Indeed, it may be through intergenerational trauma that a mouse may be born with a fear of cats. The storage of traumatic memory, it is now known, can be carried through epigenetics (chemical modifications to your genes) through two generations[61]. As I described in the original story, the little girl may be triggered into a strong fight/flight or freeze response by being in the dark, the smell of moth balls or the sound of church bells, all of these are frequently encountered in daily life.

Unfortunately, when we store a trauma in the amygdala *we also store the emotions and beliefs* learnt during the trauma, therefore survivors may be living their life *unconsciously* acting out of emotions and beliefs imposed at a moment of trauma. Said another way, trauma completely obliterates our normal 'safe base' of social and biological development. When this safe base is not available to us we may find ourselves attached to environments, people, or objects that strengthen the danger we endured in the face of the original trauma, leading us to unconsciously re-enact and relive the trauma[62].

It is very hard to identify our triggers, as when we are triggered, our thinking brain switches off. When we are triggered into a fear reaction through our senses, the amygdala activates the production of stress hormones to ensure an instant response; so, we cannot access reason and logic, or even sometimes the ability to speak. We simply react. So, until we recognise some of our triggers we can be very confused by our own behaviour or reactions. Once triggered we may react by (fight) be very angry, by (flight) needing to run away, or by (freeze) dissociating or physical pain; any of these reactions can be confusing and very irritating to ourselves, and can stop us from enjoying life[63].

How to 'De-Trigger'

The first step to de-trigger is to learn to recognise the signs in our body – to be familiar with the feeling and how it is experienced in the body – that I did feel okay, and now I do not. I will have a fight, flight or freeze (or pain) response. Fight is shown by suddenly being angry for seemingly little reason, flight can be the feeling of wanting to leave where you are, to escape, and freeze can be expressed in many different ways: physically by having a headache or body pains, or mentally by just becoming unaware of what is happening around you. Or the further state of freeze, which is called flop or fold.

You are triggered when something happens to your feelings or your body that does not really relate to what is happening in the now. Notice the next time you do not feel in control of how you are feeling – or when you are overwhelmed by a reaction to something that happens. This can be a sudden feeling of anxiety, dissociation, anger, or a deep need to run away or a physical manifestation, such as a headache. Once you have noticed that you were OK and that now you are not OK, the second step to de-trigger is to *say how you feel.* For instance; 'I feel scared' or 'I feel frightened.' The feeling will be about fear. We are triggered in relation to fear, so *fear will always be what needs to be expressed in order to lessen the release of the stress hormones and return us to a normal state of being, and enable us to think clearly again.* Fear is what controls our amygdala so recognising fear de-activates the amygdala trauma reaction and restores our sense of safety. If you remember from earlier, Broca's area is disconnected from us by the release of stress hormones, so saying how you are feeling helps de-activate the stress hormones by connecting our left and right brain.

As our strongest neurons are our optical neurons, it is very important, if possible to look at someone when you say you are feeling frightened. If there is no one you can say this to, then you can say it into a mirror. This is a feedback loop, so if you look at someone while you are triggered, their re-assurance will activate your mirror neurons and will calm you down more quickly[64].

The final step once you have said how you're feeling is to give yourself permission to feel the feeling and validate yourself that it's okay to feel scared or frightened, but it is in the past. It is not happening right now. Here are the steps in a diagram form – you may be able to photograph it with your phone or print it out so you can have it on hand – *learning how to de-trigger has been the greatest tool for all HFL guests, it is literally life-changing.* Try it.

De-Triggering

Recognise I've Been Triggered (I was ok and now I'm not) *Why?*

So, I can own my own triggers and not blame anyone else for my reactions.

Speak (and feel) the Feeling/s (Say 'I feel … scared, angry, sad etc.' to someone else or in a mirror) *Why?*

To discharge the energy in my body so I can respond instead of reacting.

Validate the Feeling/s (tell myself and my inner child/ren, 'it's ok to feel… scared, angry, sad') *Why?*

Because it is ok to feel our feelings.

Remind Myself That It Happened In The Past And It Is Not Happening Right Now.

It is so important that we start to be able to recognise when we are triggered, although it can be very hard to recognise. My suggestion, is that if you have someone at home who wants to help you, work out some sort of 'code' with your partner or friend so that when they think you are triggered they can let you know, so you can become aware as well. For example, one person might say to the other something like 'What is happening for you right now?' Or it could be something more abstract like saying a certain phrase – 'yellow roses', or 'green cheese'. You can say anything unique that you have both agreed prior as to help in this situation. If one person simply says, 'You are triggered!' it can cause the other person to act defensively. They are likely to react and say, 'No I am not!' as it can seem to be a blaming statement. This reaction only makes the situation worse, whereas a code or signal can work more effectively because it does not sound as if we are being told what we feel or what to do.

I feel the majority of relationship problems for survivors arise because we expect our partners or friends to understand us, both when we are triggered and when they are. We cannot reason logically with a triggered person so we cannot ask them to 'calm down', or to be sensible, we have to help them to say how they are feeling. We have to encourage them to de-trigger *FIRST* before continuing to discuss the issue that may have caused the trigger.

As an example, if you are furious that your partner is ten minutes late, rather than yelling at them, try to think of who kept you waiting as a child – it might be that your abuser always made you wait for them to arrive, or your mother was always late and then blamed you for her lateness. Once you have worked out where it happened in childhood, you can express your anger at that person. You will then, hopefully find it possible to have a constructive conversation with your partner rather than being blindly angry.

It is very important, but also hard, to remember when it is happening, that when we are triggered, we have no empathy. The stress hormones have cut off our pre-frontal cortex, our thinking, empathetic part of the brain. We have no ability to be aware of what others are feeling or saying or indeed how, what we are saying is affecting others. Nature makes sure we are only aware of our own needs and *not* anyone else's. This is regardless of how loving or caring we may be when not triggered. This can frequently lead to arguments, unhappiness, and misunderstandings. This is very difficult for those who love and care for us, and very difficult for us. We often do not realise that people are trying to help us and that they may be upset by something we said or did whilst triggered[65].

We cannot know what anyone else is feeling when we are triggered.

The other important point to recognise with triggering is that when we are triggered as well as not knowing what is happening for anyone else, we are also quite unable to be aware of the passage of time. The brain focuses totally on our own survival, so we can get very warped ideas about how other people might be responding to our needs. We may have warped beliefs locked into the original trauma and we may project this onto the people when we are in a triggered state.

I have learned this numerous times over the years. When there is a disagreement between two people here at Heal For Life, if one of them was triggered both their perceptions of what happened will be remarkably different. Both will be speaking their truth; however, the triggered person CANNOT be aware of what is happening for the other person, and so their perceptions are very different. In addition, once one person is triggered it can then trigger the other person, particularly in intimate relationships. Then neither will be aware of what the other person is feeling.

Most of our guests find the most useful tool they learn is not only understanding when they are triggered but also how to de-trigger. They find it life transforming. I hope you do too.

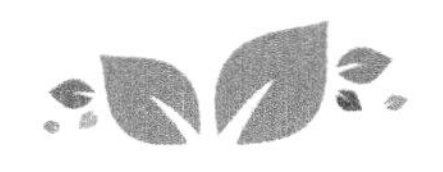

CHAPTER FIVE

How Trauma Impacts Us Physically, Behaviourally, and Emotionally

The impacts of adverse childhood experiences can still be evident 50 years after the initial experience. (Felliti, 2004)

Now that you have an understanding of the impact trauma has on the nervous system and the regulation of hormones, let us discuss how this can affect each of us physically, behaviourally, and emotionally. I am sure that, like me, you may have read despairingly of the awful and seemingly endless list of things we suffer from as a result of trauma.

Some of the long-term impacts of trauma include: depression, mental illness, suicide attempts, early initiation of smoking, alcoholism and alcohol abuse, illicit drug use, obesity, early initiation of sexual activity, multiple sexual partners and sexually transmitted diseases, adolescent and unintended pregnancy, foetal death, risk of intimate partner violence, heart disease, cancer, obesity, multiple somatic symptoms, autoimmune disease, lung disease, liver disease, sleep disturbances, problems with work and relationships, and a much higher risk of revictimisation[66]. What a nightmare!

The brain (recent research includes the gut in this) controls our functioning, so if its development is compromised, this will obviously have impact on the way we think, feel, and behave. What I have found really interesting over the years is how trauma, whatever the trauma was, has some basic similar impacts on each one of us. This has made running an organisation *by* survivors *for* survivors brilliant as we all understand each other, *and* very challenging because we can trigger each other as we all seem to react to the same things. Let's look at the similarities of effects on many of us and some of the ways towards change.

Physical Impact to the Developing Brain

The adult brain of a person who has experienced childhood trauma is significantly smaller than adults who have not experienced childhood trauma. The hippocampus, the amygdala (the fear centre), the hypothalamus, the corpus callosum (the bridge between the two sides of the brain), the left hemisphere of the brain, and the frontal lobes are all smaller[67]. In terms of personality and behaviour, this means that the thinking and analytical parts of the brain are all smaller and therefore *the ability to think through the logical consequences of actions is lessened, the ability to construct a life plan is seriously impeded, and the sense of self is impaired.*

Corpus Callosum

A smaller corpus callosum means there is less integration of the right and left hemispheres of the brain. This lack of connection between the right and left brain, I have observed both in myself and others, has a profound impact – less integration means the brain is not used at optimal capacity to make decisions.

This means those of us affected by trauma are less able to think and feel at the same time, less able to make wise decisions, as well as having a greater tendency to dissociate.

People with Borderline Personality Disorder (BPD) and Dissociative Identity Disorder (DID) have significant structural alterations in the corpus callosum, meaning people with these diagnoses have difficulty integrating overwhelming emotions[68].

Hippocampus

A smaller hippocampus is associated with the development of depression, PTSD, schizophrenia, DID, and BPD[69]. The hippocampus is connected with our sense of self, a smaller hippocampus means we have a lesser sense of self. It is not known whether a smaller hippocampus is the cause *of* depression or whether a smaller hippocampus is caused by depression. Personally, I believe, as the vast majority of people with depression have also suffered from trauma – coupled with the fact that scientists do know that stress hormones affect the hippocampus – that people with depression have a smaller hippocampus and you know from the previous statistics in Chapter Two, that the vast majority of people who suffer from depression have also suffered from trauma.

Amygdala, Thalamus and Hypothalamus

A smaller amygdala is linked to depression, Borderline

Personality Disorder (BPD), and Post Traumatic Stress Disorder (PTSD)[70]. The thalamus and hypothalamus are severely impacted when we have trauma presentations such as BPD, depression and Schizophrenia[71].

Survivors tend to have an altered 'default network', consisting of a number of brain networks related to self-relevant stimuli. *This means survivors' Posterior Cingulate Cortex may be more intuitive and aware of others' emotions and feelings, although the ability to be self-reflective in our decision making processes may be impaired*[72].

Sympathetic Nervous System

The changes from being excessively in our sympathetic nervous system can have physical effects on our health. For instance, it can lead to premature aging of the body, which in turn increases the risk of early death[73]. Levine (1997) states that trauma can cause bronchitis, asthma, migraines, fibromyalgia, chronic neck and back pain, gastrointestinal problems, paralysis, blindness, deafness, and can make a person mute. Additionally, stress actually kills brain cells that can impact our behaviours in a profound way due to traumatic experiences[74].

Behavioural Impact

Antisocial Behaviours

Feeling unsafe or stressed means we are feeling frightened (this may be unconscious). Often we are being triggered by reminders of our trauma – constantly going into a 'fear' state – and this can lead to our coping mechanisms taking over, where we can be bossy, controlling, withdrawn, 'leave' our bodies, talk a lot, or, if the fear is very strong and our sympathetic nervous system is more fully activated, we can go into a fight, flight, or freeze reactions. Once we go into the flight, fight, or freeze response we become less aware of our behaviour towards others (as stress hormones have cut off our prefrontal cortex) and we are less able to think sensibly. Learning how to know when we feel safe is the first vital step towards healing. Furthermore, feeling safe means less likelihood of being triggered all the time. The next chapter is devoted to that subject[75].

External Locus of Control

When we are young we have an external locus of control that means we believe that our successes or failures are due to factors external to ourselves. Effective parents encourage us to develop independence and they help us realise we can selfregulate our emotions with the ability to learn how to feel our own feelings. We learn from our parents that we are responsible for how we are feeling, thus giving us at around the age of 3-5 years a sense of autonomy and self-ability. This is called an ***internal locus of control***[76]. However, for many of us as children we had little or no control over what happened to us. So, for safety, we had to look to others to tell us how we could feel often far beyond the age where a child normally would. Many of us will know the feeling of looking to mum or dad to know how to behave, how to feel, rather than coming from our own feelings. We look to mother first to see how she is feeling before we speak. In adulthood, this leads us to feel that we are not responsible for how we are feeling, and hence we tend to look to others to know how we are feeling and we also tend to blame others for how we are feeling – this is called an external locus of control. This has perhaps been the hardest problem in running an organisation for survivors of child abuse: it is hard for survivors to take responsibility for how they are feeling because they didn't learn how to do that as a child. We blame others for our emotional state. Each of us is responsible for how we feel, no one can make us feel anything unless we let them. Think about what that means in your life. It's your choice.

Suppression of Emotional Expression

Some of us *try* to exist in our left brain by being busy, talking all the time, or by controlling our surroundings – anything to save us from feeling our feelings that are generated in the right brain. Some of us hide fear (as it is too dangerous) by being angry. I think I can safely say that all of us are frightened of fear because it is a sign that our survival is threatened. As adults we will do anything to avoid fear yet we will also often feel fear more strongly and more frequently than those who have not experienced trauma. Chapter Nine addresses how to overcome this problem. Suppression of overwhelming emotion is said to cause depression[77]. I certainly am aware that, from my own observation, it is the people who try to suppress their feelings that wind up suffering from anxiety (suppressed fear).

Poor Interpersonal Relationships

The vast majority of us will not have had nurturing, consistent relationships with one or both of our parents; this will have resulted in us having insecure attachment styles. Insecure attachment says it all in the title: we are insecure and find it hard to trust in relationships with others. If we had a secure attachment style, we would likely have told them about the abuse (if they were not the abusers). More information on attachment style is covered fully in Chapter Six[78].

Right Emotional Brain vs. Logical Left Brain

Those who have experienced trauma have been known to have long-term dysregulation in areas such as the hippocampus, amygdala and prefrontal cortex[79]. Trauma survivors, including myself can get stuck in our right brain and 'lose' ourselves in emotions, crying for days and unable to come through the feeling. Alternatively, we may not connect easily to our feelings at all, and spend our lives being very busy all the time focusing on logic, reason, and order. Suggestions to help change being dominated by one brain hemisphere over another is covered more in Chapter Fifteen[80].

Sexually Inappropriate

How can we know what is appropriate when we have been sexually abused? We may become promiscuous or dress in a sexually provocative way because we have no idea of sexual boundaries. Or we can go the opposite way and dress in clothing that aims to avoid attention and try to give the impression of being asexual. We chose never to wear a dress or be feminine to protect ourselves. It is very hard when we have been over sexually stimulated in early childhood.

Lack of Boundaries

This is a big issue. Our boundaries – physical, and emotional – were violated, and are likely to never have been formed, which means that we may have no idea what they are and how to keep them. Chapter Fourteen illustrates ways to work on strengthening weak boundaries and how to maintain healthy ones.

Addictions

We turn to addictions to cover the pain, to concentrate on something other than our fear, to self soothe, and try to regulate our emotions. Also, because often we did not learn that we have the right to express our wants and needs, we ignore our own needs. You will have seen from the statistics in Chapter Two that the vast majority of people suffering with alcohol and drug addictions have admitted to suffering from trauma.

Heroin, for example, is a very harmful drug, and while, unfortunately, it is an effective ameliorant for relieving the impact of trauma, healing is clearly a much healthier, more satisfying and positive alternative[81].

Self-Harming

Endogenous opioids are natural painkillers and are released during activation of the amygdala during trauma, or when we are triggered[82]. Victims of serious injuries, such as survivors of car accidents, have been known to not feel much pain immediately after the accident due to the powerful effect of endogenous opioids. Endogenous opioids dull physical pain and in turn produce a feeling of calm euphoria, which is nature's way of protecting us from physical pain when we are in danger so that we can continue to escape from the danger. Some survivors of trauma self-harm to reduce feelings of overwhelming emotional pain, or (usually for people with severe dissociation) to feel something and bring themselves 'into' their body. The beneficial effects of the endogenous opioid release associated with physical self-harm can become highly addictive over time, just as using synthetic opiates, such as heroin, is highly addictive. You do not feel the pain when you deliberately hurt yourself if you are in a triggered, that is, being in a highly aroused sympathetic nervous system. I have never met a survivor who self-harms for attention or due to outside influences, such as imitating a friend who self-harms. Survivors may scratch or burn themselves, pick or pull hair, or do anything to feel the emotional relief that endogenous opioids offer[83]. It is a quick fix much like smoking a cigarette or having an alcoholic drink. I have found that people who self-harm tend to still blame themselves for their abuse. It is important to understand self-harming is a normal coping mechanism for survivors of trauma, and to not add to the shame that surrounds this issue. The most effective way to stop the urge to self-harm is to remind yourself that the abuse was not your fault, and learn how to detrigger yourself instead. Self-harm is, ultimately, selfabuse and you deserve better. Here I want to remind you that you have suffered enough at the hands of others – you deserve to feel safe in your body – please try not to abuse yourself.

Suicidal Ideation

I did some research when I was running ASCA, (Advocates for Survivors of Child Abuse, now known as the Blue Knot Foundation) and found that 90% of our survivor members reported that at some time in their life they felt suicidal[84]. However less than half of that number actually felt like killing themselves. It is important to note that feeling suicidal is very different from actually wanting to kill oneself. I am sure if you think about it that you understand the subtle difference. It is important to recognise that it is possible to feel suicidal and also know that you are not going to actually kill yourself – the feeling provides relief from the overwhelming feeling of ***hopelessness***. This feeling of wanting to commit suicide is a very common feeling, and is a normal reaction to the feelings of hopelessness from which we suffer as survivors. Please be careful to recognise if you actually do feel that you want to kill yourself, and if you do I would ***strongly urge*** you to please reach out for help (Lifeline is an amazing support tool) before you get sucked into the belief that no one will care if you are alive or dead. ***It is a lie our brain creates*** that others will feel better if we were dead – it is not true. ***You absolutely do matter.*** Please don't let the perpetrator of the trauma you suffered win by considering ending your unique and important life.

Complete Lethargy and Connection to World

This happens when the sympathetic nervous system gets so overworked that it shuts off, and cortisol no longer activates the fight, flight, or freeze response. *It is as if the whole system runs out of energy.* When your system reaches this stage of adrenal fatigue it is very difficult to move forward – however do note that healing seems to alleviate some of the effects associated with fibromyalgia[85]. I know it changes people's adrenal fatigue as I witness it so often.

Hyperarousal

Hyperarousal is when there is consistent high arousal of sympathetic nervous system. Signs of a highly activated sympathetic nervous system and strategies to calm it down can be found in Chapter Four. Detriggering in particular will be useful for those who experience hyperarousal. It is caused by dysfunction in the amygdala and central nervous system, and leads the survivor of trauma to constantly view the world as an unsafe place. If this is something you are struggling with, you are likely to suffer from constant or uncontrolled agitation. You will startle easily and find it hard to relax[86].

Hypervigilance

Hypervigilance is also common in survivors of trauma. We tend to have a highly attuned intuition and awareness of people and situations. When the amygdala is activated, the fight, flight, or freeze response can seem exaggerated as there is no activity in the 'thinking' cortex. As a consequence, many survivors may have huge gaps in their development.

Further to this, there may be day-to-day living skills that you may have never had the chance to learn. Trauma causes profound dysfunction to an individual's sense of self, often accompanied with under- or overregulated emotions and learning deficits[87]. *'This can help us understand why survivors of trauma have low attention spans as the brain is unable to 'think' when the alarm has been triggered'.* (Levine, 1997) It is this warning system that becomes over activated in survivors of trauma and contributes to many behavioural problems.

Emotional Impact

Expecting the Worst, Feeling More Comfortable in Drama than Peace

The more a neural pathway is used, the more we continue to use it, if we have spent our childhood in drama we end up feeling, paradoxically, safer when there is drama happening around us. For years I felt safest (because my brain knew how to function) when I was feeling a bit anxious, and that is because for my whole childhood I existed in an anxious state. A child who lives in domestic violence will feel safest when in domestic violence. We tend to repeat patterns, even dysfunctional ones. In order to change this feedback loop, we need to experience different ways of being so that we can internalise a new blueprint and change[88].

Feelings of Worthlessness and Inadequacy

No one noticed what was happening when we were children, and no one intervened to save us. We then locked in the subconscious belief that we don't matter.

We do not think we can get better, or change our lives. Often, childhood messages are imprinted on our brains when parents have used phases like 'you will never amount to anything', 'you're no good', and 'you're useless'. Chapter Fourteen offer ways to address these negative self-beliefs that are born out of the deep-seated feeling of being not being 'good enough'.

Controlling Behaviours: Powerlessness

We all know the feeling of powerlessness – we were not able to be in control during trauma, so we may do anything to stay in control now, and even more so when we are not feeling safe. Feelings of being powerless can lead to controlling others as well as our surroundings, in some cases our controlling can lead to developing social anxieties such as agoraphobia (inability to leave the house).

Many of us also have a real fear of people in authority over us. I still find it really hard to make a phone call to someone I perceive as being more powerful than me, equally if someone instructs me to stand up, I will want to sit down. Powerlessness can be reinforced by some services, especially in the mental health system. This powerlessness has us accept that we are victims, and that we cannot change. This is why we need to be encouraged to take our power back to effectively heal. It is worth thinking about how this feeling of powerlessness affects your life and hopefully make the decision to take your power back. Taking your power back is addressed in Chapter Fourteen.

Inability to Concentrate Due to Stress

This is a prevalent problem in educational contexts. An inability to concentrate can result when our brains are activated by the sympathetic nervous system, and our hippocampus is not able to function efficiently due to an over-production of stress hormones. Our whole being is concentrating on a more basic instinct, that is, survival rather than other functions such as reading and writing at school[89].

Dissociation

We learned to dissociate from ourselves when the threat became too great. I am sure you have all had times when you cannot remember how you got to where you are, say when driving home or when watching a movie. Trauma is a primary cause of dissociation. Dissociation is more common in children, which is why this particular behaviour is often developed in childhood. It is a coping skill we use to separate ourselves from the traumatic event to minimise the pain and hurt. Children find it particularly easy to 'step out of themselves', as their identity is still forming. Once we have learned this coping skill of not being in our body, we tend to use it (unconsciously), particularly in times of high stress. Trauma is known as a disorder of dissociation because all of us will have suffered from some level of dissociation. This can have implications for the development of the self and can result in diagnosis of personality or dissociative disorders.

Bodily Reactions

Another problem is that our bodies can associate some physical sensations with previous abuse. A particular problem can be sexual feelings that are pleasurable, and yet we connect those feelings with trauma and our bodies and feelings may react contrary to how we want. This can prevent healthy relationships. In my experience, one cannot change the body's reaction until we process or de-trigger from the trauma the body is remembering. It is quite normal to have been sexually aroused when being sexually abused as a child. Often having these feelings leads to shame. Despite it possibly feeling pleasurable, it was *not* your fault.

Mental Illness

You may have read the statistics for people with mental illnesses having suffered from childhood trauma, so clearly there is a correlation between the two. I think the most significant statistics come from a study conducted by Read (2005) into *all* research that had been done on mental illness over a period of time. The overall statistic from all the research throughout the world over a period of time was that 69.9% of people with a severe mental illness had suffered from some form of childhood trauma[90].

Guilt and Shame

Up until the age of three we are primarily narcissistic in that we are self-focused – all children are – it is nature's way of ensuring our survival[91]. Until around the age of three to four years old, we consider ourselves responsible for everything that happens. It's why children suffer so much when something happens to a parent: the child takes responsibility for anything that happens in the family. As an example, at the age of three a child will feel totally responsible for a couple divorcing. They will think they did something wrong.

This also means survivors who have experienced trauma that occurred at a young age will more often than not take responsibility for the abuse and the actions of the perpetrator – how many of you truly believe the abuse you experienced was your fault?

Being shamed is very similar to abandonment and has a profound impact on our primary attachments, brain development, and self-identity. Many survivors can feel ashamed or guilty about how they 'behaved' during a traumatic experience, and many express sincere relief at finding they are not to blame for running away, getting violent, or doing nothing at all in a moment of sheer terror. I talk more about shame later in this book, it is such a huge issue for so many of us. The next chapter I look at the way our mother related to us impacts on how we relate to others for the rest of our lives – until we choose to heal.

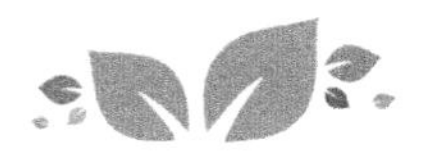

CHAPTER SIX

Recognising and Changing Attachment Styles

How we attached to our primary carer (usually our mother) affects how we relate to other people *for the rest of our lives.* That is until we start to heal. So, it is really important to discover our own 'attachment style' as it is called, and work on developing what is called a 'secure attachment' – so that we will find it easier to have satisfactory, safe, and meaningful relationships. Attachment style explains how the behaviour and relationship patterns that are established by our mother in early childhood become enduring templates for how we see ourselves, others, and the world, throughout our lives. What you are about to learn has been proven through extensive, worldwide research – the name itself has evolved to a 'style' rather than 'theory', as it now considered a proven modality of psychotherapy.

There are four different attachment styles, each with a different set of emotional needs from the others. Understanding our attachment style helps us in our relationships, because once we comprehend our own, we can recognise that different people have different emotional needs. Our partner may have quite different emotional needs than we do, all of it is dependent on their early mother and child relationship. I have chosen not to change the name of each style once we become an adult as I think it is simpler to keep the same terminology throughout our lives.

Attachment

Attachment can be understood as the emotional bond a child has with their mother (or other primary attachment figure); this is deep and enduring, connecting the infant to the mother or other primary caregiver across space and time. Attachment is a relationship that is not necessarily reciprocal in nature. In the first years, it requires the caregiver to be sensitive and responsive to the child's physical and emotional needs[93].

I have used the word 'mother' throughout, as our mother is uniquely important in this context. Of course, if you had another important caregiver in your very early years, for example your father or grandparent, or foster parent, that is to whom I am referring.

Early Theories of Attachment

Freud suggested that the infant's emotional tie to the mother provided the foundation for all later relationships (he was correct). His theory believed feeding to be the central context by which caregivers and babies built this close emotional bond. We now know that although feeding is an important component, in which mothers and babies build a close relationship, attachment does not depend on hunger satisfaction[94]. In the 1950s, a famous experiment showed that rhesus monkeys reared with terry cloth and wire mesh 'surrogate mothers' spent their days clinging to the terrycloth substitute, as being more important than the bottle which fed them. The monkeys never displayed an emotional attachment to the bottle[95].

Observations of human infants have also revealed that children become attached to family members who seldom feed them, including fathers, siblings and grandparents[96]. You may have noticed that toddlers in western countries who sleep alone and experience frequent daytime separations from their parents sometimes develop strong emotional ties to cuddly objects such as blankets or teddy bears[97]. Although, such objects have never played a role in infant feeding. Therefore, attachment must relate to something other than our feeding needs being met.

Bowlby's Ethological Theory

Bowlby suggests the behaviour of an infant can be understood by looking at the mother's history and survival needs. Behavioural systems have developed throughout history to ensure infants adapt their behaviour to give them the best chance of survival[98].

Babies have developed behaviours that enable them to have the best possible chance to receive care from the adults around them. For example, a baby will cry if put down and smile if picked up. This is because babies will be safer if they are kept close to their carer; babies need to be kept warm, fed, nurtured, stimulated, and socialised. Proximity to the mother makes this much easier to accomplish. So, when a new born baby is put down to sleep alone in a crib, it may protest this separation by crying. This crying is showing that the baby is well adapted for survival by expressing what s/he needs for survival in a way that will be noticed by the mother. Many human behaviours have evolved over the history of our species because they promote survival. You will notice, throughout the book, the importance of survival and how it has affected the development of us as humans in so many ways. Ensuring the survival of the child ensures the survival of the species[99].

John Bowlby (1969) and Mary Ainsworth (1973), who first applied this idea to the infant-caregiver bond, retained the Freudian idea that the quality of attachment to the caregiver has profound implications for the child's feelings of security and ability to form trusting relationships throughout life. At the same time, Bowlby was inspired by Kornad Lorez's (1935) research of imprinting in baby geese. He believed that the human infant, like the young of other animal species, is endowed with a set of built-in behaviours that help keep the parent nearby, increasing the chances that the infant will be protected from danger. Close proximity to the parent also ensures that the baby will be fed but, as I have mentioned, Bowlby was careful to point out that feeding is not the *basis* for attachment. Instead, the attachment bond has strong biological and relational roots[100].

This early work by Bowlby describing the evolutionary basis of attachment was a very important step in understanding how human infants form relationships.

His work recognised that for human infants, emotional security is essential for survival and having their emotional needs met is just as important as the need for food and material comfort. Bowlby was one of the first to notice that for human infants, *continuity* of care was essential for the infant to feel secure, in turn supporting the child to develop secure attachments throughout life.

The infant needs to have one or two main carers. The relationships with these carers needs to remain *stable* and *undisrupted.* If it is not stable then the baby enters a cycle that starts with protest and if ignored this becomes despair and, finally, as a way of survival the baby detaches as the repeated ruptures in relationship have threatened the infant's very basic survival. It is far easier to emotionally detach in order to survive, as that is the primary need, than continue to experience mis-attunement and lack of responsiveness from the primary caregiver[101].

Transgenerational Patterns of Attachment

Bowlby (1969) was the first to notice that insecure adults reproduce themselves. They tend to parent as they were parented. This creates a cycle where poor attachment patterns are passed on from generation to generation. So, there is no real starting point to poor parenting and **no particular person to blame.** The insecure child has had poor parenting and will likely have poor relationships throughout life into adulthood. When this individual becomes a parent, in turn, s/he will generally also have difficulty with the parenting role and in turn will have a child that is likely to be insecurely attached and share the same difficulties. Sometimes to compensate for their own poor childhood, parents overcompensate to their own child, which sadly can lead to the same insecure parenting style with similar detrimental results[102].

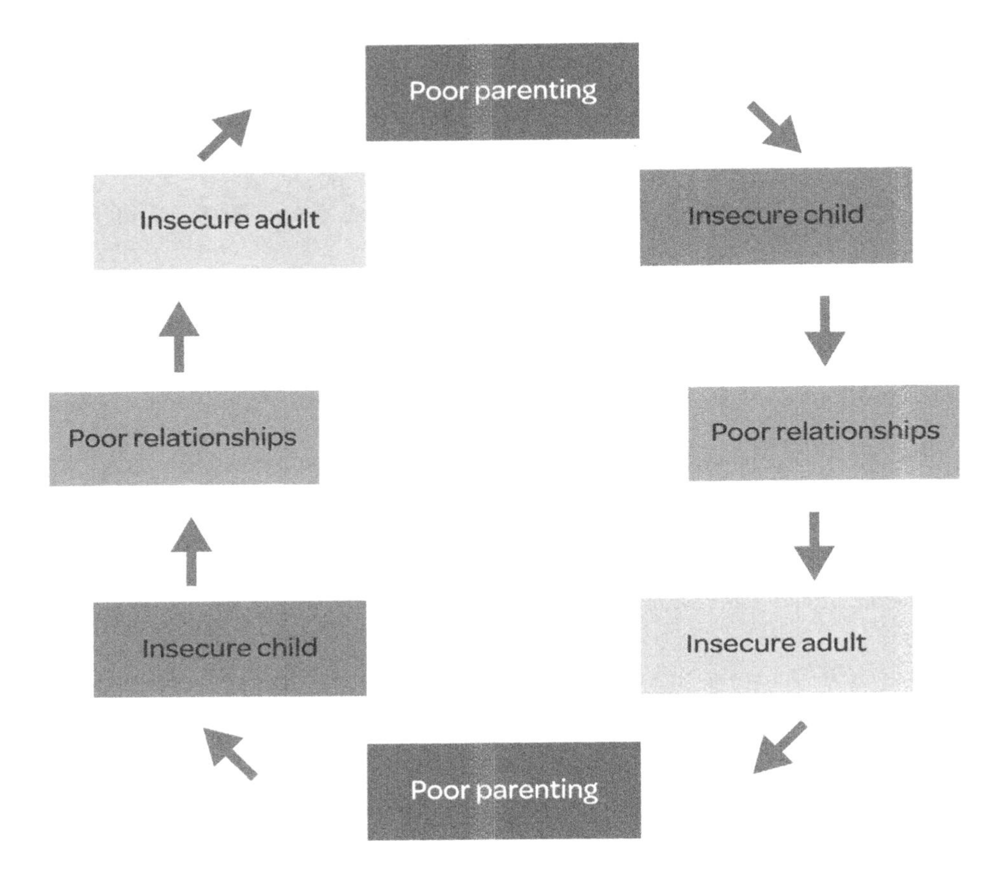

l One of Bowlby's best-known pieces of research demonstrated that deprived children often reproduce themselves. In a study of 44 juvenile thieves, Bowlby found that most of these teenage offenders had suffered significant disruptions in their early childhood relationships. These juvenile offenders were likely to become inadequate parents, in turn producing another generation of emotionally deprived and disadvantaged children[103]. All of this research was before it was discovered that the brain is plastic, so the good news is that we do not have to repeat the cycle any more. We can make the decision to change with our new knowledge on brain plasticity, and our ability to heal from childhood trauma.

Early Relationships with Caregivers

Mary Ainsworth's work in the late 1960s further consolidated the work on Bowlby's attachment theory. Ainsworth built on his foundations and her research confirmed Bowlby's idea that disruption in early childhood relationships can negatively impact on a child's emotional development[104].

Ainsworth's work found that not only was *continuity of care* important for a child to develop a secure attachment, but that care also had to be of a certain *quality*. The care had to be given by a parent or caregiver who was reasonably responsive to the needs of the child. Of course, no parent is perfect, but an adequate *quality of care* is given by a parent who is reliably attuned, or sensitive to, the needs of the infant *most of the time*[105]. This is known as attunement; the ability of a mother to detect and respond to the emotional and physical needs of their small child. Research has consistently found a link between the parents' ability to respond to the infant's needs and the level of security in the infant. In other words, sensitive and responsive caregiving by the parent predicts a more secure attachment in the child. We all want to have secure attachment so that we can enjoy meaningful and enriching relationships[106].

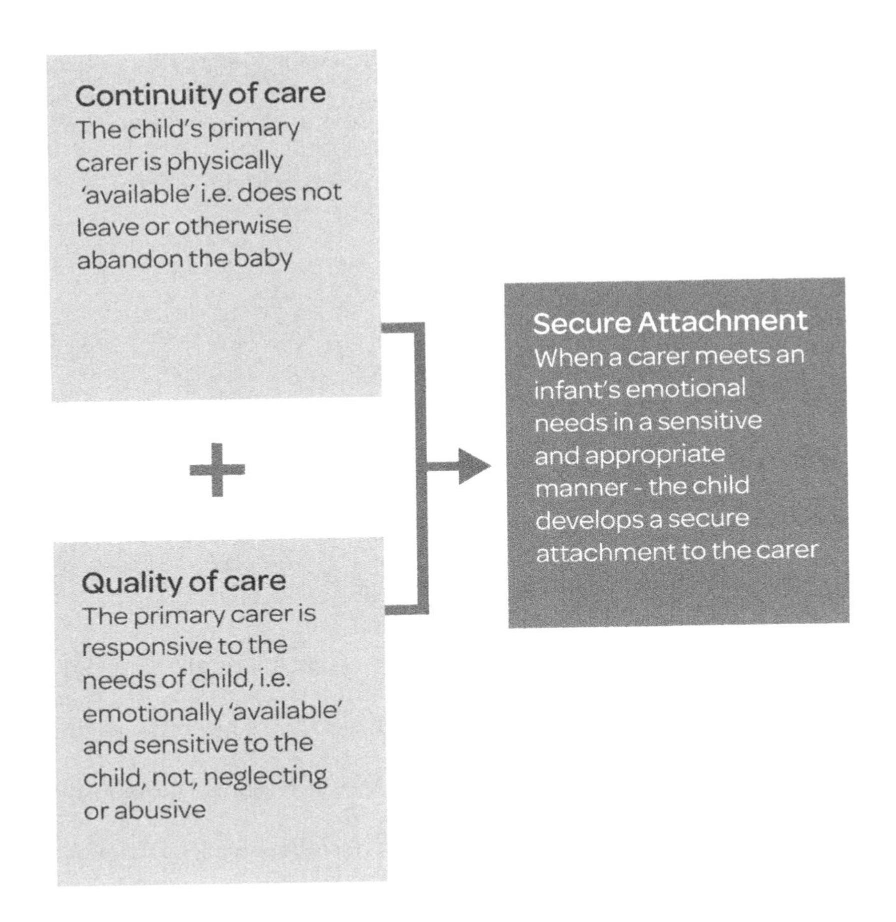

Patricia McKinsey Crittenden (2015) expanded on the work of Bowlby and Ainsworth by researching adult sensitivity within the relationship with their infant. She defines adult sensitivity as 'a pattern of behaviour that pleases the infant and increases the infant's comfort and attentiveness and decreases its stress or disengagement.' In other words, sensitive or responsive caregivers *do not control the baby or put their own emotional needs on the baby, but respond to the infant's needs*[107]. By observing infant responses to caregiver displays of emotion, Crittenden also demonstrated that infants are not easily fooled by false displays of emotion and are very good at picking up the differences between genuine and fake feelings.

In the photo on next page you will see that the baby's body language does not correspond to the loving look on the mother's face. This suggests infants are capable of telling the difference between genuine and false emotion.

False displays of emotion are very damaging to a child. Babies learn about the emotional world through their interaction with others, particularly the mother. If an adult carer's emotional display does not correspond with the child's emotional reality the child may come to doubt their ability to accurately interpret reality. On the simplest level, if a baby cries and the mother laughs at the baby, the baby will be very confused, as the baby has no ability to self-regulate except through the mother.

Types of Attachment

Developed by Ainsworth (1971,1978), the Strange Situation Test is a means of assessing and categorising different patterns of attachment in childhood. The test assesses a child's reaction to being separated from and then reunited with their mother, as well as how they react to an unfamiliar adult. Using the Strange Situation, Ainsworth and colleagues conducted research with a large sample of toddlers (around 18 months old) and found three common patterns of attachment behaviour[108].

Research tells us that the percentages of the various types of attachment are generally fairly consistent across different cultures. There can be small differences due to the different socially accepted ways of child rearing in various countries.

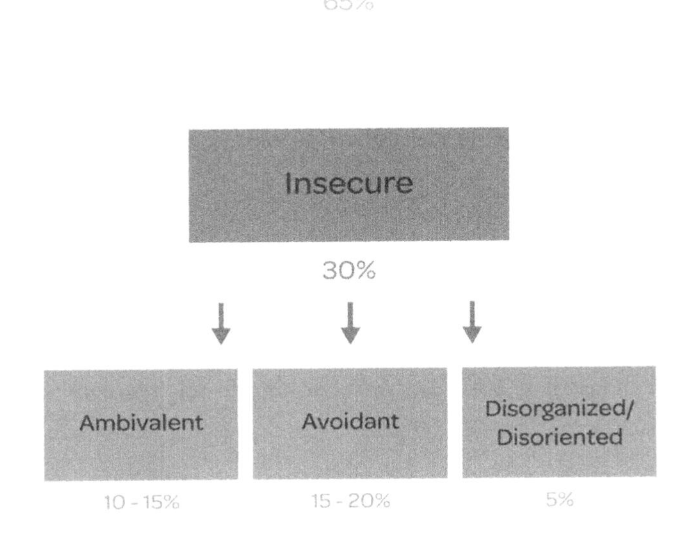

Secure Attachment

The test Ainsworth developed showed that securely attached infants used their mother as a secure base from which to explore the world. They were happy to play and explore the room and regularly checked back on their mother. When the mother left the room the secure children sometimes cried. However, when the mother returned the child was pleased, reducing their crying and approached their mother immediately[109].

Avoidant Attachment

The test showed that avoidant infants were not particularly responsive to their mother when they were present. When the mother left the room, the child did not react. Unlike secure infants, they were not distressed by their mother's absence. Nor did they react much when reunited; they avoided or were slow to greet their mother. They also did not seem to mind the presence of a stranger in the room[110].

Ambivalent Attachment

In the same test these children clung to the mother when they were present and were hesitant to explore their environment. They became upset upon separation and were not usually comforted by the return of their mother. Instead, the child was either passively or actively hostile, sometimes hitting or pushing their mother away[111].

Disorganized / Disorientated Attachment

During their initial testing, Ainsworth and colleagues found that there were some infants whose behaviour did not fit into any of the above categories. These children showed a variety of contradictory patterns of behaviour; they seemed confused, dazed, frozen or disoriented. When reunited with their mothers they might look away while being held by the mother or approach her with flat, depressed emotion. They might cry out unexpectedly after having been comforted by the mother or they might freeze when the mother returned. It is now known that these children are most at risk of developing long-term mental health problems[112].

Early Attachments and Wellbeing Throughout Life

Research consistently shows that patterns of attachment that begin in childhood seem to endure and become features of adult relationships. For example, when there is increased eye contact between parent and child, this will more often than not carry on in later adult relationships they may have. We can also observe mirroring of body language and emotional states between adult couples; adult partners – if they have been securely attached – are attuned to each other's needs. Couples can treat each other as a secure base, a safe haven and a source of comfort and support to which they return in times of stress. Just as children who have a secure attachment relationship will do better both physically and psychologically, we know that adults in stable relationships enjoy better mental and physical health than un-partnered adults[113].

Internal Working Model

Our early attachments to caregivers help us develop our own internal working model. Our internal working model acts as a framework to help us interpret what's happening inside and around us. These frameworks are built with what we have learnt from our early relationships. Essentially, this means that our caregivers teach us how to see other people, ourselves, and the world through the emotional and behavioural responses they gave to us as young children. We internalise the messages they sent us, and have created appropriate internal working models from these messages[114].

So, what kind of messages are sent by mothers, and how are they internalised to create each type of attachment style? How does this impact on our behaviour, emotions and beliefs throughout life?

I want to now discuss each attachment style in more depth. Sadly not many of us who have suffered from the impact of trauma in our lives enjoyed secure attachment with our mother. If we had been securely attached, we would have been able to tell our mother about any abuse that was happening and, as such, she would have responded appropriately and we would not subsequently have internalised the abuse as a trauma. The exception to this is when it is sexual abuse within the immediate family, then even a securely attached child may not tell their mother. The same lack of willingness to tell the mother could also be true when a child is abused by a revered and trusted person within the Church.

Secure Attachment

Secure attachment is exactly as it sounds. It makes the child feel secure in the world. The world is seen as being safe – it is consistent and predictable because the mother consistently and predictably meets the child's needs. Not just meeting their basic physical needs like food and shelter, but their emotional needs as well. Meeting these needs means that the mother is attuned to their child. Secure attachment comes from mothers that are aware of their child's emotional state and respond appropriately. If their child cries, they hold them. If their child smiles at them, they smile back. Of course, this is very unlikely to be all the time. Kids can be challenging, and no one has endless patience. A mother doesn't always respond kindly to every action by a small child. When your three-year-old is yelling and throwing mashed potato around the kitchen after you've had a tough day, you are likely to yell back. That alone isn't going to determine a child to a lifetime of difficulty trusting and interacting with others. The key thing is that the *majority* of the mother's responses help the child learn to regulate their own emotions.

A great example of this learning is the way a child who gets upset cuddles a teddy bear. The child has learnt from their mother that cuddles help them feel better. Secure attachment is formed when a mother is able to repair and re-attune when she realises she is meeting her needs, not the child's. No one is a perfect parent. The mother's ability to meet the child's emotional needs, over time, results in children learning to meet those needs themselves when their mother is not present.

They are able to learn this because having an adult consistently care for them sends the message that they are worth caring for. If they believe this about themselves, they can believe it of other people in the world. These beliefs are part of the securely attached child's internal working model. They grow into adults that view other people as generally safe, and then interact within relationships in ways that reflect this belief. They expect to be treated fairly, and they try to treat others fairly. They aren't scared of being abandoned, hurt, or ignored because this has not been their experience, they don't need to pull people in or push them away. Just like their mother responded consistently and predictably to them, they behave the same with others in their later relationships. The mother acts in place of the parasympathetic nervous system which only develops in the second year of life. The secure child's attitude to the world can be summarized as: *'I'm OK, you're OK'. The world is a safe place.*

However, sadly this isn't the case with insecurely attached children. They have no secure internal working model. And how could they have? If no one cared when you were upset, what do you learn about yourself? What do you learn about other people? Sadly, those of us who have suffered from trauma are more likely to have insecure attachment. There are three primary types of insecure attachment.

Ambivalent Attachment

The ambivalent person can be summarised as: *'I'm not OK, you're OK' – I'm not safe without you.* Individuals with an ambivalent attachment style have usually had intrusive, and sometimes emotionally manipulative mothers. These mothers are generally desperate to be loved but scared of rejection and abandonment, resulting in an intense need to manipulate their child's emotional response to them in order to ensure the mother is not rejected. They are highly likely to show love and affection for their child, but also highly likely to become upset if it is not reciprocated when and how they would like it to be. This places the burden of the mother's emotions on the child. With ambivalent attachment emotional boundaries are blurred and there is often an inherent role-reversal; *the mother attempts to have the child meet their emotional needs.* This often happens with survivors who, in their own childhood, did not have their own emotional needs met so do not know how to meet their own emotional needs. Therefore, they will unconsciously look to their children to meet their needs. Helicopter parenting (hovering over the child) comes out of the mother's own fear. If we experienced ambivalent parenting we have a higher likelihood to parent in an ambivalent style, meaning we look to other people to meet our emotional needs.

The child believes that their emotional needs are best met by others. The child does not learn to regulate their emotional responses because a caregiver that cannot regulate their own emotions cannot assist a child in developing the ability to selfregulate. A mother cannot teach a child to self-soothe if she cannot do it for herself. If the child hasn't learnt to self-soothe, they are more likely to engage in unhelpful (maladaptive) strategies to get their own needs met by others. As the child gets older, they will struggle to function autonomously because they have learnt and believe that their needs can only be met by others. They may have also learnt that they only receive love and affection from someone they care about when they behave a certain way. Because their caregivers are so intent (often unintentionally) on getting their own emotional needs met, they are not attuned to their child and will likely fail to attend to any distress their child experiences unless the child acts out and exhibits extreme behaviour. The mother will give conditional care. In addition to learning that only others can meet their emotional needs, ambivalent children also tend to learn that it is only through extreme and maladaptive displays of emotion that they will get their needs met. Ambivalent style children are often perceived as attention seeking, overly sensitive, overreacting, and even hysterical, but they simply don't *know* how else to elicit comfort when they need it because anything less than hysterical displays of emotion have often failed to arouse their own mother's attention.

Ambivalent attachment styles are likely to manifest within adult relationships as extreme displays of emotion that can often seem out of context. They are often co-dependent, and have a fear of abandonment and therefore use maladaptive (unhelpful) strategies to prevent themselves from being abandoned. They have an inability to take responsibility for their own actions, and usually display irrational anger, fear, or sadness. They do not like to be alone. Behaviour like this makes it very difficult to develop healthy relationships.

An ambivalent child will:

- Be under- emotionally regulated, in other words find it hard to control their emotions
- Look to others to know what they are feeling
- Feel they have to be in a relationship
- Trust other people rather than their own judgment
- Often be the victims of bullying
- At school, they will enjoy more of the teacher's attention than is appropriate, often being 'teacher's pet'
- Seek external validation for their emotions.

As adults, ambivalently attached people will always feel they need to be in a relationship, need constant reassurance from their loved one, and will not like to be separated from their partner for a long period of time.

If this is your attachment style, the invitation is to consciously work on building your own self-love practices, and recognize that ***you can meet your own emotional needs***. Developing your own adult self to meet your own needs is really important.

Avoidant Attachment

Can be summarised as: *'I'm OK, you're not OK' – I need to look after my own needs.*

Individuals with an avoidant attachment style have usually had unresponsive caregivers; the child's emotions and needs have been ignored or minimised. For example, rather than pick up and cuddle a distressed infant, the mother will ignore the baby crying so eventually the child will stop crying, realising that crying will not get their needs met. When a child has an avoidant attachment style, their mother has usually expected more emotional control than the age and level of brain development allows the child to be capable of. Controlled crying, which is a very popular baby-rearing tool, can easily lead to avoidant attachment style. A crying baby needs to be comforted because their developing brain doesn't have the capacity to understand that whatever is causing them discomfort will pass. When a baby cries and is not comforted, they learn that crying is pointless. They stop crying *not* because they're no longer upset but because crying hasn't served the purpose it should have, and their social engagement system has shut down. They learn for survival it is best not to feel.

A small child that seeks comfort after arguing with a young friend might be told that there's no reason to be upset, and be expected to solve the problem alone, without adult assistance. As we know, it is best for children to develop self-reliance and autonomy, however expectations put on children should be ageappropriate.

Essentially, the child's emotions are not recognised and they eventually learn that other people can't ever be relied on to comfort, protect, or help them. The internal working model of avoidantly attached persons is one of necessary self-reliance; 'no one will want to come and help me, so I won't make myself vulnerable by expecting help' is the internal message. This results in adolescents and adults that don't trust other people, are uncomfortable with intimacy, and have trouble seeking help. They're highly independent, often dismissive of their own and others' emotions, have difficulty sustaining meaningful relationships, and are more susceptible to problems with substance abuse[115]. It is clear to see how the attitude towards relationships with an avoidant person is very different to people with ambivalent attachment style.

An avoidant child will:

- Be overly emotionally regulated (they will not feel or express emotions easily)
- Often be considered a 'good' child because they do not cry or display much emotion (they have learned there is no point)
- Be the leaders or bullies at school
- Will receive less of the teacher's attention at school than others
- Be notoriously independent (Illusionary sense of self sufficiency)
- Trust no one but themselves
- Display early independence.

As adults, they will not have a great need for closeness in their relationships, may cover their pain with addictions such as alcohol, gambling work, etc., and will not trust or reveal themselves easily. People with avoidant attachment are likely to not remember much of their childhood and minimise the impact.

If you are avoidant in attachment style, the invitation is to work on trying to share thoughts and feelings with others, *try to recognise that others do want to know how you are feeling* and help you when needed.

Disorganised / Disorientated Attachment

This could be summarized as: *'I'm not OK, you're not OK' – the world and everyone in it is unsafe.* There is a general consensus that disorganised attachment is associated with very early life abuse, usually perpetrated by the child's mother or primary caregiver. The child's relationship with the mother is a fearful one – they are frightened of their caregiver. In addition to being scared that their mother will hurt them, the child's fear is also related to the inconsistency of her responses. Abusive mothers can also be capable of showing love and affection; sometimes they *do* respond appropriately to a child's emotions. However, this places the child in an impossible position.

It may not only be the mother who makes the world so unsafe – these messages may come from a significant other in the very earliest years. The child learns that the person they rely on to provide them with safety and emotional stability is scary, dangerous, and capable of hurting them. Furthermore, there is no way to escape this situation, and often no way of predicting which behaviours will elicit which responses.

For example, let's say that on Tuesday morning, mum wakes her young child with a huge smile and hug. On Wednesday, she doesn't wake him at all and doesn't respond to his greeting. On Thursday, she wakes him by yelling angrily that he has to get up right now and clean his room. On Friday, she smiles and hugs him again, then hits him five minutes later. The child has done exactly the same thing each morning; he's simply woken up. Yet mum's behaviour has changed entirely from one day to the next. Because this child has no possible way of determining why mum's behaviour changes, he assumes it must be something he's doing or not doing. If the same thing results in different responses, the child will be forever confused and fearful.

The consequences of this kind of frightening caregiver inconsistency extend beyond confusion; children begin to develop trauma responses. They are usually left almost constantly in a state of hyper-arousal because they must always be alert to any potential signs that their mother's behaviour will change.

Ultimately, they can also become very dissociative and disconnect themselves from their surroundings. Very young children need help to calm themselves when stressed, and if caregivers cannot be relied on to do this, the child is left desperately and blindly trying everything they can think of to lessen the impact of their overwhelming emotional reactions. Children under the age of two have few resources available to do this, and so patterns of hypo- and hyper- arousal, dissociation, and behavioural and emotional dysregulation develop.

They learn that not only are they incapable of eliciting a safe response from their caregiver, but that they are incapable of feeling safe within themselves and therefore within the world[116].

This makes patterns of interpersonal behaviour difficult to discern with disorganised attachment styles because it manifests as a seemingly unpredictable combination of both avoidant and ambivalent behaviour. Some children with disorganised attachment styles will indiscriminately display affection and dependence towards people they barely know, while others will seem wary and reluctant to engage with others at all, including familiar people. As children and adults, their behaviour often oscillates between extreme co-dependency and complete rejection, coupled with maladaptive self-regulation strategies such as aggression and self-harm. Due to the physical effects of trauma on the developing brain, particularly memory systems, the individual usually doesn't develop a sense of themselves as a whole or complete person. Again, because of trauma's effect on their brain, they show far higher rates of dissociation, where they experience themselves or the world as unreal, feel separated from their bodies, or in extreme cases switch between entirely different personality states. Due to all this, far higher rates of mental health diagnoses are seen in individuals with disorganised/disorientated attachment style than in any other attachment style.

The internal working model of those who have this attachment style is to trust no one, as they understand the world as an unsafe place. They are driven by a pervasive sense that they are not safe either, so if this is your attachment style, the way forward is *to work towards feeling safe as an absolute priority*. If you are disorganised/disorientated in attachment, it is more difficult to start healing because you are likely to not trust yourself or a support person. Again, establishing a sense of safety is key. Therefore, you will need to find a therapist and partner who is consistent in their behaviour towards you.

You will need to work hard on grounding, staying in your body, finding what you need in order to feel safe, and being kind to yourself. In recognising that this is your attachment style it may take a significant amount of time into your healing before you will really be able to trust another person enough to have a satisfactory relationship.

If you feel you do not fit into either the profile of an ambivalent or avoidant attachment style, then you may well be disorganised/disorientated. It is important to realise that our attachment style affects the way we relate to others for our entire lives unless we heal from the parenting we received. Also, usually our children will have the same attachment style as ourselves. Therefore, to break the cycle of abuse we need to work towards changing our attachment style.

All of us with insecure attachment will struggle to believe the world is a safe place. Learning safety and trust are keys for all of us, and our environment is of paramount importance to ensuring we are able to meet our own needs.

If you are *ambivalent*, you might find it helpful to work on the following:

- Containing your emotions by loving yourself and self-nurturing
- Learning to feel your own feelings regardless of how others are feeling
- Trusting yourself, trusting your opinions, trusting your feelings, trusting your thoughts
- Meeting your own emotional needs and learning to believe that you can and it is OK to do so
- Decide to get your needs met by being straight forward and just asking rather than using manipulative behaviour
- Recognise that others have different emotional needs, and they can love you and not need to express it all the time

- Work on developing healthy boundaries.

If you are *avoidant*, you might find it helpful to work on the following:

- Trying to let people know how you are feeling
- Trying to recognise how you are feeling and to express it, even to yourself
- Reaching out to others
- Trust, trust, trust
- Expressing your needs to others and letting others meet your needs
- Asking for help
- Allowing yourself to be vulnerable in front of others
- Being less reactive to people who openly express their needs, recognise they have different emotional needs to yourself.

If you are *disorganised*, you might find it helpful to work on the following:

- Discovering what you need in order to feel safe
- Ensuring that you live in a safe environment
- Trust, trust, trust
- Keeping grounded
- Learning to believe that you are lovable by doing some of the exercises in Chapter Fifteen
- Working on self-nurturing
- Try using a hammock and a weighted blanket to give you the feeling of being nurtured and supporting your body to feel contained.

All insecure attachment styles may find it difficult to self-nurture and self-love; it may feel unfair that you have to look after yourself as the brain is wired to need someone else to meet our emotional needs. I suggest you fight that feeling as only *we can reparent ourselves, no one else is going to do it and nor should they.* For all of us, the goal is to work towards a secure attachment.

Avoidant / Ambivalent Relationships

A big problem can occur if you have married someone who has a different attachment style to your own. If you are lucky and are in a relationship with a person with secure attachment style that will naturally help you to become more secure. On the other hand, if an avoidant attachment style person is in a relationship with an ambivalent attachment style person they will want to have their emotional needs met in vastly different ways, making life together very difficult. The avoidant does not like overt displays of emotion, whereas the ambivalent person needs displays of affection to feel safe. An ambivalent person needs to be in contact with their beloved, whereas an avoidant has no such need. It is by recognising these different needs that you can improve your relationship. *You are each hard wired with totally different emotional needs* and it takes time and patience to change your emotional needs.

I believe that I will have totally healed from my childhood when I can truly feel that I have a secure attachment style.

If you are still feeling unsure about what your attachment style may be there are several tests you can do on the internet to discover your attachment style. The best one I have found and with the best reputation is 'Gottman's: Understanding Your Partner's Attachment Style'.

CHAPTER SEVEN
The Importance of Safety

As we embrace our healing journey, the most important single thing is to ensure that we *feel safe*, and ensure that we are living in a safe environment. Safety is the most important consideration because *feeling* safe is necessary for recovery to be possible. A physical and emotional sense of safety needs to be the foundational focus of our healing[117]. Without both ***being*** safe and ***feeling*** safe, healing can only occur very slowly and falteringly, if at all, as the sympathetic nervous system will continue to be on high alert. Without a safe place to live we will react not respond, and we will utilise our coping mechanisms to hide the lack of feeling safe. Coping mechanisms tend to be not very conducive to enjoying life.

'Being' safe is not the same as 'feeling' safe. You can 'be' as safe as humanly possible from harm, even wrapped in cotton wool, and yet still 'feel' unsafe. You are not 'crazy' or 'mad' for feeling unsafe. It is a way that you may often have felt throughout your childhood because then you were often not safe and some of you may not even know 'being safe' as a feeling. This feeling of 'being safe' is the feeling I want you to discover and then be able to identify, remember, and feel willing and able to recreate whenever you need to. Those of you with a disorganised attachment style may find both feeling and being safe very difficult.

As some of you may not know this feeling of being safe, the first step in healing is to be able to identify how you feel when you are safe. It is important that you are able to recognise how it feels, what happens in your body when you do *not* feel safe, and also to know how you behave when you do not feel safe.

All of our coping mechanisms are to help us feel safe – addictions, controlling behaviour, outbursts of anger, and disconnecting from others all happen when we do not feel safe. Once we feel safe we can start letting go of the need to isolate, to be angry, to put up a wall against everyone.

When we are not grounded, it is because we do not feel safe. We cannot be happy or heal if we do not feel safe. You cannot start to release your fear or heal unless you feel safe. In the next chapter you will start learning how to heal and I talk about connecting with the inner child, however this is unlikely to be possible if you do not feel safe. Later on, once you have made the connection, you can rely on your inner child to tell you when something is not safe. It takes time, effort, empathy, and a lot of patience to create an ongoing and sustainable feeling of safety. Discovering that feeling of safety depends on how long and how much trauma you experienced in your childhood.

Feeling safe is entirely dependent on your current circumstances, and whether you are in a safe house with a safe partner or friend. To help with feeling safe, having a physical safe place is an essential first step to ensuring you are 'physically safe'.

Physical Safety

Ideally your home needs to feel and be safe. At the very least, you need one safe place that is yours alone. For me, I have a little room off my bedroom and no one – and I mean no one – may enter without my permission. When I am in there, everyone knows not to disturb me.

You might choose anywhere inside or outside; it could be a tree in the garden, your bed or a place in your home that is truly yours. No one can come into your safe place without permission, and that includes your children, partner, or parents.

Obviously, we are not physically safe if we live with physically or emotionally abusive people or people who cross our boundaries. If the person you live with is unsafe or if you continue relations with unsafe people, you will likely find it very hard to feel safe and very hard to move forward, which means you are more likely to try to survive by using old coping mechanisms. However, be kind to yourself as it may take time and support to recognize that you deserve to feel safe, and for you to find the courage to rid yourself of unsafe people, particularly if the unsafe person provides you with financial support. You could not choose as a child, but you *can* choose now. It is *your choice*.

As well as having a physically safe place to live it is also a good idea to have a safe place you can go to, maybe the beach or the bush – anywhere that feels safe when you are there. It is also a good idea to have a safe place in your imagination to use when you are away from home. The more safe places you have, the better.

To discover where might be a safe place for you, sit for a while and think about where you might feel at ease. If you cannot think of anywhere, then a first step could be to create an imaginary place. My first safe place was sitting on a cloud way above the world, I could see in all directions, and I felt very light and as if I did not have to support myself at all. It was only after some healing work that I was able to find an actual physical safe place for me.

A safe place will not be created in a similar environment where the abuse occurred; if you suffered a lot of trauma inside, you are likely to find your safe place is outside, perhaps in nature. If your bedroom was safe that may still be your safe place. If you escaped by climbing up a tree, then sitting in a tree may still give you a feeling of safety.

Examples of an imaginary safe place are:

- Sitting on a cloud
- A room with everything you want and value in it
- Deep down at the bottom of the ocean

Examples of an actual safe place could be:

- On the beach
- In your bedroom
- A favourite place in the house
- In the bush
- In your car
- In the high branches of a tree

- Near water

My safe place is at Heal For Life, on the property, on a bench that is near the dam. It is safe for me because I can see if anyone is coming from any direction, and water has always been safe for me. I was always safe on summer holidays when we stayed in a house by the water. For those of you who have more than one inner child, they may all need a different safe place. Often people with several internal children establish a house internally and create a different room for each child.

There are no rules or limitations on what our safe place is. You will know if it is right because it will feel safe. It is important that we continually check that the place we have chosen is still safe and know that we can always create a new one if we want or need to. A safe place can be destroyed if someone we don't like, or who is unsafe, comes into our safe place without our permission.

It is equally important that our safe place is not dependent on the presence of any other person, animal or object, because we must feel safe within ourselves. If we only feel safe when our dog is with us, what will happen when the dog passes away?

A crucial note to remember is to never allow an abuser into your safe place, and most people find it is best not to work on trauma memories in their safe place. It might be a good idea to view your safe place also as a place where you self-nurture.

To summarise, a safe place needs to be:

- A place where you are comfortable on your own
- A place where you can control who comes in
- A place you have easy access to.

Suggestions

Can you find a safe physical place that no one enters unless invited?

Or do you have a safe place you can go to in your imagination?

Spend time deciding on both a physical and emotional safe place you can go to.

When you think you have identified a safe place for yourself, spend some time being aware of your body and your bodily reaction when you are in that place.

When you are in a safe place you will have the physical signs that you are in the parasympathetic state, you may notice the following: relaxed muscles, slow breathing, slow heart beat, regular body temperature, a still body.

If you do not feel safe your sympathetic nervous system will be in a constant state of high arousal: tense muscles, faster breathing, fast heartbeat, fidgety, a restless body.

Emotional Safety

'While multitudes of theories and techniques to facilitate healing abound, in nearly fifteen years of clinical practice, I have found one element to be the most fundamental. To create an environment where emotional, physical and spiritual healing can take place, emotional safety is a cornerstone.' (Marks, 2011)

A lack of emotional safety means that even though you are physically safe, you are still on high alert and internally you do not feel OK. It is likely that if you're reading this book, someone you were dependent on, or someone you trusted, broke trust, and violated your boundaries and allowed you little or no privacy, choice, freedom or respect. In order to feel safe, you will need to feel that you are being granted privacy, choice, freedom, and respect.

We cannot feel safe unless we exercise good boundaries – we have to not allow people to impose on us verbally or emotionally. I repeat: ***we cannot feel psychologically safe if we continue to live with unsafe people.*** It is our responsibility to ensure that we maintain a safe space for ourselves.

Defining who is safe can be difficult. We can think someone is unsafe, although they do not intend harm because they remind us of an unsafe person. If someone does not feel safe, try to decide what about that person feels unsafe to you: is it the way they look, or the sound of their voice? That may determine the underlying cause, either that they are themselves unsafe, or that they are reminding you of an unsafe person. I invite you to look at how this might apply to you.

We have found that people cannot feel emotionally safe if key abusive people from their childhood are still in their lives. This disempowers and can really hold back healing. When one of our perpetrators is still around it is hard to really acknowledge the negative treatment or behaviour that you experienced when you were younger at the hands of this person. Give yourself permission to know that you matter, and that it is not fair to you if you have to see the perpetrator. Often it is at a family event because the family may think that somehow it will all be OK if you can 'get over it'. This is very difficult and unfair. You may choose to make the decision to miss the event to honour yourself, or go and feel unsafe and suffer just to keep the peace. I decided long ago that my safety mattered most, therefore I do not see members of my family who refuse to acknowledge that my father sexually abused me. It hurts, but I am honouring myself, and my own emotional safety in choosing to make this decision.

Sometimes, as a form of self-protection, we may protect ourselves by blaming ourselves for the abuse. For example, if your mother paid no attention to you and was very emotionally destructive to you, belittled you, and never applauded or validated you, you may subconsciously compensate by always trying to gain your mother's love, thereby denying the pain and fear of that rejection. This denial will make you feel emotionally unsafe.

Part of feeling safe is participating in activities that encourage you to be in your body. Any form of movement, particularly to music can help. Yoga is also terrific as an ongoing support as it operates on two levels – both the mind and the body. Research has shown yoga to be effective for assisting in healing for survivors of trauma[118]. However, if you find it too overwhelming to be in touch with your body, leave yoga until you find it a helpful resource.

What Safety Feels Like

For some of you, the feeling of safety may be so foreign that it might be helpful if I offer some ways you can know that you are safe.

You are safe if:

- You can breathe deeply
- You can express your emotions
- You can fall and stay asleep
- You can express gratitude and feel loved
- You are able to notice others and have the ability to separate your emotional space from other people
- You can be your authentic self.

Suggestions on How to Implement Emotional Safety

- Do not allow others to impose their emotional needs on you
- Maintain healthy, safe, relational boundaries, especially around sexual behaviour
- Do not allow unsafe people to be with you

- Have clear boundaries and be able to say NO when you want to
- Have the ability to ground yourself. You will find a few grounding exercises at the end of this book
- Work out what you need to in order to feel safe and HONOUR this
- Know who you can trust with your story and who will keep it confidential
- Allow yourself to acknowledge your feelings to yourself. It is not essential that others do.
- Always work on keeping your left brain in charge and present
- Be honest and ensure those you choose to surround yourself with are able to do that too
- Avoid having anyone exert abusive power over you
- Remember that you always have a choice in how you act and respond in any circumstance.

Safety in the Workplace

Safety in the workplace is a tricky one because it is outside our control, and that can be very triggering for survivors of trauma. If we have an abusive boss or workplace colleague it can be very, very challenging. What can be very difficult in a workplace environment is that we may not feel listened to, accepted, validated, or honoured. This can be triggering with disastrous consequences.

Some people's behaviour can be manipulative and tricky to navigate in the workplace. Additionally, survivors of trauma can often be triggered by those in authority, particularly in an authoritarian workplace as a result of their own feelings of powerlessness. However, an ***authoritative*** workplace can feel safe. As workers, we actually feel safest when we have a superior who is clear in their requirements and observes healthy emotional boundaries (that means they do not ask you to be involved in their personal lives, or comment on yours) – this is an authoritative leader.

All of this is why Trauma Informed Workplaces are the best places for survivors. They will state what is required of workers without using power over their subordinates in the workplace. An authoritarian leader is arbitrary in using power and imposes their demands without fair consideration of others. Here is a chart we have drawn up to determine the difference.

NOT TRAUMA INFORMED	TRAUMA INFORMED
Power over	Power with
You can't change	The brain is plastic
Judging	Observing
People need fixing first	People need safety first
Operate from dominant culture who are right	Cultural humility
People are out to get you, don't trust	People will live up to the trust you give them
There is Right and Wrong	Multiple viewpoints
Helping	Learning
You're crazy	It makes sense from your experience

NOT TRAUMA INFORMED (cont.)	TRAUMA INFORMED (cont.)
Obedience / Compliance	Empowerment / Collaboration
Need to know is the basis for communication	Transparency
Deal with the presenting issue	Consider whole person and their history
Us verses them	We're all in this together
Labels / Pathology	Acceptance
Fear-based	Empathy-based
I'm here to fix you	Supporting healing

People make bad choices	People who feel unsafe do unsafe things
Behaviour is viewed as a problem	Behaviour recognised as indicative of child
What's wrong with you	What happened to you
Blame/ Shame	Show respect
Difficult behaviour needs to be contained/controlled	Difficult behaviour is a sign of not feeling safe
Object is to do things the right way	Object is to connect
Prescriptive	Choices
People are bad	People are doing the best they can
Consider only research and evidence	Consider lived experience

Working in an unsafe environment can be very detrimental to healing, and be very invalidating to your inner self. If you are querying whether your workplace is safe it may help to ask yourself questions such as the following:

- Can people discuss their own opinions knowing they will be listened to?
- Are staff members blamed when anything goes wrong rather than it be considered as a possible system failure?
- Are staff members asked for their opinions? Or is the boss' viewpoint the only one that is acceptable?

If you do not feel safe in the workplace you can try to create your own internal safety to minimise your reaction to the environment. Although difficult, where you work is a choice, you can always choose to find another place of employment. However, before making any hasty decisions, the best course of action is always to try to de-trigger yourself, ensuring you are using your left, rational brain when communicating, and use non-violent communication.

When we do not feel safe, it is often because we are frightened by something that reminds us of our childhood and then we may become reactive in order to protect our wounded self. We may turn to anger, often with disastrous results. Try to learn to recognise when you do not feel safe and take it as a warning signal that you have become triggered and try to detrigger as outlined in Chapter Four.

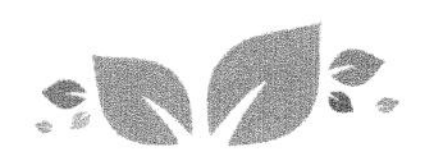

CHAPTER EIGHT
Connection With The Inner Child And Inner Self

Based on my experience as an early childhood educator and art therapist, I have concluded that we cannot eradicate child abuse in our culture without healing the wounds of our own Inner Child. We will never cure the epidemic of child abuse in the outer world until we stop abusing the Child in our inner world. (Capacchione 1991, p. 22)[119].

The inner child or inner self is that part of ourselves that holds the emotions and feelings from childhood.

In the chapter on Transactional Analysis (TA) you will also read another perspective of understanding the child self; there it is called the 'child ego state'.

The greatest change happened in my healing when I realised what this 'inner child' stuff was all about. As I mentioned in the first chapter, reading Lucia Capacchione's book, and other books on the subject, helped me realise the importance of this concept, and this realisation led to the successful development of our Heal For Life program. When I first read about the inner child I certainly recognised that this was a part of myself that I had totally ignored. A highly recommended first step, as suggested by Capacchione, was to draw a self-portrait of my inner child using my non-dominant hand[120]. When I saw what I had drawn, it convinced me of the importance of recognising my own inner child. This is what I drew:

This indicated to me that I had imprisoned my child self, and that she wanted to be free. Her feet were outside the prison I had built around her.

I have certainly learned over the years that the longer I spend with my inner child each day, the greater the results and personal benefits. When I connect with this part of myself I discover how I am feeling and what is happening in my ignored internal world.

There are many words that can be used to describe the inner self, the wounded part of ourselves that has been traumatised: the inner self, inner child, the wounded self, the emotional self, other self, feelings, intuition, or even the right brain. *The terminology is not important*. However, it is important that you use the word or words that work best for you. Recognising, and trying to learn how to relate to this wounded part of self is, I believe, necessary for healing. I believe that it is essential to recognise this part as a specific separate component of ourselves, with different motivations and often different feelings to those of our adult self. When we avoid connecting with this wounded part we suffer from dissociation, disconnection from self and body, and other symptoms that reinforce our original trauma. If we ignore this part of ourselves we can go into depression and constant anxiety and generate the onset of physical ailments. However by recognising our feelings we can help ourselves to stay healthy in mind and body.

To recognise this part of ourselves encourages us to acknowledge rather than deny our childhood and the associated painful emotions. Joy and the thrill of being alive is also a key part of this emotional child part of ourselves.

Connecting with our inner child is the hardest part of healing for many of us, as we have often denied or are fearful of our child self, given the suffering from childhood we have needed to suppress in order to survive. This avoidance is natural: our brains are designed to avoid re-visiting painful emotions such as, fear and horror. It is natural to not want to connect with the painful memories of what happened, however, I have found connecting with this child part of myself is the most effective and simplest way to heal[121].

If you have recognised that your attachment style is avoidant and you are rather disconnected from your emotions, then you may have difficulty connecting with your inner child. Be patient and, importantly, try to not let your left brain think whatever you do is nonsense or is just your imagination, instead try to discover what your inner child is trying to say. If you have a more ambivalent attachment style you may not find the connection as difficult, though you may find it difficult to contain the emotion your inner child is expressing. Those with a disorganised attachment style may find this connection very difficult or very easy[122].

Whether ambivalent, avoidant or disorganised we all have a smaller corpus callosum so it is hard for us to connect our left and right brain so our adult self can support our child self.

A few people find that they have several children inside them, some find they have hundreds, some find they have two, some discover they have a boy and a girl, or one child at different ages. I have met survivors who have an animal as well – it is likely that this happened when, for them, being human was proving very unsafe. Each of us had a unique way that our brain coped with the awfulness of what was happening, so please be understanding of yourself with whatever you discover. Essentially, it may be said that trauma experienced early and often, demands that individuals need to build more sophisticated internal structures to be resilient in the face of extreme adversity[123]. There is no norm. Some people dissociate and switch from one child part to another. *What is always essential* is to ensure that your adult self is always present and stays present when you connect with your inner child, there is no healing in regressing or totally becoming the child, as this is *unhealthy and unsafe.*

I believe that learning the truth of what happened to me in my childhood was essential for me to understand myself. I have found listening and learning about what really happened in my childhood has made sense of ME as a person in the world.

As explained, trauma is contained in the right hemisphere of the brain, in our unconscious, therefore we can only connect to our inner self through our right brain to do healing work and ***only when we feel safe.*** Paradoxically, we can also find a perfect way to connect with our fear-based emotions and child self is when we are reminded of a traumatic event by being triggered, and then, if we chose to, we can unlock the original trauma that the trigger is trying to remind us of by connecting with our inner self and remembering the trauma.

In order to connect with our inner child or children, we need to find a safe way to access the right brain. It is critical that we keep our left brain engaged as well, otherwise we would be regressing, and if this is the case the child is at risk of being re-traumatised rather than healed. As mentioned above, ***it is key to our healing that we connect with our inner child with our adult self always present*** so the adult self can offer support, listen, and nurture afterwards. Sounds odd, I know, but trust me it works! This way of working also helps to build a stronger connection between the right and left brain.

How to Access the Right Brain:

1. Through Music

Consciously try to connect to your body while listening to loving music. Also using music as part of a visualisation can be wonderful.

2. When You Are Triggered

Rather than just de-triggering, if you are in the right place you can allow yourself to discover what has triggered you and identify when this happened before, in childhood. This can give you an easy access to a trauma and your inner child.

3. Through Your Body

If you notice you are holding your body in a particular way you can bring your awareness or talk to that part of your body, for example you may have a pain or sensation in a part of your body that is similar to the original trauma. Start to practice becoming aware of your body and your own movement.

4. Writing With Your Non-dominant Hand

This can be helpful. Write a question to your inner child with your dominant hand (the hand you usually write with) then, with your non-dominant hand, write an answer (without judgment). As a left brained dominant person, I have found this method very effective.

5. Through Drawing

The first and simplest thing to do is to draw your inner child with your non-dominant hand. Or by just letting your non-dominant hand draw whatever he or she feels like, again try not to judge or think 'how stupid' or 'what nonsense' because these are all left brain thoughts, and you will never get anywhere if you judge yourself as you try to make this important connection.

6. Play

Doing childlike things or playing, while of course keeping your adult self present to observe (ensuring safety).

7. Be Creative

One way is to use clay, just feeling it, holding it, kneading it, not thinking about creating something specific, just seeing what comes up. Seeing what feeling is created by the action and then connecting with the child self that felt that way as a child.

8. Sitting in Silence

This is helpful as it allows you to stop and connect with your emotions (the right hemisphere is non-verbal).

9. Through Nightmares or Flashbacks

Instead of being terrified of nightmares or flashbacks, try to welcome them as an opportunity to heal. Allow yourself to remember what was in the nightmare or flashback and then follow the process in the next chapter. Always love and nurture yourself after a flashback or nightmare and allow yourself to recognise the feeling and fear.

10. Through Visualisation

Visualisation can be achieved by listening to someone leading a guided meditation. Do not worry if you cannot see anything during a visualisation as that is not important. Often as survivors we will not see in pictures, particularly if we are avoidant in our attachment style. In my experience, those with an ambivalent attachment style are more likely to see in pictures than those with avoidant attachment style, and a disorganised attachment style can be either. The point is that we are all different, so try not to be hard on yourself if you find visualisations difficult. They are extremely effective and can be incredibly useful even when we don't feel as if it is doing any good! You can use music in the visualisation to further enhance engagement of the right brain. Some people with many children however find visualisation very difficult and unhelpful as their brain cannot decide who is doing the visualisation.

Here is an example of an effective visualisation:

Close your eyes if you feel safe enough to do so (if not, find a place to concentrate on the floor). Feel your feet on the ground and your body where it connects to the chair or lounge.

Be aware of sounds around you. The sounds will come and go, just as your thoughts come and go; just accept them. Be aware of your breathing – there's no need try to change your breathing. Give yourself permission to be here... this is your time, and you deserve it.

Notice anything that may get in the way of relaxing (e.g. negative thoughts), and put them aside. Notice any sensations, tensions or pain in your body... accept that they are there.

You might like to picture yourself surrounded by a bubble of light and love. Imagine a warm, healing light full of love (or God's love) above your head. Imagine this light entering your head and slowly flowing down through your head making your head feel soft and warm.

Feel the softness around your eyes, your cheeks, loosening your jaw. Feel the light slowly moving down through your neck to your body; let the love soften your shoulders, flow through your arms and down through your chest warming your heart, then down through your chest and into your stomach and hips, flowing down through your thighs, your calves and through to your feet. Feel all the love flowing through your feet connecting you to the wonderful earth.

Picture yourself beside a wise old tree. Hug, hold or look at the strong tree. Gain strength and courage by being with the tree. Let the tree give you the strength to put aside your fears or anxieties.

You might like to hang on the tree any negative thoughts, or concerns – look around from the tree.

You see a path going through the grass into the bush; it is inviting you to follow it. You follow the path enjoying the bushes, trees and flowers on either side of the path. You can feel the sun on your back as you walk along the path; a rabbit scurries across the path. You can see an open gate in front of you. Beyond the gate is a beautiful garden.

Walk through the gate into the garden, close the gate and lock it, if you want to, so you feel safe. Do anything else you want to ensure this is your safe place.

Observe the garden, trees, plants, flowers, and birds. Smell the plants, see the bright colours, the butterflies floating between the trees and plants, the beautiful flowers. Hear the sound of water right at the heart of the garden; walk through the garden to its very centre there you see the most perfect, clear water. It is so pure and inviting.

Maybe find somewhere to sit, a bench or chair, and pause quietly for a moment.

You feel someone is with you in the garden – you look up and see a child in the garden with you.

Notice what the child is doing. Notice how the child is feeling. Notice what the child looks like; notice the age of the child. How do you feel about this child? What do you want to do? Are you going to reach out to greet the child? Or are you going to wait for the child to come to you? Do you want to sit close or hug your child?

Take the opportunity to spend time with your child.

PAUSE

PLAY soothing music that you have chosen if you find it helpful.

Slowly bring your awareness back into the room, open your eyes, wiggle your fingers and toes.

Be present to listen to your child. Do whatever you would like to do in order to discover what your inner child is feeling, needing or wanting to communicate.

Whatever kind of visualisation you choose to use, it needs to engage the senses (smell, taste, sound, sight, touch), as this is the way trauma memory is activated in the amygdala and right hemisphere brain areas.

Particularly in the early stages of healing, try to commit to spending time each day with finding out how your inner child is feeling. The more time you spend the faster you will be able to process and integrate past traumatic events. You can honour your inner child and do each week (or as often as possible) something, that you feel your inner child or children want to do, however silly it may seem. This process is compensating or correcting what we missed out on in childhood. We are listening to ourselves in a way that did not happen in childhood. We are honouring our feelings as being important. Remember this connection with our right brain self is necessary because we have a smaller corpus callosum, which means that we have less integration between our left and right hemisphere, making it difficult to know what our inner child wants to do or feel. Very often we do not know how we are feeling even if the inner self is affecting our behaviour. If you are ambivalent or disorganised in attachment style it will also be very important to continually work on developing your adult self to comfort and support your inner child[124].

If You Find You Are Resistant

If you are resistant to connecting with your inner child there will be a number of good reasons for this, including:

- You are not feeling safe.
- You are absolutely terrified of accessing the fear in case it is too overwhelming – you have spent so long surviving by not remembering that it is difficult for the brain to change and start to remember, feeling all the hurt and pain.
- You do not think what happened was bad enough to justify connecting and healing, it may be easier to blame yourself than your (mum, dad, friend, brother, etc.) whom you may feel loving towards. You may not want to risk damaging this relationship.
- It feels safer to stay in your left hemisphere and talk a lot, hoping that will somehow help (it won't).
- If you suffered from less than adequate mothering in your first year of life you may not know how to be loving enough to yourself to connect.
- You may have several children inside you and one may be protective of the others, and not let you connect with others.
- Fear, fear, fear.

There is another way to start if you don't want to start with a visualisation. This is particularly important if you feel out of control and overwhelmed by your emotions. Give love to your inner self, think loving thoughts, and stroke the top of your left arm with your right hand. Hug yourself while picturing hugging your inner child – healing cannot start while we are frightened of, or have hateful or angry feelings towards, our inner pain/child. This will help you stabilize and strengthen your adult self[125].

Resistance is natural, however connecting is your choice. I have found that if I give love to my inner child it helps me profoundly. If abandonment is the issue, there are exercises specifically designed to support this – see Chapter Thirteen for the doll exercise. Allow yourself to try to accept that if you are feeling an impact from your childhood in your adult life, something did happen that needs your attention, and you do deserve to heal and give your inner self love.

Healing takes time and patience, and most of all it takes a daily commitment to love and care for our inner child/children. I believe we need to listen to our child, and accept what the child may say happened to us or how he, she or they are feeling. Ignoring or pretending it didn't happen is like leaving a wound bleeding and unattended and then wondering why it's not healing.

When we start to heal by addressing these painful wounds, just like physical wounds initially they need to be tended to every day, they need soothing and attention otherwise the wound becomes infected and spreads, causing enormous hurt. Don't let your wounds worsen – nurse them, help them, love them, and heal them by consciously giving them love. It is necessary you acknowledge to yourself how much your childhood events hurt you and allow yourself to make the choice to heal.

Every time someone rings me in crisis who has attended a healing week my first question is usually 'when did you last connect with your inner child?' the answer invariably is, 'Oh not for ages, I've been too busy, too distracted, been feeling so low'. Once I have suggested they spend the evening re-establishing contact, change occurs for them and I know they are back on the path of healing. ***We cannot heal unless we devote time and love to our inner child.***

How empty would the sky appear, if there were no stars at night?
No shooting stars to wish on, or moon to shine its light.
The ocean would be incomplete if it did not touch the land
No weathered rocks to crash on, or waves to wet the sand…
All elements to creation are dependent on another
How strange, my special child should live without a friend or mother
I long so much to know her and to feel that she is dear
Though no matter how I wish or pray I cannot hold her near
The shame I hide weighs heavily, she feels it every day
Yet all she dreams is for my voice to tell her… 'It's okay'
She gives her love so openly and seems to understand
Why sometimes I can't pick her up or hold her tiny hand
Her words are too young to express the pain my mind now knows
But patiently she smiles and waits for seeds of love to grow.
Though I cannot say I love her or tell her of my fears,
I shall offer her my empty arms; assure her that I'm here.
I will comfort her and guide her, help her through our pain
I'll answer any questions and shelter her from rain.
It's a hard path, that I know but to myself I will be true
And though I'll daily struggle, one day we will break through!
Although we are now incomplete, I will crawl… 'til I can run
And her patient love will reap reward when two hearts meet, as one.

Leigh

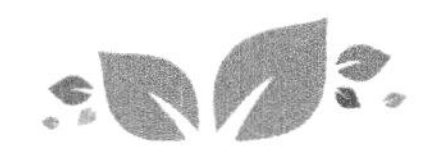

CHAPTER NINE
How to Overcome Trauma

Memories Permanently

The great success of the HFL program has been survivors discovering that they can rid themselves of triggers *permanently* by processing trauma memories. This means that survivors have been able to reclaim their lives from being dominated by childhood events and beliefs. We encounter many of our triggers on a daily basis – so, releasing even *one* trauma makes our lives so much better.

Heal For Life calls this process of healing from a trauma 'The Heal For Life Process'. Some people find they can do this process on their own at home, others find they need support. I think it is very important to include The Heal for Life Process in this book, even if you can only achieve healing with the help of a therapist, as it is the core of our work. It is a very effective, proven way to release the fear that is affecting us through our triggers. The process involves, in simplistic terms, moving the trauma from the unconscious (right brain) amygdala to the conscious (left brain) hippocampus. Do discuss this approach with your therapist, if you have one. I, as a survivor, have found this method to be the very best way to heal myself.

The impact that triggers have on our daily lives provides motivation for many of us to heal. The 'triggers' from our trauma impact us deeply and, dependent on what they are, can totally affect our enjoyment of life. These triggers activate the flight, fight, or freeze mechanism that (if sustained over long periods) is *so* detrimental to our physical and mental wellbeing. ***I believe triggering is the single greatest problem for survivors.*** How often have you been upset with yourself because you have been very angry without real cause? (fight) How often have your emotions from your childhood affected your relationships in adulthood? How often have you fled from an event you wanted to enjoy or even moved to a new house without understanding why? (flight) How often have you found your brain to be elsewhere (freeze) or been sick with no apparent cause (freeze) or just felt endlessly on high alert without understanding why (fight, flight, or freeze response).

Unlocking specific trauma is very beneficial as it means we free ourselves from any reminders (triggers) of childhood trauma that are held in our amygdala. These trauma memories are invoked via the senses, touch, smell, hearing, taste, pain, and sight. Often, we are unaware that we have been triggered, as triggers come in so many different guises.

Let me give you some examples. My sister historically believed she was allergic to cheese. One day I mused that it might not be an allergy but rather a trigger; she reacted to such a suggestion, as I am her younger sister, and she retorted, 'Not everything is related to trauma, you know, I might just be allergic to cheese.' To which I responded, 'Yes but you can drink milk and eat butter so it would be a very strange allergy.' So, that night she decided to use The Heal For Life Process to find out if the cheese allergy was in fact a trigger. She connected to her right brain via doing the visualisation (previous chapter) with herself, and then she asked her little girl why she hated cheese so much. Her little girl told her that when she was five years old, her father had tried to strangle her using his bare hands, and that he had just washed his hands with a special gardener's soap that smelled of cheese. She then helped her inner self to release the fear, and followed that with an empowerment visualisation (she visualised her father being eaten by a goanna). That evening she enjoyed pizza with lots of cheese and she is now able to eat cheese without any physical reaction. The trigger no longer exists as she has released the fear, therefore the amygdala no longer reacts to the smell of cheese.

We can be mistaken in the reason for a trigger. Another example: one of our male guests was triggered by touch – he could never let anyone hug or hold him – and he thought that this trigger was due to sexual abuse at the hands of his grandfather when he was young. However, when he asked his little boy what had created this awful trigger, the answer was quite different. As a child in a very dysfunctional family, his only ally was his older sister. One day she ran out on to the road and was killed by a car, but when the little boy heard the sound of the crash and rushed outside to see her the adults stopped him, and physically held him back from seeing his sister. To his amygdala, the death of his sister was life threatening – stress hormones were released, and his flight, fight, or freeze mechanism was fully activated. Through his senses, he connected touch by the adults to this event and was triggered whenever anyone touched him. Once he had released the fear and re-empowered his little boy, he spent the rest of the week asking for all of us to give him hugs. It was beautiful.

There have been guests who were allergic to smells such as certain perfumes or after-shave, others reacted to oil – all of which were traceable back to a traumatic event.

One person was triggered by the sound of someone eating an apple, as that was what her perpetrator did on one particularly traumatic occasion. Another person would get angry and leave if anyone watched her work. Some people are triggered by things that happened to them while riding in a car, and as such they hate being in a car, or can only be in a car if they are in charge by being the driver.

Triggers come in so many different forms. Can you recognise something you always react to?

You can heal from triggers, as well as ***the beliefs*** that may have been imposed on you at the time of the trauma, by using The Heal For Life Process. These locked in beliefs can have a profound negative influence on our lives until we unlock them and are able to expose them as lies imparted to us by our perpetrator. The sorts of beliefs that can be locked into the amygdala with the original trauma can be as simple as, 'This is your fault, you invited me to do this', or 'you're a bad girl or boy'. These are beliefs we can carry as truths throughout our lives until we heal, when in fact these messages were unfairly imparted by the person who abused us. We live our lives based on false beliefs imposed by a perpetrator.

It is very common to have no idea what the trigger relates to, as trauma is stored in our unconscious brain. The only way to unlock what happened is to connect with the right brain. We can also use the process described below when we have had a nightmare, a panic attack, or are feeling very emotional for no apparent or obvious reason. I use this process when I cannot sleep for several nights in a row, as this is the way my inner child tells me there is something from my childhood she feels ready to release. Each of us has to learn the signs that we have been triggered, that a new memory from childhood is ready to be released.

It is very common for us to disbelieve what we start to remember. Allow your disbelief, and don't fight it. You will soon know if it is the truth. If we are making it up from our imagination there will be no fear attached to the event and no release from a trigger. The truth *will* set you free. My suggestion, which works for me, is to just explore the memory and then see if there is any emotion connected with the memory, if there is then I consider it to be true – what matters to me is releasing the fear connected with the memory, as that means the symptom, or trigger, will disappear as well. Our recall of the event may not be fully accurate as our trauma memories are stored in the amygdala which only stores what is remembered through our senses and what seems important to the child (at the age they are at the time), therefore it may be fractured or incomplete, and all the facts may never come to light because the amygdala does not store chronologically. The amygdala won't necessarily be a factual account, but rather a snapshot of what was important and scary to the child at the point of trauma. I believe that what matters in healing is the release of fear so that the amygdala can release the trigger, therefore making it possible to live life to the full.

I have observed over many years that we only remember what we are ready to deal with. I first remembered abuse not connected with my family and I thought that was my entire story, then as I healed from this trauma over several years, new triggers occurred. My brain kept telling me my father sexually abused me throughout my childhood. It took me months to feel prepared to look and accept that possibility with the help of my psychologist. Years later I remembered the cult group abuse in my father's churches. I have been very lucky as I confronted my father when he was very sick, because I wanted to give him the chance to say sorry before he died. This he did. So then I was able to accept the truth. Each new reminder of my past has come to me via a new trigger.

After all the work I have done, all the triggers I have processed that once affected me, I now have no emotional connection to those memories or the people involved in my abuse in those memories. I so often see survivors of horrific abuse who are still hurting from the events that happened, and I feel sad that they have not been given the opportunity to fully heal.

Sometimes, of course, it is possible to release fear without remembering a specific time of trauma, particularly if there were a lot of traumatic events. However, just releasing fear with no story can be an addition to the work I am going to recommend, not a replacement for the work itself.

I am also no longer interested in sharing details of my story because what happened is no longer important to me. My truth is my truth for me alone. Your truth is your truth. If you find you want to tell people your story, stop and consider this: do you want your past to determine your future? Of course, it is important that our story is heard and validated perhaps once or twice, however there just is no healing in repeating multiple times. *Each of us is worth so much more than what happened to us as a child, despite how hard it is to move beyond that.*

Of course, all of this is very problematic for those of us who are brave enough to try to take our abuser to court. The process of prosecution requires you to repeat your story multiple times and this can be very upsetting and retraumatising if you have not healed the hurt sufficiently. I have heard from so many of our guests that they were glad they did a healing week and worked on the impact of their trauma with a therapist before their case went to court as then they had the ability to not be overcome by the proceedings and could say their truth fluently and without being so overcome by fear that the defense could overwhelm them with their questions and attempts to prove the person was not abused.

Let me now go through our six part process. The first essential step for healing is safety and trust.

1. Safety (feeling safe)

A person needs to feel emotionally, physically, and spiritually safe for effective healing to take place. You need to feel completely safe before trying to process any trauma memories. If you do the work with a therapist you must feel that he or she is walking alongside you, not telling you what to do, and that it feels safe.

After all, it is ideal to do this work with another person, as social connection changes the brain.

It is imperative for safety as well as healing to always have your Adult self with you as a witness, and to keep you grounded. To feel safe before you start you may need to first ground yourself, using whatever grounding technique works for you. Some people use prayer as a part of this grounding process. The grounding used at Heal For Life is at the beginning of the visualisation in the previous chapter. Do what works for you. As long as your adult self is there and in charge of the process, you will not be overwhelmed or remember more than you want to, or are ready for. The need to feel safe is what stops us from ever being overwhelmed, as we will only remember what it feels safe to remember.

2. Connect

You access the trauma, as described in the last chapter, through right brain activities such as visualisation, music, creativity, movement, and non-dominant hand drawing and writing – this connects you to the inner child or inner self, the part that holds the unconscious memory of the trauma.

3. Recognise

Once this connection is made, recognising what happened in whatever detail is available is essential. Some of this needs to be spoken out loud to involve the left brain and to aid integration. If there is a person with you, they should ideally be a caring person who validates and listens, as no one may have listened before. An external, empathic witness can be very validating, as usually it's apparent that at the time no one did acknowledge the event in the way your inner child needed. That is why it is a trauma memory. It is important that your adult self validates and believes the memory that is coming up for you.

4. Release

It is not the detail of what happened that matters for healing (legal requirements are quite different), it is the release of the fear that it was not possible to release at the time. It is fear that is the key emotion – of course there may be other emotions covering our fear, such as sadness, anger or confusion – however to heal and release the trauma from the amygdala it is essential, in my experience, that you have to recognise and release the fear. As an example, if your mother or other close relative dies, when you are a child, the event may be stored as a trauma memory and internalised as fear; fear of not being able to survive without a mother. As well as a feeling of loss and grief but it is the fear that has made the trauma. In the case of a sibling, the fear that created the trauma might be the child thinking they were responsible for the death (remember a child is narcissistic before the age of about five or six). *If it is trauma there is not just sadness but fear involved.* Releasing the fear can be done in many ways, you can wring the fear into a towel, you can run the fear away, you can shake the fear out, you can scream out the fear (often hard in a city but can be done while driving or into a pillow). You can release the fear in whatever way your inner self chooses.

Movement is really helpful, as *emotion* is energy in *motion*. Speaking the fear out loud is also important to re-activate the Broca's Area that is always disconnected during intense trauma. Having said all that, it is possible to successfully release fear in your imagination – you can visualise it moving from your body any way that seems right to you.

Young people at Heal For Life often like to make what we call 'gloop' – flour, water, and (usually black) food dye – and then they can actually choose to get rid of the symbol of their fear by burying, throwing, or otherwise disposing of it. If you use your imagination to get rid of your fear, it is important to verbalise using an 'I' statement that you are feeling and releasing fear.

You will discover that once you have released the fear it will not be necessary in the future to tell others about what happened to you (except where you have to for legal reasons, etc.), as repetition of the story is not helpful, and actually re-affirms you as a victim rather than as a victor. If you still want to tell others or still feel great anger, you haven't yet finished the process, or in other words you haven't yet released all the fear. Sometimes this also happens when there is another aspect to the trauma that also has to be explored.

5. *Empower*

Once the inner self has remembered what happened and released all the fear surrounding the event, it is then time to ask the inner self what they would like to do to take their power back. This is an *essential step* that I originally learned from Peter Levine's (1997) book 'Waking the Tiger'. If we do not re-empower, we store the memory as a victim, whereas we store the memory as a victory if we do re-empower the child.

This re-empowerment can be done in the imagination, or physically, or by imagery. For example, if the inner self wanted to burn the person who abused them, they might make an image out of cardboard and then put the image into a fire. Being violent is allowed because it is the child not the adult self who leads this – sometimes people choose to have an angel take the abuser away, or have a pack of wolves chase the perpetrator away. It could be as simple as saying no, or telling the adult involved that their behaviour was NOT OK. Your inner child self can do whatever they like and will enjoy doing. Finding a voice during this reempowerment is very important to ensure full integration of the right and left hemispheres of the brain. Often releasing anger can be an important act of re-empowerment, allowing the child to be very angry that the person betrayed their trust in such an appalling way.

6. Nurture

After re-empowering it is equally important to nurture the inner self. This step can be very hard if you were not nurtured as a child. It can be easier if you have had a child (as hopefully you managed to nurture your own children), as you can nurture your child self just as you nurtured your offspring. Just lying down and hugging yourself may be more than enough. Certainly, rest is very important, just for twenty minutes or so, to support brain integration. Holding a doll representing you, giving your child self lots of love in whatever way feels right, is also a powerful way to self-nurture.

Here is the model in summary:

1. *Safe: feel safe and in my body*
2. *Connect with my Inner Child* (by visualisation, art, writing, etc.)
3. *Feel the feeling* (I feel… scared, sad, angry, etc.)
4. *Release the energy around the feeling* (crying, screaming, going for a run, punching a bag, etc.)
5. *Re-empowerment* (ask your inner Child what they need to do to take their power back)
6. *Nurture or have fun with my inner Child*

Healing from trauma is hard and is most easily done with a supportive therapist or on one of the HFL programs. You will find great opportunities to heal if you can notice when you are triggered and then allow yourself to discover, through some sort of internal dialogue, the cause of the trigger. We look at triggers, flashbacks, and nightmares as opportunities to learn more about ourselves and to heal. Triggers are treasures, even if they don't feel that way at the time.

This model has evolved from 20 years of work with over 8,500 guests at Heal For Life's Childhood Trauma and Abuse residential healing retreats. The outcomes we achieve are born from weaving neuroscience and psychological understandings with knowledge gained from the last 20 years of people using and working with this model in healing from trauma.

CHAPTER TEN
How To Recognise and Enjoy Emotions

Feeling is healing (J.Fell)

In my experience, the understanding and the acceptance of feeling all emotions is *the key to successful healing.* I believe that therapists too often concentrate on talking, and helping you think about what is happening in your life, rather than getting you to express how you are feeling. It is true that the expression and release of emotions can be very difficult for many of us. Some of us feel our emotions are out of control, and for others feeling emotions is something we just can't do! Whether we are emotionally under-regulated or over- regulated is dependent on our attachment style (see Chapter Six), however we still need to allow ourselves to *feel if we want to heal.*

Healing allows our emotions to be a self-expression of what is happening both in our internal world and external worlds, rather than the two worlds being in entirely different spaces. Often the 'external self' does not allow the expression of feelings, to try to protect ourselves from what was, or is, happening. Over the years, this self protection and subsequent disconnect from my true internal feelings grew so strongly that before I started to heal I very seldom allowed my-self to feel at all, regardless of what was happening in my life. This meant I was often not able to really enjoy happiness or indeed sadness. This is a great pity, as I believe that life is made worthwhile when we experience emotions.

Taken to the extreme, this shut down of emotions can lead to physical illness, anxiety attacks as well as flashbacks, depression, anxiety, panic attacks, and nightmares – all of this is our internal self (our right brain) struggling to be acknowledged and to be listened to. If you remember, the right brain is *dominant*, therefore it *will insist* on being listened to. I have met many survivors who have spent their time trying to deny their emotions, not realizing that is what has led to their depression and anxiety[126].

Allowing ourselves to *feel and* express emotion is critical. *I encourage you to accept that all emotions are important to your healing:* there are no negative emotions. When we release an emotion, it cannot overwhelm us. It is when we try to suppress an emotion that it feels overwhelming and great damage is caused to ourselves.

Anger

I remember I found it very hard to accept when my psychologist first told me that there is no such thing as a negative emotion, as my parents had taught me that anger and fear are bad emotions. This meant I had great difficulty in expressing either of those feelings. Anger is only a 'negative' or an inappropriate emotion if we take our anger out on others. Physically or emotionally harming people with our anger is not OK. However, it is very healthy to feel anger at injustices or anger towards people who have done us wrong. Releasing our anger from childhood events is critical to healing. Recognising that what happened to us was not

OK, and that it should NOT have happened, is a very important part of healing. Releasing anger lowers our sympathetic nervous system. Decreases stress hormones, and brings us back to a calm state[127]. Anger often has a profound impact on our physical well-being, depression and migraines being the most common physical representations of suppressed anger.

There are many safe ways to release anger. Punching or throwing a pillow, wearing boxing gloves and punching a boxing bag, hitting a solid object with a swimming pool noodle or a rubber sword, stamping the feet and expressing with words how you feel. There is no need to hurt oneself when releasing anger, as that is unkind and unloving towards the self. Many men have said to me, 'I have so much anger inside of me I am afraid of what will happen if I let it out'. Releasing anger is not the same as raging, or holding on to the anger. I have never witnessed, or been afraid, that someone will go too far when releasing anger. It amazes people to discover the difference between raging and releasing. One is holding on to the anger, the other is letting the anger go; letting the anger leave the body. I believe many anger management courses would be better off if they taught safe release of anger and then also recognition of the origin of the anger itself.

Emotion is *E*nergy in *Motion*, using energy to express anger is important – screaming inside a car can be used effectively for anger release as for fear, as mentioned before. Yelling at the person who hurt you (where you will not be heard) is a good method, usually easiest while in the car, preferably away from people. Remembering that a majority of all emotion comes from childhood, it is a really good idea to check whenever you are angry if it is about what is happening right now or is it reminding you of someone or something from your childhood. Fight is part of the fight, flight, or freeze response, taking it out on the person who you are angry with in the 'now' may be a bad idea as well as being very unfair. We do tend to take our anger out on a safe person, it can often, quite unfairly, be a partner. Anger is usually covering fear.

Fear

Fear is a necessary and very important emotion; it keeps us safe from danger and helps us to stay alive.

Feeling and releasing fear is also an essential part of healing. Feeling excessive fear or being frightened of things because of my childhood is what I really needed to heal from[128]. I could not allow myself to feel fear as a child, because there were too many terrifying things happening. So, I would be naughty (mostly at school) or daydream. What did you do to hide your fear from others?

When you de-trigger by saying 'I feel frightened' or 'scared' or 'terrified' (whichever is the right word for you) you are helping yourself release the fear. You can release fear in the ways I mentioned in the previous chapter. Acknowledging you are feeling frightened will stop you becoming anxious or having panic attacks.

Sadness

Sadness, and really deep grief, can often be the first emotion to be experienced. Many children are not allowed to feel sad. Parents mistakenly believe that children do not need to grieve or feel sad. Releasing deep sadness was the first emotion I connected with. I was able to allow my inner child to cry and cry, releasing so much sadness about my childhood. I cried for two days, that was really the start of my healing.

Grieving connects us to our parasympathetic system and relief from stress. I was lecturing one day when a father came to me and said he was very worried about his thirteen year old son and sixteen year old daughter as their mother had died the previous year. They were both endlessly sick and failing in their grades at school. He was in despair. When I asked the children if they had grieved their mother's death, if they had felt and released their sadness. They replied 'Oh no, we have to look after Dad, he has suffered so much' I explained to the father that the children were in their sympathetic nervous system and still highly stressed. I suggested they spent the weekend remembering and grieving their loss. A month later the dad told me the change had been extraordinary. As the children had allowed themselves to release their sadness, they had reverted to their normal selves, their grades were back and they were in good health. The sympathetic nervous system was no longer in charge! Feeling your sadness is essential for good health. However, remember that sadness is usually covering fear.

Joy

Healing from childhood trauma is not just about the fear, anger or sadness we may not have been allowed to feel, it is also about discovering the wonderful person we were each born to be. I think it is really important to choose to pursue joy and happiness with as much determination as we pursue any other aspect of our healing or any other emotion. We want to fully experience all our emotions. To be able to really allow ourselves to know the feeling of joy is not easy, but it is *incredible* when we do discover its true essence. Joy is incredibly important and yet we so often deny ourselves joy in our day-to-day lives. This is so sad.

Many of us are not experienced at feeling and expressing joy. It is as if we think we don't deserve to be happy. Or for some of us it is such an unknown feeling – that it doesn't feel safe to feel happy, or we don't even know how to feel happy. Those of us who did not receive nurturing love will find it particularly hard to think we deserve to feel joy. However, it is just as important to feel joy as it is to feel fear, anger, or any other emotion, especially when healing. Healing without the re-discovery of joy is just *too* painful.

I have found it important to find joy for my Adult self separately from finding joy for my Child self. Both parts of me deserve to truly know the feeling of joy.

If the thought of having fun brings up a lot of fear, part of your trauma may be connected to an occasion that was meant to be a joyful experience. On our healing weeks we have a joy day when we invite our guests to a party, and I find it sad that there are always a few people who had a traumatic experience connected to a party. One person had been raped during a party, another was embarrassed by wetting her pants at a party and the other kids made fun of her. Another had all the kids at the party fall on top of her and she was terrified and thought she would die as she was so enclosed by the bodies. This last person had been terrified of going underground or going in an elevator as a consequence of this trauma. Sometimes no one can be blamed for the trauma, like in the last example, however it didn't lessen the terror to the small child and the damaging long-term consequences.

For all of these people it was necessary for them to use our trauma release process and uncover where the connection to fear and attending a party had come from. Then they were able to enjoy a party. In the last case, the survivor was also able to go underground and travel in lifts – this was a huge relief. For all of them they were now free to enjoy parties, and to feel joy.

Trauma is temporary but joy is permanent

-Josie (HFL team member from the Philippines)

Suggestion

Answer this question:

'What do you most enjoy doing?'

When did you last do that? Sometimes when I ask a trauma survivor that question I find they have not allowed themselves the time to do what they most enjoy for many years, if ever. I suggest that every day you consider what you want to do to find joy, even if only for thirty seconds. Practice is what makes those neurons grow. The invitation is to make pursuing happiness part of your daily life.

It might seem impossible when you are very depressed, but do please try. Think of things that make you joyful. Personally, I love to travel so, to give myself joy I read about places I want to visit.

Another idea is to make a joy box. Think of anything in your childhood that did bring you joy. It could be nature, playing hopscotch, or dressing up in your mother's clothes. Think about how you can put representations of things that gave you joy into a joy box. Creating this box may help you connect with the things that did and could bring you pleasure. Or you could make a box of all the things you couldn't or didn't do in childhood that might give you joy that you now richly deserve to experience.

It is important to make a commitment to do the things you enjoy, and not feel obliged to do the things you don't enjoy doing. If you hate cleaning your house, you could try giving yourself permission to not do it – just for the joy of it – how your house looks is your choice.

Joy also means setting healthy boundaries so we do not spend time talking to, or being with, people we do not want to spend time with. You will learn more about that in the chapter on boundaries.

Now let's think about our child self and joy. Our child self needs encouragement to find joy too, as part of the denial of the pain of childhood includes the denial of the joy of childhood as well. The child is born creative and free and as the child holds all emotions it needs to feel able to express joy, freedom and love. I suggest spending time with your inner child, discovering what she or he really likes doing, and then working to find ways to do those things. You might want to spend more time playing freely, taking up a hobby, or simply bringing more colour, excitement, or music into your life. Obviously, our child self is part of our adult self, but sometimes we have disconnected from what it is that we really enjoy, so some of us need to do this work in two parts for a while.

An important step in your healing is also to do the things you could not, or were not permitted to do as a child, allowing you to feel free. My mother always poured scorn on Painting by Numbers, so the other day I bought a Painting by Numbers book and my inner child loved filling in the numbers and doing what I had not been allowed to do!

Suggestion

With your dominant hand ask your inner Child what she or he would like to do or like to eat, then do that or eat that! Remember to always ensure that the adult is very much present, keeping the child safe.

Some of us find it hard to even know what we are feeling; we have suppressed our true feelings for so long, or we never learnt from caregivers that it was OK to feel and to express our feelings. Some of us are so inexperienced at feeling that we cannot even recognise a feeling or name it. A first necessary step maybe to learn ways to recognise what the feeling is.

How to Identify What You Are Feeling

If you have difficulty recognising what you are feeling, you might find the chart below helpful. You can look at it whenever you are not sure what the emotion or feeling is. It could be a good idea to print it out and put up on a wall or on your fridge. Some people have found it helpful to draw their emotions in their own pictorial form.

HOW DO YOU FEEL TODAY?

Suggestion

When you cannot identify a feeling It can help to ask yourself: if the feeling had a colour, what colour would it be? Does the feeling have a shape or texture? Sometimes trying to visualise helps us to connect to our right brain and to the feeling, just as drawing the feeling can also help.

You could try drawing the feeling with your nondominant hand, letting your right brain inner child choose the colour for the feeling. Then it may be possible to release the feeling while drawing it.

Another way is to take deep breaths to connect with what you are feeling – and a word may come to you, like 'frightened'. If you say out loud 'I am frightened' the feeling often follows. Try it. It might sound silly, but it works for me. Once you have a word for the feeling, you can acknowledge the feeling release it and then comfort yourself, often with reassurance that the feeling is from childhood and not from what is happening in the present.

Also asking yourself 'In what part of the body am I feeling this emotion?' and then, 'What happened to this part of my body?' For some people, questions like these will bring up an emotion which can then be released using one of the suggested methods or whatever else you might think of doing to release the feeling from your body.

Let me remind you of the different attachment styles and how they affect the way you manage your feelings.

Secure Attachment Style

People lucky enough to have secure attachment style will find it easier identifying and feeling. They will be able to feel safe enough to express their emotions and share them, where appropriate with safe people in their lives.

Avoidant Attachment Style

Those of us with an avoidant attachment style will have learned from a very early age to suppress our emotions; we discovered it was safest not to feel and so we suppressed our emotions as a child[129]. For many people who have an avoidant attachment style, emotions are expressed physically through pain in the body, as this is safest. I almost physically died when my memories first surfaced, as I was unable to allow myself to feel or release the actual emotions from my childhood. I spent five weeks in hospital, my body literally shutting down, while doctors looked for a logical reason for this malady. The doctors were at the point of implementing exploratory surgery when a wise friend suggested that there might be a psychological explanation, and indeed there was.

For those of us with an avoidant attachment style, working on allowing ourselves to feel, and learning how to express what we are feeling to a safe person is incredibly healing. I like to describe it as though we have too strong a container around our emotions and that we have to feel safe enough to loosen the lid. When we decide to ignore our feelings, we come into conflict with ourselves. If we had to suppress our emotions in childhood to survive then we became accustomed to doing that, however it is NOT helpful as adults and it is not conducive to healing, growth, or brain integration.

Ambivalent Attachment Style

People with ambivalent attachment style will often feel overwhelmed by their emotions, and sometimes feel unable to cope. They have under-developed emotional regulation. It seems impossible to control emotions or to know what to do when in the middle of feeling emotional – they may cry or feel sad without knowing why[130]. Their emotional contents are not being held within a container. People with ambivalent attachment will find it helpful to develop an adult self to contain their emotions, so that the emotions aren't overwhelming.

When stuck in an emotion try to provide a container for your emotions. Try to bring in adult thoughts, such as 'it isn't happening right now', 'there isn't anything happening to me right now for me to be sad about'. Try mentally putting your arms around yourself (as you would have loved your parent to have done) and comfort little you. This can be very hard if you were never nurtured, but it is important to try.

Disorganised Attachment Style

Individuals with disorganised attachment style will fluctuate between being over regulated (feeling everything) and under regulated (feeling nothing).

Essentially, there is an inability to self-regulate emotions as no containment was given by the mother figure in the first three years of life[131]. It helps for these people to understand that it is safe to feel sad, angry, frightened, or happy.

Feeling emotions is vital to recovery. As described earlier, the emotions associated with trauma are locked in the amygdala and other associated right hemisphere areas[133]. As such, traumatic memory cannot be accessed through talking about the experience alone, unless the talking is to lead you into the feeling. Talking about trauma without the associated feelings will not change brain structure or release the trauma from the right hemisphere of the brain. There is even a danger of re-traumatising.

Re-traumatising occurs when we remember what happened without allowing ourselves to fully release the feelings and, also most importantly, without reempowering the child self. There is, amongst health professionals, great anxiety about re-traumatising a survivor, and rightly so, we do not need to re-live our trauma without relief. In my experience, retraumatisation can occur when the therapist is frightened of the client's emotions, so they do not ensure the client fully releases their fear. The therapist can, out of their own fear, unintentionally encourage the client to suppress their fear. An example of this is when the client starts to share something from their childhood and they become overwhelmed by their emotions, and instead of helping the person release the emotion the therapist will try instead to contain the emotion. This leaves the client stuck in the emotion rather than being helped to fully express it. When this occurs in therapy, we can leave a session feeling worse than when we went in.

It is also not helpful to tell our story without emotion – even being asked to tell our story to a new therapist is potentially re-traumatising for us as each time we tell it without feeling the emotions connected to the events, we are strengthening the feeling of being a victim, and we are reinforcing the helplessness we felt when the trauma happened.

In my experience, there will not be an issue with retraumatisation if we are allowed, or allow ourselves, with our adult present, to always fully express what we are feeling as we tell our story.

Always remember that the core feeling that is suppressed from a traumatic event is fear. Even when we are feeling sadness or anger when remembering a traumatic event, fear will always be the underlying emotion. We can choose how to release this fear through action. *EMOTION is ENERGY in MOTION.*

When trying to express an emotion, or validate how you are feeling, it is helpful to know that the optical neurons are the strongest neurons in the brain and that by looking in the mirror you can engage your optical neurons and thus provide yourself with your own much-needed validation. The brain grows and changes through interaction with others – and that 'other' can even be through your own rational, adult self.

Developing an adult self brings self-control back into life. It is worth practicing developing this adult self to look after you every single day; ***being the parent to yourself that you would have loved to have had.*** If you have an overdeveloped adult self who suppresses all emotion, try to recognise when there are physical signs that you are suppressing your emotions. Such signs include feeling sick or having a bad headache or just wanting to sleep[133]. Try asking yourself 'What am I feeling?' and then express that feeling out loud, even if you are not actually feeling the emotion – even saying the words will help.

No one can make you feel anything, you are in charge of your emotions, but if you ignore your emotions they may cause you to become unwell.

Head said: 'I contain the law',
Heart said: 'I am full of feeling'.
Head said: 'I am logic, I am structure.
I am the stake that supports the young plant'.
Heart said, 'I am love. I am mystery.
I am the creative force of life'.
Then Head and Heart began to quarrel.
Head said: 'You are emotional and irrational.
You live in a world of chaos'.
Heart replied: 'You are cold and unfeeling.
You do not live at all'.
So Head and Heart went to God
and asked if they could be separated.
God laughed at them and said
'Not even God can do that.

You two belong together.
Apart, I'm afraid you're nothing.
Head, you are the container.
Heart, you are the contents.
The container without the contents
is as hollow as a drum,
all noise and no substance.
The contents without the container
will disperse and be wasted,

good for nothing at all.
There's no way you can be separate
and lead useful lives.'
Head and Heart grew anxious.
'But we are so different.
How can we find peace?'
God said: 'Draw close and become lovers.
Respect each other. Nurture each other.
Help each other to be equal.
You will come together as one,
and when you are one,
a truly amazing thing will happen.'
Head and Heart sat up at that.
'What kind of thing?' they asked.
But God only smiled
and said: 'Wait and see.'

- Joy Cowley's poem 'Head and Heart', from her wonderful book 'Aotearoa Psalms'.

In this book, you will constantly find connections that all point to the same conclusions in relation to healing, that *feeling is essential to healing*, and that the way we regulate our feelings relates to our attachment style.

Feeling is how we connect with our hidden, wounded self and feeling is what makes us authentic and real. Never allow yourself to forget that the vast majority of all emotional reactions come from childhood[134].

Working with survivors of trauma, I see examples of this every day. If you hate someone for doing something, such as being late for an appointment, look at who was always late in your childhood or whether it mattered if you were late. Recently I was working with a man who was furious because his wife had not returned $100 that she owed him; he was in a great state about it, proclaiming 'How can I ever trust her again?' When I asked him, 'Who took money from you as a child?' his response was, 'My mother, and she never ever gave it back.' However, it was hard for him to recognise that his anger was really related to his mother rather than his wife. If you can release the feelings you're carrying from childhood, you will not burden yourself or your current relationships with the weight of these past feelings, in the present.

Suggestions

Each morning and evening identify and validate how you are feeling – look into the mirror and tell yourself how you are feeling, knowing you can choose to change how you are feeling if you really want to. Notice when something really upsets you and then consider where this may have come from in your childhood. If you want to lessen the emotion around these feelings in the future, allow your child self to express how they felt on the original occasion (this will include fear) and follow the Heal For Life process to avoid feeling upset by a similar situation in the future.

There are other helpful ways of releasing the emotions trapped from the trauma in our bodies such as:

- Bowen therapy
- Reiki
- Yoga
- Movement
- Massage
- Somatic Therapy
- Kinesiology

Allow yourself to release your emotions. I found Emotional Focused Therapy (EFT) quite helpful as well, but not as the only way of healing as it was not allowing me to know what had happened to me, and that is the part that I have found incredibly important.

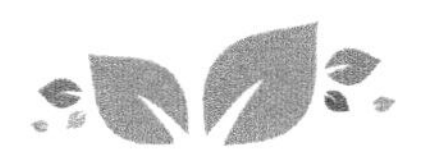

CHAPTER ELEVEN
Transactional Analysis and Behaviours

This chapter is about how we can discover how many of our day-to-day decisions and interactions with others are influenced by what Eric Berne (1957) called 'ego states'. Recognising where our self-beliefs come from can help us change the way we think about ourselves. Developing a healthy adult internal dialogue is also critically important if we are to take control of our lives in a positive, empowering way.

I have also found, during the Heal For Life healing programs, that it has profoundly helped our guests to recognise that what they have believed as negative truths about themselves are not truths but rather ideas imposed by their parents, or abusers, and these negative self-beliefs can, once recognised, lose the power to influence behaviour and self-beliefs.

Introduction to Transactional Analysis

Transactional Analysis (TA) is a theory of personality and a systematic psychotherapy for personal growth and change that was established by Eric Berne in the 1950s. It is invaluable as it provides the opportunity for us to observe that what happened in our childhood, and how we were treated, is still subconsciously affecting the way we think and act today.

Eric Berne's book and 'TA Today' by Ian Stewart offer a lot of useful information, and I will explain how I have utilised Berne's theory to be specifically helpful to survivors[135 136].

TA is seen by many as a reasonable and realistic model because it confronts you with the fact that you are responsible for what happens in your future, despite the impact of negative experiences in your past.

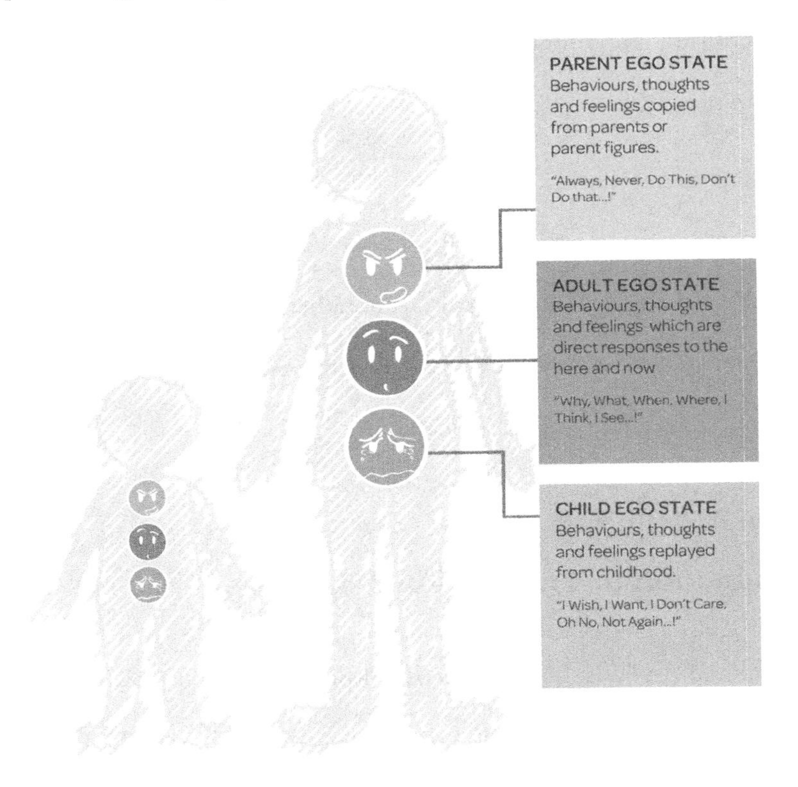

Parent-Adult-Child Ego State Model

TA is founded on the belief that everything that we have experienced from the moment of birth (and it is now believed even before birth) is recorded in detail and stored in the brain. These recorded 'tapes' are capable of being 'played back' in the present.

Berne discovered these ego states from working with a client. During his treatment, a 35-year-old lawyer stated to Berne, 'I am not really a lawyer, I'm just a little boy.' Berne experimented with talking to the 'adult' and the 'child', addressing separately the two parts the client identified. Later, Berne and the lawyer identified a separate 'parent' part. This part appeared to be reproducing thoughts, feelings, beliefs and behaviours that the lawyer saw and heard his parents do when he was growing up. Through continual observation of many more patients, Berne proposed that the adult, parent and child ego states exist in all people. *Berne believed that these states of being were not roles but actual psychological realities*[137].

The Parent

The Parent consists of a massive collection of recordings of imposed, unquestioned, interactions perceived by a child between the ages of birth (or before birth) to five. The greatest influence at this time of life is a child's parents or parent substitutes. The parent ego state is an internal recording of everything the child sees his or her parents say and do. Importantly, data from the parent is taken in and recorded, without editing, because the young child does not have the intellectual ability or language skills to construct meanings, modify, explain or correct what she or he, has perceived from the parent. For example, if a parent continually tells a child that they are hopeless, the child will believe that she or he is indeed hopeless, and will likely carry that belief as a truth for the rest of their life unless this belief is critically examined and exposed as being untrue. The adult is likely to believe that as they are hopeless they can never achieve anything and may well self-sabotage, therefore the parent's message does become the truth. Equally, if a child is told they are wonderful and perfect they will grow up believing that as fact, regardless of input from others when an adult.

The parent state also includes all the spoken and unspoken rules, laws, warnings, or advice children hear or see from their parents. The parent ego state records all the non-verbal body language, such as the disapproving look that reflects punishment or the smiling face for approval. The parent ego state also contains the 'how to' messages. For example, how to make a bed, eat food correctly, put on shoes, or blow your nose. Parent ego statements often start with 'Never eat with your mouth open', 'Always speak when you are spoken to'; 'Don't forget that big boys don't cry.'

It is important to know that what a parent says or does is perceived as being correct by the very young child. Whether the rules are good or bad is irrelevant to the recording. At such a young age the child is totally dependent on its parents for survival so it is important to the child's survival to please and obey the parents. Other sources that can become part of the parent ego state include older siblings, other authority figures and, often in today's world, television or social media.

The parent voice is a permanent recording. Berne believed that the recording cannot be erased and is likely to be replayed throughout the rest of the person's life. However, I know these recordings can be re-written and how to do that will be described later. Whether parent data is helpful or not in the present depends on whether the imposed beliefs were positive or negative. The parent state also includes the nurturing, caring parent's voice, holding, cuddling, and lovingly supporting the child when in need.

Visual Examples of Parent Cues

Furrowed brow, pursed lips, pointing index finger, head-wagging, a 'horrified look', foot-tapping, hands on hips, arms folded across chest, tongue-clucking; sighing, patting another person on the head, or any behaviours or mannerisms particular to your parents.

Examples of Parent Verbal Cues

'I'm going to put a stop to this once and for all…'; 'I can't for the life of me…'; 'Now always remember…'; 'How many times have I told you…'; 'In my day…'; and 'Why can't you just…?'. Positive nurturing voices are also part of the parent state such as…'Oh poor you, what can I do to help?' or 'Let me give you a hug.'

Some words may indicate the parent state especially if they reflect an automatic, unthinking use of the word, combined with the physical cues. Examples of such words are: 'should'; 'ought'; 'stupid'; 'ridiculous';

'disgusting'; 'shocking'; 'lazy'; 'nonsense'; 'poor thing';

'no!'; 'how dare you'; 'not again!'

These parent messages are so locked in that I am sure many of you, like me, will hear yourself repeating a phrase used by one of your parents even if, as a child, you did not like that phrase. It is one way poor parenting can inadvertently be carried from generation to generation.

The Child

While the *parent* state records all the *external* learnings from birth (or prior) to five, the child state records all the *internal learnings*, or responses, to what a very young child experiences. *The emotions felt by the child as a result of parental input* are all carried in the child ego state.

A very young child is small, dependent, and unable to analyse. The child has demands and needs to explore, touch, and discover their world. On the other hand, parents have demands and need to curb a young child's behaviour, either for their own safety (e.g. 'Don't touch the hot stove') or to meet the parent's needs (e.g. 'I need you to sleep now because I am tired'). A young child is not able to figure out cause and effect and often feels frustrated, angry, and rejected when s/he is not able to do what comes naturally to them. This begins the process of experiencing negative emotions and the early conclusion 'I AM NOT OK.'

Harris (1967), in his book 'I'm OK – You're OK' stated that this permanent recording of not being OK is the residue of having been a child, *any* child, including the child of kind, loving, well-meaning parents. It is the *situation* of childhood and *not* the intention of the parents that produces the problem. When even the children of 'good' parents carry the NOT OK burden, one can begin to appreciate the load carried by children whose parents are guilty of gross neglect, abuse, and cruelty[138].

At Heal For Life we do not believe these recordings need be retained for life. We can examine and identify our different ego states and discern which of those messages are real, and which can now be re-organised or discarded.

The child ego state may be triggered at any time in our adult life. Many situations can remind us of similar moments experienced in childhood and bring on the same feelings we experienced then. When a person is totally overwhelmed by feelings it could be said, '*the child has taken over*'. When anger dominates reason, it can be said that '*the child is in command*'. The child also has a very positive side. Contained in the child are all the feelings of curiosity, wonder, awe, happiness, excitement, freedom and joy. The child contains the 'aha!' moments, all the feelings associated with 'firsts' – the first step, the first word, the first time you tied your shoelaces yourself, the first time you stroked a cat. *The vast majority of all strong emotional reactions or responses are said to come from the child state.*

Examples of Child Physical Cues

Tears; quivering lip; pouting; temper tantrums; highpitched whining voice; shrugging shoulders; constantly saying 'sorry'; downcast eyes; teasing; delight; laughter; clinginess; hand-raising for permission to speak; nail-biting; squirming; and giggling.

Examples of Child Verbal Cues

Baby talk; 'I wish…'; 'I want…'; 'I don't care'; 'I guess…';

'bigger, biggest, best'. Little children also say 'what'; 'when'; 'where'; 'why'; and 'how' a lot, however this can also be the Adult ego state beginning to operate in the young child analyzing situations.

So, when do the parent and the child stop recording? I have observed that although traditional TA considers the child will have felt all conceivable possible attitudes prior to school, the impact of trauma and abuse means that these internal messages can continue being encoded throughout childhood. We know that the right brain is unconscious and the left brain does not develop until the second year of life, so the early messages will be lodged in the unconscious right brain (see Chapter Three and the appendix). Therefore, they will not be as easy as the later ones to recognise and change.

If the recording of parent and child are permanent and vast, how can we unhook from the parent and child tapes from the past? The answer is to develop a functioning adult part of ourselves to critically evaluate the self-beliefs that were encoded in childhood.

The Adult

From the age of about 10 months, a child starts to become more independent, is able to move around and explore and do things for him or herself[139]. This self-actualising process is thought to be the beginnings of the adult ego state. Adult data comes from the child discovering for themselves about life and how it may be different from what the child has been taught by his or her parents. For example, a child who is yelled at for touching something can react initially by crying, but then a few moments later reach out and touch it again anyway. This process of collecting data independently from the parent is the function of the adult state.

The adult state is like a data-processing computer, analysing information from three sources: their parent ego state; their child ego state; as well as data gathered independently from the outside world. Unfortunately, the development of the adult can easily be squashed by a strong parent or child state, or under situations of extreme stress. For example, when a young child is harshly punished for thinking differently from its parents the child may learn to survive by putting their adult aside and complying with parental demands. This makes it much harder to develop a strong adult later if the child was not allowed to be independent in thought or action. It is why many of us do not have a strong adult self so find it hard to be analytical about what is happening for ourselves when we are adults. We often seem unable to know how to help ourselves. We want to lean on others or let others tell us what to do. Our parent and child states dominate our lives.

The adult's most important function is to examine data by asking questions such as: 'Is that information true?'; 'Does that information apply today?'; 'Are these feelings appropriate to the present or are they in response to old data?' A young child who is encouraged to explore, think and test the information parents give them is, in fact, developing their adult. If the parents' information is grounded in reality then the child learns, through their own developing adult, to feel secure, because their findings are supported by what they were taught in the first place.

It is important to note that the process of verifying parent or child data does not eliminate the 'NOT OK' recordings. For example, if a mother spanks a three-year-old child for running into the street, the child feels fear, confusion, anger, and frustration. The three-yearold doesn't understand the concept of danger, and does not understand that the mother is trying to protect the child. The fear, anger and frustration are recorded in the child state as being NOT OK. The recordings are not erased later, when the child is older and understands why the mother punished him unless one accesses their implicit (unconscious) memory. TA can help people understand how the original situation of childhood produced so many NOT OK recordings. This understanding does not erase the recording, but can give people the choice to turn the recordings off or change the thought.

The adult's other functions are reality testing, probability estimating, and updating child and parent data. For example, the adult updates the child data, determining which feelings may be expressed safely in different situations. The adult gathers data from the outside world and determines, by way of example, that it is appropriate to cry at weddings but not to scream in anger at weddings.

The adult grows and increases in efficiency through training and use. It is normal to practice being an adult. However, under too much stress, the adult can be impaired to such a point that child emotions take over inappropriately. As Harris explains, 'The boundaries of parent, adult and child are fragile and if signals from our environment remind us of situations we experienced in the helpless, dependent days of childhood, our adult can be reduced to an onlooker[140]. In this situation people often say, 'I knew what I was doing was wrong, but I couldn't help myself.' In extreme situations, triggering the child can lead to people regressing to feeling tiny and helpless.

If there is little conflict between what was taught in childhood and what is real, the adult is freed to be creative. The child provides information about what it wants, what makes it happy, and the adult provides the 'how to' information to make it happen. However, if the adult computer is cluttered with unfinished business, confusion, or conflict, then there is little time or space to be creative.

Many decisions in the adult are automatic because they have been checked out. For example, parent data such as: 'Stop at red lights'; are found to be true and therefore do not need to be assessed repeatedly. Many survivors whose problems originate from poor parenting have a weak adult state, and thus find it hard to feel in control of their lives because there is no discerning adult state present to help them make decisions or move through their emotions.

Examples of Adult Physical Cues

The adult face shows that it is listening by responding appropriately to the listener, showing that they have heard the person they are listening to. The adult face is straightforward and open, allowing child expressions to show naturally, if appropriate.

Examples of Adult Verbal Cues

'In what way'; 'Comparative'; 'True'; 'False'; 'Probable'; 'Possible'; 'Unknown'; 'Objective'; 'I think'; 'I see'; 'It is my opinion'.

Often people expend lots of energy making decisions with common difficulties being 'I always make the wrong decisions'; 'I keep going over and over the same thing'; or 'I'm afraid of making any decision.' This displays a lack of adult ego state present.

It can be helpful to recognise that in each decision three sets of data must be processed: the parent, the child, and the adult. In particular, understanding the child's feelings is essential to enabling the adult to process new data. If fear of the parent tapes is too strong, the adult may not feel free to examine the parent and the adult may become prejudiced by the parent or child data. When we start to use the adult state to make decisions using both the input from parent and child state we will be able to be more effective. Freedom of the adult comes from recognising what is the truth in the parent and the child information.

Sometimes we need to make decisions even when we don't have all the data. We already do this every day in many ways, for example, we get married without being sure it will last; we vote without being sure of the outcome; we decide our priorities and values without being sure they are exactly right for us. While the child in us requires certainty and security, the adult can accept the fact that this is not always possible.

When the parent or the child dominates, the outcome is usually predictable. We either repeat the behaviour of our parents, do the very opposite, or keep living as a servant to the feelings from the past. This is how many of us live our lives before we start to heal: we are dominated by our parent or child ego states. If the parent ego dominates, we will believe and live by all the parental messages such as 'I am hopeless', or 'I will never amount to anything.' If we are dominated by the child states, we will not be able to move through our emotions, and will feel 'stuck' in them. However, when the adult is in charge the outcome is not as predictable there is a possibility for change. If we have received dysfunctional parenting, then the parent voice and the child voice will tend to dominate, and the adult voice will not be running our lives. *Therefore, developing the adult voice is crucial to healing.*

One of the primary aims of healing is to make the shift from feeling powerless (like a 'victim') to feeling empowered, with choice as to how to live life. This definitely requires an awareness of, and commitment to, developing a strong adult ego state that challenges 'tapes' from childhood that are no longer useful or supportive. The development of an analytical adult state assists the process of learning to 'respond' to life, rather than simply 'react' from old parent and child tapes.

For most of us, our childhoods were not normal and we did not learn to develop a strong adult and many of us are dominated by parental negative messages. To help you, I have slightly modified Eric Berne's model to more specifically meet survivors' needs. I like to think of three dominant different parent states: a nurturing parent, a critical parent; and a rescuing parent. This is because many survivors have experienced an extreme form of parenting.

Critical Parent

The 'critical parent' state occurs when we copy or accept the critical behaviour of our parents of blaming, judging, lecturing, or shaming ourselves and others. 'Negative critical parent' is easy to recognise as it is the loudest voice in the mind. This ego state behaviour reflects parental behaviours that blame, shame, putdown, batter, insult, and injure the child. This parent ego state is often the key player in how we then parent ourselves before healing – we unconsciously play out this behaviour against ourselves and others, perpetuating the cycle of abuse and violence.

I have found, while working at Heal For Life, that a person's negative self-beliefs are not truths, but rather they are beliefs imposed by a parent, community, school or Church. They can be changed by the adult state by examining the facts. In my own life, my negative voice (imposed on me by my father) said 'I am stupid', and I believed this voice so I left school at age 16 and only went to University at the age of 50 (after I had started my healing work). Even now I feel surprised if someone describes me as intelligent.

Pause for a moment and consider your most critical self-belief. Some examples to help you, taken from our many guests who have felt this way, are: 'I am not good enough' – think about it: everyone is born good enough without needing to do anything. 'I am stupid' – think about that: no one is stupid, we all do the best that we can with the brain that we have. 'I am a slut' – this can be imposed by a sexual abuser on their victim:

no one is born a slut. 'You will never amount to anything' – anyone can achieve in life.

Remember sexual assault is NEVER the victim's fault, regardless of any behaviour. 'I am bad' or worse still 'I am evil' – these are messages that were directly imposed upon us by the perpetrator to make us feel responsible for the abuse. Each person determines what they make of their lives, and does so even more fluently once freed from negative parental messages.

It is a very good idea to share with your therapist, or trustworthy friend, your own critical self-beliefs, as they can offer you an outsider's perspective, and with that a way to challenge your negative self-belief. This takes great courage to do and it is hard because we believe these negative thoughts to be true, so we may need to be helped to gather evidence to prove to ourselves that it is a lie. We do not want to tell anyone these negative self-beliefs because we believe they are true. I challenge you to discover that they are not true.

Suggestion

A good way to remove negative self-belief/s is to write down a negative belief that you have on a sheet of paper. An example: 'I am useless', then, using your adult self, consider why this might not be true. Sentences such 'I am useful to my friends' or 'I often help others' and 'I look after my children' – or whatever is true for you. After all, no one is useless. You may find writing positive sentences against your own self-belief very difficult, as we believe these statements as truths, even though they are not. Just keep on trying! After you have written as many positive statements as you can read them back and consider the evidence before you. Hopefully, you will have enough courage to say aloud, to engage both parts of the brain, the opposite of that negative self-belief – so, for example 'I am useless' the opposite would be 'I am useful and worthwhile.'

It can be really helpful to take the writing and symbolically destroy the belief by burning the paper it is written on, or tearing it into pieces, or scribbling over it –

do whatever you want to do to destroy that piece of paper, as this will help take away the power of the negative belief. This is a very hard activity as we believe the lies we were taught. Therefore, working this through with the help of a therapist or friend can be very beneficial.

An extension of the critical parent is the absent parent.

Absent Parent

The complete absence of a parent sends a very strong negative message to the child state. It gives the child negative messages. The belief 'I have no value', 'I have no worth', 'I am unlovable', 'I don't exist'. These are strong messages to overcome, and if you suffer from a lack of any parenting, the first step is to try to develop your nurturing parent state by doing kind things for yourself. It is very hard to overcome the total lack of a parent, which can happen so easily if your mother was addicted to drugs or alcohol. If this is your history, you deserve and need a very good therapist who can start to teach you how to self-nurture and self-love. You will need external help because it is very hard to learn something of which you have no concept. A person with a very weak or absent parent ego state will tend to live very much in their child ego state.

Rescuing Parent

This kind of parenting is when we were too cared for, and held back from resilience and personal self-belief by the actions of our parents. 'Rescuing parent' behaviour is doing for the child what the child can do for themselves (e.g. homework, cleaning their room, decision-making) and never allowing the child to learn by their own successes and mistakes. This is a difficult state to recognise because you may think the 'rescuing' was very loving, you may consider your mother or father was wonderful and blame yourself even more for your inability to succeed in life. However, rescuing parents lessen your own self-belief and acceptance of your own value as a person. They lessen your ability to think for yourself and make your own decisions. This is often caused by parents trying to overcome their own trauma by giving too much protection and loving care to the child. These parents, through their own pain, may have gone to great lengths to shield their child from the 'dangerous' world by controlling situations to fit what the parent felt was 'right' for the child. Rescuing parents may also have been too lax, wanting their children to be happy, neglecting to set limits and boundaries for their child that help them to take responsibility for their lives. This parent may discount a child's own feelings, or try to change them. Rescuing parents are often overly anxious parents who transfer their anxiety on to the child. The ultimate in rescuing parent I have witnessed was when a young woman continually tried to suicide because her mother always told her 'you will not survive without me.' The mother had died, and so the young woman believed that she could not survive without her mother. Rescuing parents are looking after their own needs (and fears) and so they unintentionally emotionally limit the development of their child.

Typical rescuing parent behaviour may include not letting the child cross the road, stay overnight with friends, experience negative emotions, or explore the world themselves. This behaviour makes the parent happy and the parent feel safe, but the child is not learning resilience or the capacity to self-nurture, and ultimately this can cause damage in the same way as the more obvious critical parent. The rescued child will never feel safe without their mother advising and helping them.

Nurturing Parent

The Nurturing Parent can be almost non-existent for those of us who had very rescuing, critical, or absent parents. Fortunately, if you are reading this you are still alive, so someone in your childhood did validate you enough for you to survive. Maybe a teacher, a grandparent, or a neighbour? Someone will have shown you some nurturing love. A very little love goes a long way!

When we copy behaviours from our parents that showed us they were looking after us, we are said to be in our 'nurturing parent' state. For example, a parent reads bedtime stories to their children because their parent did before them.

Many survivors find it challenging to recognise 'nurturing parent' behaviours – the 'critical parent' can be so loud they 'drown out' memories of anything positive in childhood. Given enough reflection and healing, survivors can find they gain a different perspective. Learning how to nurture our inner child leads to a strengthening of the nurturing parent, and aids in mitigating or even losing the negative, critical voice. Some words to describe the nurturing parent are: caring; consistent; attuned; validating; allowing the child to make mistakes; warm; supportive; and loving. We all need to develop a strong nurturing parent within ourselves to compensate for what we missed out on when we were children.

Suggestion

Write out all the words you can think of to describe the ideal, caring parent. Then write a letter to your inner child and try to tell them how you will nurture them and show them love. Try to include words you wrote out to describe how you will nurture your own inner child. This is a particularly difficult thing to do if you received very little nurturing, however definitely not impossible.

Now I have outlined the three dominant parent states, I will identify three strong child states for survivors of childhood trauma. They are the wounded child, natural or free child, and rebel/protective child.

The Wounded Child

The wounded child state contains all the hurt, sad, lonely, guilty and fearful feelings associated with the trauma and pain we experienced in childhood. Those situations when the emotion was awful and unbearable. This wounded part of ourselves is the part we want to acknowledge and help to heal. Throughout our childhood, and even adulthood, we have developed coping strategies to hide this part of ourselves from the world. If we had not we would not have survived. The world is not kind to frightened, lonely and scared children.

Suggestion

A good way to start healing is to write down all the words that you feel are relevant to the wounded child part of yourself ideally using your non-dominant hand. Read back the words, noticing the words you wrote down, as they will be significant. If you wrote 'lonely' as the first word that is probably the dominant feeling you had as a child. Sit for a moment and let yourself acknowledge how hard it was for you when young to feel such loneliness, and allow the adult part of yourself to listen and comfort you. Recognise that you have no need to be lonely now as how you live your life now is your choice. It is your choice to go out and meet more people, socialise and connect with others.

I live in fear.
Fear of discrimination.
Fear of abuse.
Fear of pain.
Fear of being misunderstood.
Fear of being shunned.
Fear of being ridiculed.
Fear of not being accepted.

I live in torment.
My demons haunting me.
My monsters taunting me.
The voices in my head saying,
'You are worthless, useless.
Your existence is pointless.
Your life is meaningless.
You should just die.'
And the agony is just too much to bear.
You have to divert it somewhere else.
So you take a cigarette,
Inhale, exhale the poisonous smoke
That slowly kills you.
You take that stick
And push it against your skin.
Oh, the release is addicting,
The pleasure in seeing your pain spelled out.

I live in self-loathing,
And self-blaming
As the night wears on,
The voices get louder.
'You are a monster.
You are a demon.
You are a hurricane
Causing destruction
Everywhere you go.
You wreck your own life.
You are a sole-bearer of your mistakes.'
And there is no voice to contradict and refute them.
You are alone.
Alone in your darkness.

Alone in your hell.
You can't see a way out.

And it's just too much to bear.
You surrender, succumb and
Let the anguish and despair overcome you.
Where is the hope?
There is no more hope.
There is nothing left you.
You are too broken to carry on.
Too damaged to repair Too corrupted to heal.
Is there really no hope?
Maybe there is.
So you start searching for it.

- *Denise M. 'The Wounded Child. (A HFL guest, 2014).*

The more we heal and release our fear and hurt from the wounded child, the less we will need the rebel or protective child who I will now describe for you.

The Rebel / Protective Child

This part of ourselves is the part we developed so no one would see how much we were hurting inside. It is the part of ourselves that we developed to protect ourselves from our pain. Without our rebel/protective child we would not have survived. It contains all the behaviours associated with protecting our pain from the world. For some, the rebel/protective child will have been overly people-pleasing to mask the wounded child, or perhaps very competitive, or highachieving in order to excel at school work or in sport. They may have been very naughty at school, to have some power somewhere in order to hide the wounded child within. Or been the comedian, or been a bully?

What did you do as a child to hide your pain from the world and are you still doing it?

I was the naughtiest kid in the school – I gave myself some importance by being the worst behaved child possible. Fortunately, I have found as an adult other ways to protect my wounded child.

Many of you will also have changed your coping methods as you aged. Usually, this rebel part of ourselves as grownups is a behaviour that is not serving us well. For example, someone who rebelled in a passive way by simply not doing what they were told when they were a child may find that ignoring work requests in order to 'show them who's boss' isn't really helping their career. Ignoring our feelings through drug and alcohol abuse usually becomes destructive over time too, with more and more alcohol needed to keep the wounded child's feelings repressed. Always putting others' needs before our own, continuing to be a people pleaser, is not healthy either.

Suggestion

What are you still doing to protect your wounded child? Pause for a moment to think about this. Then write it down. What do you still do now to protect yourself from pain? Do you employ any of the following, most common, ways of hiding the wounded child?

- Addictions: alcohol, illicit and legal drugs, gambling, sex, work, shopping, excessive exercise, food
- Isolation: Agoraphobia, or avoiding getting into relationships
- Humour: the joker at events (have you noticed how many of the world's top comedians have had difficult childhood experiences?)
- Anger: when you are feeling vulnerable
- Self-sabotage: to try and avoid being hurt again
- Depression: the ultimate rebellion being to stop feeling everything and anything
- The People Pleaser: always wanting to care for others, do what they want and not think of your own needs
- Obsessive compulsive behaviour
- Victim role playing: 'poor me' behaviour, drawing attention to yourself by telling everyone how hard life is and how much you have suffered
- Rescuing others: helping anyone in need, while never attending to your own wants/needs
- Perfectionism: the house has to be perfect, you have to dress / present yourself perfectly.
- Being compliant, always doing what you are asked to do.

As we heal, the extremes of the wounded child and the destructive habits of the rebel/protective child will lessen and we will grow closer to being the free child we were born to be.

Free Child

This part of ourselves represents the feelings, attitudes, and behaviours we experienced as children that were independent of parental pressure, limits and rules; these are the times when we were free to simply 'BE'. Maybe it was playing freely when our parents weren't around, or times we spent with people who allowed us just to be ourselves. For some survivors, there is little recollection of being safe enough to have the experience of their 'free child.'

The free child is able to feel what they want when they want to, they can laugh, giggle, be free of parental internal voices and discipline, they can change their feelings in an instant just because they can! Make daisy chains, run in the grass, splash in puddles, get dirty without caring, be FREE. The free child has no 'should or 'must' in their vocabulary!

I have noticed with joy that the more a person heals the more they feel free to uncover this wonderful part of themselves. One word of caution: as we develop this part of ourselves, it has to be in conjunction with the development of the adult self, as the free child knows no limitations to behaviour or danger. The free child always needs an adult ego state present to keep them safe.

Suggestion

What did you enjoy doing in childhood? What were you not allowed to do in childhood? Why not allow yourself to do it? Maybe it's eating ice cream or playing hopscotch. Perhaps, it is singing, playing or lying out in the sun. Consider allowing yourself to relive any happy, 'free' childhood moments. You may find this very difficult, as it may not feel natural to indulge yourself, however strengthening the free child while working with your wounded child is so important. We need to provide balance and to ensure healing is not just about pain but also about having fun.

The Importance of the Adult Ego State in Healing

The adult is the essential part of ourselves that we develop to effectively manage our day-to-day life. The adult's function is to take in information from the other ego states and the outside world, give information to the ego states and make responsible decisions, instead of allowing ourselves to simply be reacting to life from our history-based child or parent states. For example, the adult can listen to the wounded child and determine whether their feelings are in response to a real, here-and-now situation, or a trigger from childhood trauma, and then decide what is the most beneficial thing to do rather than ignoring the wounded child leaving them stuck in pain.

The adult has the ability to access the reality of the 'here and now.' When the adult is functioning well, we can feel relatively stable and can take into account the present context and situation to decide and implement the most appropriate behaviour for each moment of the day. However, as mentioned previously, healing survivors often feel 'out of control' and that they are not functioning 'normally'. More often than not we are hampered by the physiological (physical) effects of the trauma that make it difficult to feel grounded and keep life in perspective. The adult is often under-developed and overwhelmed by the wounded child and the dysfunctional parent. I cannot list the number of times I have listened to a survivor in immense distress about an emotion that is from childhood rather than from the present time. Emotions such as sadness, fear and anger, when examined by the adult state, are seen to be relevant to something from childhood not the present moment. As soon as I ask, 'Where is your adult' the ex-guest usually laughs and admits they hadn't remembered to allow their adult to review what was happening.

I hope that you are beginning to realise the intended message of this book is this: how we feel today, or any day, is our choice. What we do with our life is *our choice*, however making the right choice is very difficult without recognising and confronting the child messages or stored parental beliefs that we all carry. Furthermore, it is highly likely we will self-sabotage and not reach our true potential if we do not confront our negative self-beliefs inherited from childhood. How can we make the right choice if I believe, for example, that I am worthless? The aim is to become fully functioning adults who consciously respond to reality and interact with others in the world. As adults, we are able to make informed choices and decisions about the way we live our lives. To recognise the lies imposed on us in childhood and no longer allow these lies to dominate the way we think and behave. Whenever you are feeling overwhelmed or emotional a good question to reflect on is, 'is this emotion relevant to what is happening today.

Suggestion

Spend a small part of each day developing your adult self. Use your adult self to connect with your child self to see how the child self is feeling, then comfort the child. One way to do this is to use the right arm (the left side of the brain) to stroke the left upper arm (the child self-right brain), saying loving words[141]. I have found that having an understanding of TA theory has been and is incredibly beneficial to aid me in my healing journey.

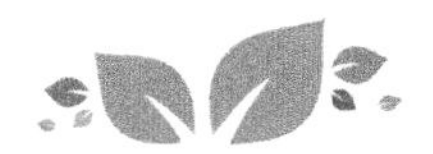

CHAPTER TWELVE
Learning To Love and Nurture Yourself

There are only two feelings,
Love and fear.
There are only two languages,
Love and fear.
There are only two activities,
Love and fear.
There only two motives,
two procedures,
two frameworks,
LI,two results.
Love and fear.
Love and fear.

- Michael Leunig's poem 'Love and Fear' in 'When I talk to you'.

Once we have started to examine our internal selfcritical parental voices, and reject these beliefs, it becomes possible to start to genuinely love ourselves more. I believe that healing is about finding more love in my life. Both self-love and love for others. Our childhoods were directed and governed by fear, which was needed to protect us and keep us safe, our brains grew and developed ruled by fear and self-protection in order for us to survive. Now we can start to release that fear and replace it with love.

As adults, we have a choice: we can continue to let our lives be ruled by fear, we can continue to protect ourselves by using anger, by isolating ourselves, or living in anxiety. That way of living feels comfortable and familiar; it is predictable and manageable. Each of us knows how to live in fear. *Often covered by anger.* Or we can choose to challenge and face the fear and turn life around. We can choose to re-focus and realign our brains to live in *love*. This is not easy, as we have kept ourselves alive by being directed and controlled by fear. Love is, for many of us, an alien emotion.

How do we do this? How do we live in love, love for ourselves, love for each other, and love for the God of our understanding? Re-programming ourselves is not easy, and all our instincts fight against living in love. Each time I succeed a little bit, I live a little more, I grow a little more, and I become happier and I enjoy sharing that happiness with others.

I am not talking about forgetting or ignoring my pain, overcoming my trauma by forgetting it and just feeling love. I am now inviting you to use that sense of love to give yourself the courage to face your childhood fears and pain, and by doing so, release the fear, to allow space for love.

To truly love is a huge challenge. To love the people who do us wrong in the now; to love the people who have not cared that we suffered trauma. To love the world that does not seem to understand us.

If you are reading this book, I know that you do have self-love deep within you – if you did not, you would never have decided to embark on the hard road to healing.

When we truly love ourselves then we will truly heal because we will know that we deserve to heal and that we have the right to a good life. I love myself and want to give myself the best life possible. Do you?

Suggestions

Here are a few suggestions you might like to try each day (add your own).

- Spend five minutes each day (or when you think of it) writing down what you love within yourself. Be kind to yourself, and each time you have a negative thought, make sure to lovingly correct yourself.
- Write down the names of anyone you really dislike or are angry with, in the now, not your perpetrator (that is quite different). Then think what there is to love about them. If you do choose to do this about someone who hurt you in childhood, let your adult do this exercise because your child has to always have the opportunity to express their anger until it is all vented, which can only really happen once we have fully remembered and acknowledged what happened.
- Concentrate on anything in the present, or in your childhood, that fills you with positive thoughts. Allow yourself to concentrate on that positive image (it might be your loving grandmother, a kind teacher, a wonderful moment when you felt safe, any moment at any time that gives you a happy, positive feeling). Embrace and grow that feeling.

- Read books about self-love; a particularly good one is 'How to Fall in Love with Yourself' by Amanda Donner (there are lots of others as well).
- Go for a walk, smile, and behave warmly to everyone you meet: the person in the shop, the person on the street – anyone and everyone you meet.
- Every time you feel that familiar feeling of anxiety or fear or anger, stop, take deep breaths, and say to yourself 'I choose love, I choose love'. I CHOOSE LOVE.

Finding love is not easy – sometimes it is easier to hate, be anxious, or think negative thoughts about people, and it is hard work to love unconditionally. However, the rewards are endless. If you choose love, love determinedly and love despite the obstacles. You will be amazed at how you will change your world and the lives of the people around you. It is that hard and also that simple.

Nurturing By Self-Parenting

Finding and feeling love goes hand in hand with selfparenting by nurturing myself. Self-nurturing is giving love to myself. My wounded inner child needs a lot of love and nurturing from an adult. This is something the child missed out on. Who better than myself to love and parent my inner child?

Sadly, we tend to parent our inner child as we were parented so, as my mother did not give me much attention, that is my natural way of parenting both my own children and my inner child[142]. In consequence, it is a constant fight to give my inner child enough time and love. How did your mother parent you? Did you parent your children the same way? Or did you try to do the opposite? If you did the opposite, then parent your inner child as you hopefully have parented your own child or children.

Learning to take care of our inner child's needs, wants and desires, and loving unconditionally that inner child, are all necessary for healing. It is virtually impossible, and actually quite abusive to ourselves, to try to force external change without first addressing our core issues and healing our wounded child. The first step towards healing is learning to love that wounded, hurting child. Healing from the original trauma is one issue, learning to love and support the inner child in an on-going and committed way is the next area to be addressed.

We may heal from the effects from trauma, but then what? If we have not developed a strong, loving parent, it is very hard to permanently change those original negative parent messages, so we are at risk of sabotaging our own healing. Our healing will be very hard if not impossible if we do not explore and work on developing self-love and self-parenting. Self-parenting is much easier if we work with a therapist to learn how to do it – we each have different negative messages from childhood that can impede our own healing and knowledge as to how to be an effective self-parent. Simply paying attention to the parenting voices within ourselves, and the hurting child self, is a very productive start whether on our own or with a therapist. Giving love to our child in a nurturing way is incredibly helpful. As I mentioned this can be ridiculously hard if you received no parental love, as you will *not* have the neural connections or memory to know what to do[144].

As a start, try to trust and validate your inner child's feelings about little things. Remembering all emotions come from our child self. Try to notice what you are feeling asking and validating yourself with reaffirming questions like, 'What are you feeling?' or 'What do you really feel like doing today?' and listen to the emotional response. *A very basic rule is to be kind to yourself.*

What is really important is to become aware of blaming, scolding, lecturing, commanding, criticizing, judging, threatening language from your inner parent to the inner child, and work on changing that. Listen to what you say to yourself internally, review and think 'is that kind or true?', and 'would I say that to anyone else?' This process is really the journey of learning to unconditionally love yourself, and to find the way to re-parent yourself that suits you best. The process of self-parenting also involves the process of setting new boundaries and guidelines. Our child needs boundaries just like our own children do or did. Selfparenting does not mean allowing your child self to do what they want when they want, that is not loving yourself or others!

A basic problem can be a result of many of us coming from dysfunctional families is that we really *do not know how* to be a nurturing parent to our child. Our wounded child is often over-disciplined or underdisciplined by ourselves. We need to employ our adult to inform our nurturing parent, to source information about what is healthy parenting, including limits and boundaries. Some people have found watching a TV series with a 'happy family' can be helpful, talking with your therapist, sharing with friends, and reading parenting books without self-judgment can also help. Sometimes these new parenting guidelines are very difficult to incorporate as they go directly against family rules learned in childhood, and directly against what you needed to do as a child to survive. It can be very difficult for survivors to venture out and learn new ways of being in healthy relationships. It requires the inner child to trust that the inner parent has the power to 'go against' the family rules and really protect the child.

I believe that while only we can be responsible for our own parenting, we also need validation and contact with other people to support our healing. For a lot of survivors, families and perpetrators are not in recovery and it is not safe to involve them in the healing process – in many cases they don't want to know. Many survivors feel isolated because they have to leave their family of origin completely. I would encourage you to try to build a strong support network through counselling, support groups, and friendships. It would be ideal if some of this network were securely attached and non-traumatised people. It is important for your adult to find new, healthy people to mentor and support your growth. However, letting your wounded child choose these people alone could be tricky, as the child is likely to have over-glamorised expectations. For many survivors, it takes a lot of healing in order to distinguish what was truly nurturing and what was not. For example, a child who was repeatedly sexually abused by parents may have been told or believed that that was how parents show their love. Healing will require examination of the many destructive mixed messages contained in this behaviour by a parent against a child. Additionally, abuse tends to be intergenerational and survivor's parents are often also survivors, often resulting in minimal healthy nurturing role modelling within the family.

It can be very empowering for survivors to know that by healing they are giving themselves permission to learn how to love and be loved. There is so much hope for previously dysfunctional families when one or more parents choose to heal their own childhood pain and become more attentive and loving to their own children. This is how we can each stop the intergenerational impact of abuse.

The positive, nurturing parent is present when our needs are met, when we take care of our health, and when we can provide ourselves with the love and affection that we require to feel safe and secure in the world. Our nurturing parent will also encourage us to explore the world.

Points to Remember

- It takes time to develop trust. Avoid judging your inner child. For example, if you say to yourself 'Inner child, I love you' and your inner child responds with 'No you don't, you liar! You've never loved me!' be sure not to get into an argument about it. What your inner child believes is their truth.
- Aim for a win-win for parent and inner child, where both parties have their needs met. If conflicting needs between the two selves are strong enough, you might experience an inner conflict, which can create a major problem in your life. Physical, emotional, mental or social paralysis, panic, inability to make decision/s, and somatic illness, usually indicate an inner conflict is happening. *Start listening.*

- Be consistent – try not to stop and start, don't work on loving yourself every day for a week and then leave it for ten days, if you do this the child learns not to trust the parent.
- Be there for your child because you want to – doing it out of duty, or because it makes you feel good, is not enough. Your child needs to know you are there for them *no matter what.*
- It is the responsibility of the parent to initiate and maintain contact. The parent must take responsibility for their half of the conversation first. Just as in outer parenting, the child may become even more rebellious and distant when the once neglectful parent starts showing concern, however, be consistent because the child will naturally change in response.

Suggestions for Nurturing Our Inner Child

- Try a weighted blanket, expensive to buy but I have found are wonderful for survivors who were not held; try just the feeling of a heavy blanket first. The weight holds you in a nurturing way. Weighted blankets are often used for Autistic children to help them feel safe. In my experience working with survivors, some people have a huge reaction from trying one. This actually can be helpful, as it may be the rebel child expressing anger that they haven't been loved and held.
- Lie in and wrap yourself in a hammock.
- Stroke your left arm with your right arm.

- Look in the mirror and try to say words from your own nurturing parent list of words.
- Ask a therapist or safe person to hold you so you can experience the feeling of being safe and nurtured (because if you don't know the feeling of being held you cannot start self-parenting and nurturing).
- When you are feeling overwhelmed by your emotions, try to imagine that your parent is holding your hand, keeping watch over you so nothing bad will happen. Use your right hand as the parent to hold the left hand as your child, as the body is the opposite of the brain's hemispheres.

It is paramount to recognise the importance of healing both the inner parent and the inner child. If you do not develop a loving inner parent who can nurture and protect the inner child, healing is almost impossible and certainly very slow.

Here is an exercise I recommend for each of you to do, the harder it is to do the more you need to do it! If you have suffered from abandonment at any stage in your childhood then it will be both particularly difficult and particularly helpful.

Abandonment is the ultimate feeling of not feeling deserving of love. It is accompanied by profound hopelessness. Often, survivors of abandonment will look to someone else to make life better, when in fact it is only ourselves who can make life better by showing love to ourselves.

Abandonment is one of the hardest traumas from which to heal, and abandonment and neglect have the greatest detrimental effect on the development of the brain[144]. If we receive no input at all from our primary carer, then our brain cannot fully develop, as our neurons grow from interaction with others.

Suggestion

This exercise appears to be simple, yet it is very effective. The harder you find it to do this exercise the more you will gain from it. If you think the exercise is silly, leave it and come back to it when you feel ready and able. I have known people who take years before they can start to love themselves enough to start this exercise.

Choose a doll to represent yourself as a baby; take time with your choice, make sure the doll looks and feels right. This may involve several trips to shops and how much you spend is dependent not just on your own personal finances, but on how much you value yourself. You can buy a doll from a thrift store for a few dollars, or have one made at great expense – it is your decision how much you want to spend on yourself.

Once you have chosen the right doll for you and taken it home, observe your own reactions. Do you hate the doll? Do you want to hide it away? Do you want to hold it? Try not to be judgmental, but just observe your own reactions. The idea is to hold the doll lovingly as if he/she were you as a baby. However, it can take months before you can do this. Be kind to yourself and know the more you don't want to hold that doll, the more you do need to do this exercise. So, please do persist. At first you may be more comfortable just talking to your doll from a distance.

Slowly work up the length of time you can feel comfortable holding the doll in your arms. I repeat, this can be very hard to do, and the harder it is the more important it is to persevere. While holding the doll in your arms you may feel many different emotions – just accept whatever you are feeling; remember that there are no 'bad' feelings. It doesn't matter what comes up, just acknowledge the need to recognise that particular feeling in relation to yourself as a baby. When you can hold the doll as if it is a baby (yourself), spend up to 20 minutes a day talking, holding, giving love, and feeling your emotions in relation to this baby doll.

We have found for many people that the need for this exercise continues for several years, so I suggest that you keep doing this exercise for as long as you need it. It is important and far more effective if you can work with a doll rather than a stuffed animal or teddy. After all, you were not a stuffed animal when you were a baby, and this doll is a representation of you as a baby. It is also important to take care of your doll. Do not allow anyone to make fun of him/her or hurt him/her. If you have to start with a teddy this is still better than nothing, but a doll that represents you as a baby would be much better.

Social Media and How Destructive It Can Be to Self-Love

I have heard from many people how they have used social media, such as Facebook, as a form of connection or to gain validation. The problem is that often there is little to no validation or real connection from Facebook, but rather a constant stream of highlighted moments of other peoples' lives. Some may argue that we are now more connected than ever through social media and other online relationships, but research has shown that virtual interaction with others generally does not improve your mental health, and can actually increase your risk of depression[145].

A 2017 study investigated over half a million U.S. students in grades eight to 12 after the introduction of smartphones (which first came on the market in 2007). By 2015, two out of three US teens owned a smartphone. The researchers found that depressive symptoms in teens increased by 33% between 2010 and 2015. The suicide rate for girls increased by 65% during the same period[146]. Researchers determined that the rise in depressive symptoms even matched the increase of smartphone use year by year. They concluded that increased time on new devices, such as smartphones, can lead to significant increases in depression and suicide.

Other studies have shown similar results. A study of over 1,780 adults aged 19 to 32 found that those who spent the most time on social media sites had the highest risk of developing depression. Whereas, those who spent the most time on 'non-screen' pursuits, such as socializing face-to-face with friends, had the lowest risk of depression[147].

Ask yourself how are you using social media? Does it bring you pleasure? Does it validate your feelings? If the answer is yes, then that's great. If the answer is no, or if you don't know, or if it's only a maybe, then you could consider putting it aside for a week or two. Check in with yourself after a few days as to how you're feeling without using it. Then ask again after a week. A few members of our community who have done this found an extraordinary difference in their sense of wellbeing when they didn't use Facebook.

Social media can be a great tool in our healing (enhancing connection with others, etc.), but it can also be very unhelpful. Make sure that you know how you're being affected emotionally by your use of social media, and proceed with caution when deciding whether to continue using it.

Loving yourself and nurturing yourself are very important and you are worth it. Remind yourself of that. You deserve love in your life.

The one thing in life that's definitely true, your life will improve when love breaks through

When love breaks through your spirit soars high
You spread your wings and begin to fly
When love breaks through you take back your power
Your life becomes sweet when once it was sour
When love breaks through you begin to believe
There's nothing in life that you can't achieve
When love breaks through you see the truth
You recapture the freedom you lost in youth
When love breaks through you learn how to live
You release old resentments and start to forgive
When love breaks through you let go of shame
You embrace the past and no longer blame
When love breaks through you become less defensive
You feel more outgoing and less apprehensive
When love breaks through your answers become clear
You trust in yourself and let go of fear
When love breaks through you break out of yourself

You start to create emotional health

When love breaks through your future becomes bright

As your being is filled with more and more light

When love breaks through you can go with the flow

Feel good about yourself and allow it to show

When love breaks through you feel good enough

You'll develop a mind that's courageous and tough

When love breaks through you're filled with hope

Whatever the challenge you know you can cope

When love breaks through you fight for a cause

You achieve many things without needing applause

When love breaks through you wear a big smile

You realise your value and know you're worthwhile

When loves breaks through you're finally free

To be anything you've ever wanted to be

So, if you wish life was like this for you, keep chipping away 'til love breaks through

- Jonti Fell 2003. 'When Love Breaks Through'. Written as a gift to Heal For Life.

CHAPTER THIRTEEN
Setting Boundaries

As survivors of trauma, each of us has suffered boundary violations in our childhood that will have impacted on our ability to develop and maintain good boundaries in our adult lives. If you were emotionally abused, you are likely to have poor emotional boundaries because you were not allowed to have your own feelings, and you probably found it safest to be told what to feel. You learned from experience to only express feelings that would help you to be, or at least to feel a bit safer. If you were sexually or physically abused, you are likely to have poor physical boundaries as your physical boundaries were crossed.

For each of us, learning boundaries is a critical part of our healing. People with poor boundaries *say yes when they mean no, and no when they mean yes.*

They often cannot recognise the needs of others or themselves. They also may not respect or understand other peoples' boundaries.

We all have to learn how to set limits, *how to honour our own feelings,* and how to make choices that are in line with our own beliefs or wishes. Having good boundaries keeps us safe and helps us to know who is responsible for what, especially when there is conflict. Setting good boundaries helps us to develop a good sense of self. Generally speaking, developing good boundaries is particularly hard (and therefore very important) if the trauma started very early in life[148]. When I develop good boundaries, I recognise that it is only myself who is responsible for meeting my needs and wants, and it means that I find it easier to ask for help from others when I want it.

Definition of Boundaries

A simple definition comes from Cloud and Townsend(2017) who state that, 'Boundaries define us, they define what is me and what is not me.' Cloud and Townsend go further to state that, *'Any confusion of responsibility and ownership in our lives is a problem of boundaries. Just as homeowners set physical property lines around their land, we need to set mental, physical, emotional and spiritual boundaries for our lives to help us distinguish what is our responsibility and what isn't'* [149].

Our boundaries are set by us. Our boundaries are flexible, and by our own choice, changeable – if they are rigid, then they are no longer boundaries but rules. Physical boundaries of inanimate objects and geographical borderlines are easy to recognise. Most people immediately know when someone intrudes on the boundaries of what they physically own, for example when a thief breaks into their home or steals their car.

It is not always easy for us as survivors to recognise that we also have the right to own our thoughts, feelings and beliefs. These psychological boundaries are not as apparent as physical boundaries, yet they are just as real and certainly just as important. Healthy psychological boundaries help us to feel safe and comfortable in relationships, ensuring at all times that *we care about our self and our own needs and wants.*

What is within our boundaries? Another way to ask this is, 'What is within my control?' In addition to our physical body and health, we are responsible for our feelings; attitudes and beliefs; behaviours (and their consequences); choices; values; limits; talents; thoughts; desires; money; and giving and receiving love. The development of internal boundaries is important. Examples of internal boundary questions include: 'What do I like?'; 'What do I believe?'; 'What do I need to feel balanced and happy?'; and 'What do I think?' *Do you know the answers to those questions about yourself?*

When we have clearly-defined boundaries, we begin to communicate openly and directly. We establish guidelines for what we expect of others and what we will give them in return. We become clear about what we are responsible for, and we can allow others to be responsible for what happens in their lives. With good boundaries we can feel safe, make informed choices and feel free to live the way we want to.

Healthy boundaries are not meant to be walls to keep everything outside of us – boundaries are meant to be flexible. They are what we want, not what anyone else asks of us. This means boundaries are different for all people and we can choose to change a boundary at any time. Like walls with gates, we can choose what flows in and out. Good boundaries are clear and protective of our self, our values, and our beliefs. Good boundaries allow us to get close to others without the threat of losing ourselves or smothering, invading or trespassing on their lives.

Without clear boundaries, it can be challenging to develop mature, healthy relationships. This is often because, without awareness of our boundaries, it is difficult to recognise what is appropriate behaviour and what is not. It can be challenging to distinguish our needs and wishes from those of others. It can be difficult to make decisions and we can become too reliant on others to tell us what to think and feel. People lacking healthy, clearly-defined boundaries can also end up in difficult or even dangerous situations because they are not even aware that a line has been crossed, and that their boundaries have been violated. Without healthy boundaries, we are at risk of allowing dangerous or exploitative relationships.

Boundary Development

We develop healthy boundaries as we attach and then individuate (separate) from our primary caregiver[150]. Developing healthy boundaries can be very difficult when we have not had good examples of boundaries in our childhood. We may have had our boundaries broken so often that identifying safe boundaries is a new world for us, and our brain will try to tell us we don't have the right to do what we want.

We develop healthy boundaries by recognising that we matter, that *we have a right to how we are feeling*, and that we have a right to choose what we want to do and when we want to do it. As we learn boundaries, we can also recognise that sometimes it is ok to do what we don't want to do, because it matters so much to someone we love. We realise it is all a choice. Healthy boundaries make life so much simpler and so much more enjoyable because we do what we want to do and not what we *should* do. Better relationships are more likely because we don't look to other people to meet our needs, nor do we become disappointed if relationships fail because we have not been clear about our needs. Life is wonderful with good boundaries.

Suggestion

A starting point for developing boundaries is to ask yourself:

- What do I want?
- What do I need?
- Am I doing this because I want or because I feel I have to?
- Do I want to do this? If the answer is No. Will I do it anyway because it matters to someone I love?

The Effect of Trauma on Boundary Development

How does abuse and trauma in childhood affect boundary development? Why do many survivors have limited knowledge and understanding of boundaries? Boundaries are largely formed in childhood. How others treat a child shapes how his or her boundaries become defined. When a young child's needs are met appropriately and he or she feels safe and secure, the child develops a sense of personal boundaries[151].

In stark contrast, abuse and trauma in early childhood can rob a child of the sense of safety that is needed to explore his or her own identity. Any type of abuse, physical, emotional, or sexual, is a boundary violation. Victims of abuse experience a loss of control over their own bodies and lives. Children who grow up in homes that don't function well in terms of communication or understanding, where physical, mental, and emotional boundaries are not respected, are often confused, vulnerable, and feel insecure. These children often do not even attempt to defend their rights to individuality, as their parents' behaviour has taught the child that they do not have any rights[152].

Cloud and Townsend (2017) explain further that, *'Attachment is the foundation of the soul's existence. When this foundation is cracked or faulty, boundaries become impossible to develop'* Why? Because when we lack a sense of security in relationships, we do not know what to do when in conflict. We feel we only have two choices: to set limits and risk losing the relationship; or to refrain from setting limits, and remain a prisoner of the dynamic we have co-created. We feel dependent on other people's needs to make decisions about ourselves.

When a caregiver fails to meet a child's needs, the child does not learn to experience his or her own needs, but rather they experience only the needs of others. This blurs the boundaries between the child's and other's needs. Parents who have unmet needs of their own may use the vulnerable child to meet their needs, further confusing the identity of the child. For example, mothers who suffered their own boundary violations when they were very young may find it distressing and acutely painful when their infant wants to move away and develop their own self. The mother may demand closeness and dependency from the child to fill her own unmet emotional needs[153].

Violent acts of assault or trauma, and extended periods of emotional or sexual abuse, have significant, enduring negative effects on the development of boundaries[154]. Children who have been abused often are not allowed, or are never given the chance, to learn their boundaries. For example, when a child is sexually abused this leads to confusion over the very basic rules of ownership of the body. Instead of learning that their body is their own and no one else is allowed to touch it without the child's permission, they learn that their body is to be hurt, abused, or manipulated by others. They have no control over their own body. Their physical boundaries are likely to be variable or nonexistent.

Cloud and Townsend (2017) also describe some common boundary injuries that occur in development when growing up in a dysfunctional family. Generally, the severity of the trauma or dysfunction in the family deepens the resulting boundary problem.

Boundary injuries may occur when:

- Love or safety is withdrawn by caregivers when a child states a boundary

- When caregivers react with hostility, rage, or violence to the child's attempts to separate and have boundaries
- When caregivers are over-controlling and try to prevent children from making mistakes
- When children are not given limits or boundaries by caregivers (therefore growing up without respect for other people's limits)
- When children are given inconsistent limits (e.g. caregivers are overly strict then overly lax, especially in alcohol or drug addicted homes)
- When children experience trauma, they do not develop two very necessary foundations of development: the belief 'the world is reasonably safe' and the belief 'I have control over my own life'.

The most extreme representations of inadequate boundary formation often come in the form of mental illness. Steele and Van der Hart (2011) describe clients diagnosed with Dissociative Identity Disorder, schizophrenia, or personality disorders as fundamentally needing help to repair, form, and manage their boundaries[155]. This is because they had no examples of good boundaries to learn from and they have no knowledge of how to set good boundaries. ***Severe trauma at a very early age usually means poor boundary development***[156].

Other problems survivors of trauma may suffer with due to poor boundaries include 'co-dependency' issues; intimacy issues; addictions; and domestic violence.

Or alternatively, they repeat the cycle of abuse, abandonment, or neglect toward their own children. Friedman and Boumil (1995) share some examples of how under-developed boundaries can be experienced by an individual. See how many apply to you[157].

With under-developed boundaries, you will find:

- It is difficult for you to ask for what you want and need and hard to say 'NO' to others when you would like to
- It is easier to take care of other people's needs and desires than your own – it is also easier to go along with them than express your own opinions
- Other people seem to know you better than you know yourself – they also seem to know what is best for you
- It is hard to make decisions because you frequently don't know how you are feeling or what you think about important issues
- When feelings are present, they are so strong that they are overwhelming – it is difficult to control the 'volume', to turn feelings up or down and still be in touch with them
- Relationships seem to be one-way and you always put more into them than you get out of them, and even though you're not getting what you want, you stay within the relationship
- Other people's moods have a big effect on you because you feel responsible for them or because to be aware of other people's feelings is the only way to stay safe – when a friend is happy, you are happy; when a friend is sad or angry, you blame yourself

- Concentrating and paying attention are often difficult – you are too easily distracted or influenced by things going on around you
- Learning from your own mistakes is not easy – you seem to keep making the same errors in judgment repeatedly, and you have little confidence in your own experience
- Other people seem to have a better grasp on reality than you do, so you depend on them to tell you what is true and real
- People can take or borrow things from you without returning them or repaying you – what's theirs is theirs, and what's yours is theirs.

Over-developed boundaries can lead to:

- Isolation – not letting anyone be a part of your life so as to keep yourself safe
- Having no friendships because you can never accommodate the needs of your friends
- Inflexibility and rigidity – when boundaries become rules, you are at risk of both of these ways of behaving.

Cloud and Townsend (2017) elaborate further by describing common problems with boundaries. They suggest that boundary problems can be categorised into four key areas: compliance; controlling; avoidance, and non-responsiveness. Of course, it's likely that boundary problems can be a combination of more than one of these. It's also possible to have different boundary problems in different areas of life, or within different relationships.

Compliants – Say 'YES' to the Bad

Cloud and Townsend (2017) state if parents have blocked a child's ability to say 'No' this can handicap that child for life. These children can become compliant adults who do not feel they have the right to say 'No'; 'I disagree'; 'Stop that'; 'It's wrong'. People who are compliant can become chameleon-like, changing to suit others because of their many underlying fears. They are completely disempowered. They do not think they can make their own choices or decisions. Is that you?

Avoidants – Say 'NO' to the Good

These are people who avoid situations or people so they won't have to set boundaries. They often find it difficult to ask for help; to recognize their needs, and to let others get close to them. As Cloud and Townsend (2017) explain *'Individuals with walls for boundaries can let in neither good nor bad. No one can touch them'*. It is common to be both compliant and avoidant, i.e. say 'yes' to things that aren't good for you, and 'no' to things you really want and need.

Controller – Don't respect others' Boundaries

Many, if not most, survivors find in adult life the only way they can feel safe is to be controlling. Controllers don't respect another's limits. As Cloud and Townsend (2017) explain, *'They resist taking responsibility for their own lives, so they need to control others. People who feel the need to control can do so aggressively, through verbal or physical force, or manipulatively by talking others into saying 'yes' through guilt or seduction.'*

It is possible to be controlling even though you are seen to be compliant or avoidant. For example, doing things for others you don't want to with the unspoken expectation 'I'll scratch your back then expect you to scratch mine', without telling the other person what you expect in return.

Non-Responsiveness – Don't Hear the Needs of Others

Some boundary problems manifest by simply not responding to responsibilities in our lives. As Cloud and Townsend state (2017) 'We are responsible to care about and help, within certain limits, others in our lives. To ignore needs of others or be narcissistic and exclude others' needs is non-responsive.' This becomes problematic when others tell us they have a problem and we don't respond. For example, if one person in a marriage is unhappy and their partner does not hear his or her feelings and does not participate in helping solve the problems, that partner is not holding up their responsibility to the marriage.

Survivors are often very good at unconsciously creating boundaries, in the form of coping mechanisms. Sometimes our boundaries are the opposite from what would be helpful. Sadly, we reverse the function of boundaries and keep the bad in and the good out. This is evident when survivors hold on to negative feelings and beliefs (keeping the bad in) and find it almost impossible to ask for help, love, affection or validation (allowing the good in).

An essential part of healing is acknowledging and correcting violated boundaries. It is also necessary to create boundaries that are flexible and permeable enough to allow change, growth and interdependence, and strong enough to retain the essential sense of self as separate from others.

The issue of 'boundaries' is often new to survivors when they begin to heal. I suggest you start by trying to make small changes in your life. The first step is often to become aware when boundaries have been violated.

Summary of Boundary Problems

	CAN'T SAY	CAN'T HEAR
NO	*THE COMPLIANT* *Feels guilty and/or controlled by others; can't set boundaries*	*THE CONTROLLER* *Aggressively or manipulatively violates boundaries of others*
YES	*THE NON-RESPONSIVE* *Sets boundaries against responsibility to love*	*THE AVOIDANT* *Sets boundaries against receiving care of others.*

Ask yourself some basic questions:

- Who don't I trust? And decide if you can work out the reason and if you really want to keep them in your life
- What makes me unhappy or resentful? And decide to make changes

- What makes me angry or sad? Do I want to feel these feelings?
- What makes me uncomfortable or shames me?

How can I change the situation?

The process of taking action to repair, rebuild and manage boundaries is often challenging as patterns of a lifetime may need to be changed and this change can initially feel uncomfortable.

Boundaries cannot be developed in isolation, they are about relationships, so reading, studying, or practicing boundary setting alone will do little to help. Start to think about your relationships and try to be clear about any individual decisions that you would like to make, and then go about implementing these boundaries.

Healthy boundaries are essential to living a life that is truly of your own making. Clear boundaries can lead to more loving relationships, clarity about your life, and more energy to spend doing what you really want.

Trauma and abuse can have devastating effects on boundary development. Survivors often do not know they have choice, feel like victims, and are vulnerable to continued exploitation and abuse. A core element of healing is the development of a sense of self-worth, wholeness and individuality. Learning self-worth means that you recognise that you are unique and your boundaries deserve to be respected[158]. Here are some specific types of boundaries so you can consider how good your boundaries are in each area.

Physical Boundaries

Your physical boundaries not only include your skin, but also your comfort zone – the space around you, and the invisible circle of energy that surrounds you. Your zone is fluid, and how close people can get to you usually depends on how well you know them, or how you feel about them. Do you allow people to touch you even when it feels uncomfortable? Do you claim your own physical space? You can change your physical boundaries depending on how you are feeling. No one should ever touch you without permission. That is your right. A healthy physical boundary is when you can say no to a hug or a kiss if you don't feel like it. Holding out your hand for a handshake is a good idea when you don't want the person to try to give you a hug. Try it.

Emotional Boundaries

We are responsible for our emotions and how we feel at any time. You have been reading all about reacting to reminders of trauma and these are reactions and not controllable. However apart from trauma related triggers (which will decrease with healing), your reactions and feelings are your choice not dictated by what you have experienced in childhood but what you want as an adult. A person crosses our emotional boundaries when they tell us either how to feel or what we are feeling. When a mother says to a child, 'Don't be frightened,' she is violating the child's emotional boundary by telling the child what they are allowed to feel or not feel, therefore weakening the child's self-belief and ability to allow themselves to feel fear. It is important to always acknowledge an emotion the child is experiencing, rather than invalidating the feeling – to invalidate the feeling is to invalidate the child. Does your mother still invalidate your feelings?

Sexual Boundaries

Sexual boundaries are the boundaries that you decide what is appropriate sexual behaviour for you. Sexual boundaries mean that you recognise that you can choose your level of sexual engagement with another person. If you do not feel like having sex, that is your right. You are under no obligation to have sex or sexual contact as a result of another person's needs. Do you determine how far you go with a partner? Do you stop people from making sexual remarks that illicit an uncomfortable reaction? Equally, are you so frightened that you have set sexual boundaries that are so rigid that you say 'no' to any sexual involvement even when you really want to say yes?

Mental Boundaries

Mental boundaries are your thoughts, attitudes, beliefs and values. Do you allow others to influence the way you think? Influence you in what you value? Are your values your own values or your parents? This is really interesting to think about in relation to Transactional Analysis in Chapter Eleven and any unconscious parental influence. Many of us carry our parents' values as if they were our own.

Time Boundaries

Deciding how much time you will allow for various activities in the day and deciding how long you might wait if a friend is late for a meeting, or deciding how much time you will give to a friend on the phone. Poor time boundaries are when we allow someone to take up our time when we don't really want them to. Equally damaging is having overly strong time boundaries; this is when we have no ability to allow for minor lateness by a friend.

Spiritual Boundaries

Spiritual boundaries are not letting others define our spiritual beliefs. My spiritual boundaries are being crossed when someone states their religious belief as a fact, such as 'Jesus is the son of God'. That is a belief, not a fact, and if anyone tries to tell me otherwise they are crossing my spiritual boundaries. It is important to separate beliefs from facts in order to set up, maintain, and respect spiritual boundaries.

Christian Boundaries

Many survivors, as we live in a predominantly Christian country and especially for those who have suffered religious abuse, are further challenged as they struggle with what are 'biblically appropriate' limits to set. For example, the biblical commandment, 'Honour your mother and father', taken literally may mean a survivor remains in an abusive relationship with his or her parents even after they have become an adult and can leave. Christian values have tended to become social norms so people may have the belief that 'family is everything.' Cloud and Townsend (2017) recognise the common struggles many Christians have with setting limits and boundaries. Allowing our own belief around forgiveness is another important boundary we have the right to set.

Financial Boundaries

Financial boundaries are the ones that we set around finances. It is our decision whether we lend money or not, and if, when, and how much money we choose to spend on ourselves or on others. If you never have any money and have debts, ask yourself if that is the way you want to live. Or do you have poor financial boundaries? A weak boundary is when you lend money to someone when you don't want to.

Suggestion

Consider when or how did you display unhealthy boundaries today? Did you say 'yes' when you really didn't want to? Did you say NO when you really wanted to say yes? Did you let anyone do or say anything to you that upset you today?

You might like to check in each of the types of boundaries and decide whether you are happy with your boundaries. So, for financial boundaries you might like to ask yourself, 'What do I want to happen in relation to finances? Am I happy to lend or borrow money?'

I need to add that feeling bad is very normal when we first start to try and set boundaries. You have the right to alter your boundaries whenever and however you choose.

A good idea to help you with recognising who you want to spend your time with is to draw the diagram below on a large sheet of paper.

In the 'Me' circle, write the names of anyone you feel completely intimate with, to whom you would tell absolutely anything. There may not be anyone in this circle.

In the next 'Cuddle' circle, write the names of anyone you feel very close to, people with whom you would happily share a cuddle. In the 'Hug' circle, write in the names of people you would give a hug to (people you are close to but with whom you are not very intimate). In the 'Handshake' circle, write the names of friends who you like, but with whom you are not very close. In the 'Wave' circle, write the people you would say hello to, but not invite home to dinner.

Everyone else goes in the outer, or 'Others' circle – these are people you do not want to acknowledge or do not want to be an important part of your life. When you have done this exercise notice where everyone in your life is placed. It is a good way of visually seeing how you want your relationships to be, and having done the exercise then try to stick to your own decisions.

It is recommended to do this exercise on a regular basis, as boundaries are not rigid but changeable – just as our boundaries change, so too do our relationships.

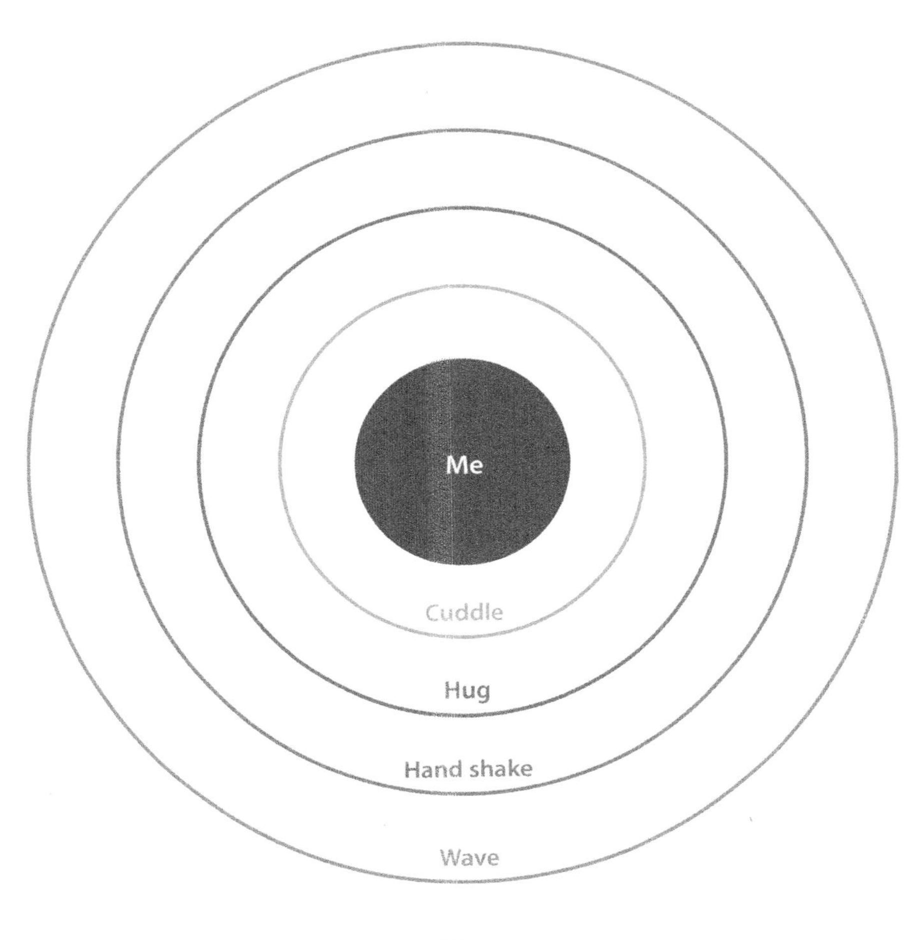

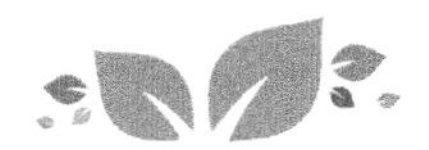

CHAPTER FOURTEEN
Overcoming the Impact of Powerlessness; How to Change Thought Patterns, and the Impact of Shame

One of the major effects of childhood trauma is that in our adult lives we often feel powerless, worthless, and unimportant, and this has a major impact on our ability to heal ourselves and impedes our ability to love ourselves. The brain is plastic, we take on messages that we receive from our parents, and our brain develops and changes as a result of these messages. Chapter Eleven explored how we can divide these messages into ones that we received externally (parental ego state), and ones we decided on internally (child ego state) as a result of our childhood experiences. The fact remains the biggest and deepest impact of trauma is a feeling of powerlessness because we could not stop what was happening to us.

Recognising the way this feeling of powerlessness had impacted on my own development was, I found, a very important step. Why did I begin to feel so worthless? It is certainly *not* because I was worthless, it is because as a child, on countless occasions, I learned through the actions of the adults around me, that I *was* powerless.

For you it might have been as a combination of poor parenting (whether a critical or a rescuing parent) as well as the powerlessness we all inevitably felt at the hands of the person who perpetrated our abuse. This message of powerlessness is internalised 'I am powerless when my parent (or perpetrator) decides something'; 'I have to do what they tell me because the consequences are not endurable.' Trauma is lifethreatening (to the child at that age) because there is no choice, it is not possible to disobey. The sense of powerlessness is absolute. The depth of the feeling of powerlessness may be exacerbated by the parental messages we received, but it will always occur to some extent from any trauma. It will depend on the type of parenting we received, as well as the age we were and the type of trauma we suffered, as to how deeply affected we are by the feeling of powerlessness.

The feeling of powerlessness is pervasive and debilitating. It is the feeling that we do not have control over decisions that we make, that we do not have control over our bodies, that we are not in charge, and that we do not have the right to have our needs met. The feeling occurs because indeed it was true: we had no control at all. We were totally powerless to determine the outcome of what was happening to us. This is huge. I can remember when I first recalled the moment of absolute powerlessness and hopelessness I felt when I realised I could not escape from the doctor who was abusing me, nor could I open the door and get away from him. The door was seared into my memory and I used to be triggered by locked doors. This sense of powerlessness is what holds us back from reaching our true potential in life. If we have suffered trauma, often we don't believe we have the power to be anything or to control our own destiny as adults. It is why we need to be reempowered by our therapist or by any healing we undertake for ourselves.

I had parents who, apart from the sexual abuse, in my daily life did not disempower me as badly as some of you may have been. I did not suffer from the daily debilitating emotional abuse that some of you might have experienced. I did not have parents who constantly made me feel inadequate with their words or actions. However, I learned from being sexually abused that I could not escape when being abused, therefore I was powerless to prevent the abuse. This meant that in my daily adult left brain life, I felt in charge of my destiny and was able to do whatever I wanted to do in a work sense, however, the trauma of the sexual abuse meant that the feeling of powerlessness from my trauma overrode my ability to accept and internalise any positive feedback I received.

This inability to accept any positive feedback was felt even as a successful businesswoman. Particularly, whenever I had an important phone call to make or needed to assert my rights in a situation, I would falter badly, and often to my detriment. I always felt I had to prove myself.

A large part of the powerlessness comes from the fact that no one helped us, or perhaps no one noticed what was happening to us – no one did anything to stop the abuse. Naturally, we will feel powerless or worthless when no one did anything to help us when we were little. We will undoubtedly have issues around power.

We will try to overcome this feeling by some of the following actions.

Controlling Others

We all like to control others or some area of our lives to counteract this feeling of powerlessness. I mean all of us. Many guests at Heal For Life have argued the point, however I can always help them find an area in their life they determinedly control. What area of your life do you control? Who you see? Where you live? What you eat?

To recognise that this need to be in control comes from being made to feel powerless, is really helpful. I discussed it already in relation to boundaries, now let us explore it further. Acknowledging that because of this powerlessness we may not let others tell us what to do can be a great start towards changing this boundary. It may help you to start to try to listen to others. Have you ever been organising an event with another survivor? It's likely that both of you will try to organise it your way! In an attempt to overcome powerlessness, we tend to organise and control everyone around us. I, and only I, will know the right way, and everyone must do it my way – coupled with that need, it will also feel like a very personal attack if they have a different view to mine.

We see this controlling behaviour often in the workplace. I believe that demanding, unreasonably authoritarian bosses will almost invariably have suffered abuse or trauma, now they need to control others in order to feel okay about themselves. All bullies will have suffered from feelings of powerlessness, so that now they need to overcome those feelings by bullying others. Those of us who were bullied have the feelings or powerlessness reaffirmed by being bullied. As you read in attachment styles, bullies tend to have avoidant attachment styles, while those who have been bullied tend to fall into the ambivalent attachment style. This is not an excuse for bullies – it is an explanation. Some of the children who come to the Heal For Life kid's camps are bullies, and when they are safe enough to acknowledge that their bullying behaviour has come from fear and from the need to be in control, that is when change can, and does, happen. When they process some of their original trauma, lose their fear and sense of powerlessness, then change is rapid and *permanent*.

While bullying behaviour is unacceptable, it is unfortunate that we blame the bully, because this behaviour stems from hurt that happened to him or her. If the bully is helped as a child to understand why they are behaving the way they are, and not blamed for their actions, they can be supported to heal from their trauma, then they are more likely to be able to change their behaviour.

Here are some of the ways we assert control in our lives.

Controlling our Environment

Often, we control our environment by choosing to stay at home and not go out very often, if at all. This is one of the main impacts of trauma, for people to isolate, so much so that they can become agoraphobic. It is one way some people's brains cope with powerlessness as it at least gives the person power over their environment. If this is a problem for you, then I suggest you spend time with your inner child, explain that you will protect them when you go outside, and extend love to that terrified little person inside. Then try a very short trip and gradually extend going outside as you feel safe to do so. As when helping a little child, you will want to be very kind and gentle with yourself in this process, and avoid any kind of self-blaming.

Controlling our Eating Habits

Many of our guests have suffered from some form of eating disorder. Anorexia and bulimia are two very obvious ways we take control of our body, often when we have no control over anything else. I have noticed that the reasons for choosing to exert control over the body are varied. In some cases, it is to exert control over something, and the amount this food control annoys others adults can be subconsciously quite satisfying; an act of defiance. It can also be a form of control over something that was said – the abuser may have labelled the person skinny or commented on their size, or perhaps meal times were traumatic at home. Among the teenagers with whom I have worked eating issues usually relate to the teenager determinedly showing they have control over their body and no one else does. Interestingly, I think the reason teenagers want perfect bodies is often so that they will look 'normal' and look like the models in magazines. They think if they look perfect then they will no longer have such painful self-doubts about themselves. Further to this, many believe they will then be treated normally and not as a misfit. Other reasons reported to me have been very clear and specific relating to instances from their abuse and their own need to control what their body takes in as an act of defiance. Sometimes the food issues are from internalised parental messages, the parent telling a child 'you are too fat' or similar judgmental comments about the child's body.

Of course, the societal expectation that a woman should be slim is implicit in our culture, so obviously some element of that exists but, in my experience, I have not found it to be the primary reason. Conversely, being overweight is generally a protective mechanism, so as not to be as provocative, to provide a protective layer over the inner child[159]. I have found that it is women who have been sexually abused who do this, and it is very hard to shift prior to healing. However, I have noticed that as people heal and no longer have a need to protect the wounded child that the weight just disappears, regardless of eating habits.

Interestingly, stress can lead to holding weight around the mid-section of the body. The main, deep, abdominal fat contains five times as many cortisol receptors as other parts of the body. When cortisol is released, it signals the liver to release more glucose into the bloodstream, which then causes an increase in insulin production. If this continues to happen not only are we storing fat, but you begin to develop insulin resistance – a precursor to diabetes[160].

Refusing Commands

Survivors often react, as mentioned previously, if they are told to do something, especially if it is instructed without good reason. We are very likely to react and do the opposite! This is a particular problem for traumatised kids when at school, as traditional discipline can make them more reactive. Boot camps are usually the worst possible solution for children who have suffered trauma as it imposes behaviour and demands obedience without questioning. This is retraumatising. Similarly, survivors who go into the armed forces can suffer terribly. The training to have a successful army is discipline without explanation and to be accepted without question. When discipline is imposed in this way, survivors of trauma may turn to coping mechanisms of either being totally compliant or by behaving rebelliously. If this rebelliousness is destroyed through the powerlessness of the situation, the result can be very destructive. It will be like being abused all over again.

Some survivors find the concept of a very disciplined environment appealing, and that is why they turn to the services; however, it can be very harmful to survivors[161].

We are very careful at Heal For Life never to order anyone to do anything as generally people will not feel safe and their willingness to heal will be impaired.

Looking After Others to Feel Good About Ourselves

It is arguably a good thing that trauma exists, because a very high percentage of survivors exist in all helping professions. However, it can be done to the extreme, and there are many survivors who care and do more for others than they care or do for themselves. Could this be true for you? This is particularly true for the child who had to act as parent for his or her parents. Who may have then developed their identity and sense of self- worth around looking after other's needs. In doing so, we feel in control because we are looking after the other person.

Being Angry

Disempowered men often take their pain out on women with violence, and, to a lesser degree, vice versa[162]. Men release testosterone in a sympathetically aroused state to give them the ability to fight the danger. When this powerful hormone has been released men may turn to violence to cope, more so than women[163]. I wonder how many violent men had abusive mothers? Or as a child they were not helped to learn to self-soothe or to express their emotions. Certainly, many of our male guests admit to being violent. I have always wondered if road rage is the reaction of a person who felt powerless in childhood and so takes out their pain on others. Of course, anger is also a reaction to being triggered.

There are other behaviours caused by this feeling of powerlessness.

Powerlessness Expressed by Constantly Apologising

For some people, this is a very difficult trait that is hard to shift. Some individuals cope with powerlessness by apologising for everything, or taking responsibility for anything that happens or that goes wrong. I have noticed this is very obvious in people who have grown up in domestic violence situations.

You only need to apologise if you have done something wrong, and that will not be all day, every day (which is how often the 'sorry' word is used by many people). Your parent may have blamed everything on you, but you can now take power back by not apologising for everything. I invite you to try to notice if this is your challenge to overcome. Try saying 'excuse me' when walking past someone in a crowded room and to say 'thank you for calling' rather than 'sorry I missed your call'. It is hard and takes patience when your core belief is that you need to apologise for existing. You don't have to apologise: you are worthwhile and brave. Remember, you reading this book, therefore you are consciously working towards change.

Feeling Obliged to Always be Helpful Regardless of Personal Circumstances

As survivors, we may neglect our own needs first in the hope that if we go above and beyond to help a person then they won't notice how terrible we really are. This is a type of behaviour that often occurs before healing.

Victim Behaviour

We become a victim when we think that someone else determines how we feel, or when we allow anyone to tell us what to feel or think. Powerlessness equals being stuck in victimhood. It is victim behaviour when we say things like, 'I always get it wrong', 'the world is so unfair', 'nothing ever goes right', 'It's my fault', etc.

We are a victim when we do not believe we can heal ourselves, and blame our perpetrator for the ways our life seems to have failed. Victim statements such as, 'I feel abandoned,' 'I feel attacked' or, so often used by survivors 'I feel blamed.' A victim phrase is one that we use to describe our feelings in a way that implies that someone else needs to fix us, or that we can't do it for ourselves. The chances are high that if we use victim phrases, the other person will react in one of two ways: they will either go into rescuer mode and comfort you, or (depending on your choice of words) react strongly against you. It is best to refrain from using these victim phrases, particularly when you are trying to resolve conflict with someone, as they are blaming statements, and blaming is a way of maintaining powerlessness.

I invite you to notice if you are taking responsibility for your own behaviour, emotions and actions, and recognise that *no one can make you feel anything.* We can choose how we feel at any time, which we couldn't do as children. Blaming and being the victim is the well-worn pathway for so many of us, and it is totally destructive. Blaming is the use of an external locus of control, looking outside myself to find the reason as to what I am feeling. Blaming is allowing myself to continue to be powerless.

It is possible that we received attention by being a victim in childhood, therefore we develop a belief that we receive the most support from the world by continuing victim-like behaviour. Is that true of you? Do you look to friends and family and others for support because you feel you are a victim and cannot help yourself? This is very easy to do and difficult to change. This type of dependence on others is more likely if your attachment style is ambivalent or disorganized (see Chapter Six). We often do not recognise that we are behaving like a victim, and in the end, it can lead to us losing friends, as healthy relationships have to be based on equality and want, rather than need.

It is worth remembering that only *we* can help and heal ourselves: no one can do it for us. *No one*. We have to believe in ourselves and our ability to heal, and to do that we are required to encourage and strengthen our child self with our *own* adult self. It is up to us, through the strengthening of our adult self, to allow our inner child to feel, to express, to be constantly reminded that it was not our fault that we experienced trauma – we did not ask for it, and certainly we did not deserve it. Of course, there is a difference between acting helplessly and asking for help when needed. The ambivalent attachment style will feel helpless, while conversely the avoidant attachment style will find it difficult to ask for help. Friends are there to support us in need, are you as available to all your friends to hear their pain or do you feel your pain is so big you cannot help anyone else? That is when I suggest you start working on supporting yourself more or you may lose your friends.

As we take our power back by making decisions, addressing our 'sorry' behaviours, and taking charge of our lives we find that we are also developing our adult self, it means we will stop needing to control everyone and everything.

Here is a suggested list of aspirations we can work towards, to change from being a victim to being a victor, to living *your* life as you want to live it.

As I continue my healing journey I aspire...

To love myself – this needs no explanation, it is what I believe we all truly want to achieve

To genuinely believe the abuse or trauma was not my fault – I achieve this by working on the critical parenting voice, by constantly stating it to myself so as to change the neural pathways. Often I had to believe it was my fault rather than blaming my parents, which would have been even more dangerous as a child as I needed my parents support to survive *To give and receive in life, with balance* – this involves developing good boundaries. To not try to gain love by giving so much love to others. Knowing that we each deserve to express our love and to feel loved.

To truly know that I do not have to be powerless any longer – this also means I take responsibility for my life and my healing.

To be fully responsible, at all times, for my behaviour and decisions – I cannot blame others for anything in my life; my life is my choice. I can't control how others treat me, however I can control my responses.

To choose my own input into situations created by other people – I am not responsible for anyone other than my inner child/children.

To strive for quality and leave the need for perfection behind – it is empowering to recognise perfection is just me trying to prove to myself that I am okay, and that I am in control.

To honour my own feelings and values even when others don't agree with them – I can feel anything I like, and it does not have to be what others are feeling; I can create and maintain good emotional boundaries.

It is okay to feel my feelings.

To know that I must work towards not fearing rejection, as my fear will work very hard toward creating it – if I think I will *not* get on in a group, I will behave in a way that inspires people to reject me; I have to *move towards* people, *not* hold back because of my fear.

To be able to trust and allow myself to feel my emotions, knowing they cannot destroy me – feelings can be contained and released safely once I develop a strong adult self. There is nothing to fear but fear itself!

To know that no one can make me feel anything unless I give them the power to do so – I can choose how I respond to anyone, and if they are angry at me I can choose to be angry or I can choose to stay calm.

To know that I am responsible for the way I feel: that I cannot blame anyone else – how I feel is entirely my choice.

To practice tolerance and respect at all times – many people tend to hide their pain with anger or unsuitable behaviour, however being kind to others is a much more pleasant experience. Hurt people hurt people.

To succeed, I must first of all believe that I CAN succeed – focus my attention on positive messages and remove ones that tell me that I cannot succeed. Particularly critical parent messages. Remember that the brain is plastic.

To regard problems as challenges, and mistakes as opportunities to learn – know that mistakes are okay, everyone makes mistakes – that's how we learn. *To become the cause of my future and not just the result of my past* – To feel genuinely free from living my life as a victim.

These are the Heal For Life Aspirations which we all commit to in our community.

How Do We Acquire Shame and How Do We Heal from It?

No one is born ashamed. No baby or tiny child feels shame. Shame is acquired from the behaviour of the adults around us. We learn shame once when we get to the age of being aware (at around the age of six), when we begin to comprehend language and selfimage, a sense of knowing who we are[164]. We learn from the adults around us what to be ashamed of – we do not know what shame is without their input. Adults either actively teach us what to be ashamed of, or we learn from observing their behaviour. Some children learn to be ashamed of their bodies and always want to cover them up, other children are happy with their bodies, and are happy to be seen naked – this is just one example of how we learn to be ashamed depending on the reactions of the adults around us.

When children have dysfunctional parents, they typically believe there is something wrong with them that caused the parents to be behaving the way they are. Some parents shame their children by saying 'you're a bad girl or bad boy', as a way of controlling them. They use constant criticism rather than praise with the result of a greatly increased feeling of shame being imposed on the child.

For those of us who feel shame in relation to some aspect of our abuse, it is usually because we have taken responsibility for what happened to us because of how the abuser shamed us. Often perpetrators will use statements such as 'you made me do this because you are so pretty' or 'you made me do this because you flirted with me.' Therefore, the child takes responsibility for the abuse and feels great shame.

The grooming that the perpetrator may have used to make us comply can make us feel as though we encouraged the abuse. The abuser may make friends with us first – they might tell us we are special, if we think that what they are doing is bad, or we feel uncomfortable, we decide that it must be in our minds because we have been trained to believe that the abuser is 'nice' and/or 'kind.' If he or she is sexually abusing us in a way that may feel good, often will lead to a dreadful feeling of 'I must be bad' or 'I must be wrong' as part of me is enjoying this and part of me is not. This is very confusing and shaming. Sometimes an abuser will become great friends with our parents and our parents may speak highly of that person, complicating the already confusing situation.

Shame is acquired from the impact of the adults around us. The more the person is perceived by adults to be good or important (particularly if our parents have that feeling) the more shame the child will take on. Leading to a higher likelihood of taking responsibility for the abuse. When a child is abused by a respected person of the Church or by someone the parents admire, they will be very confused and think it must be their fault, or their shame to bear. Research has shown that shame is more deeply felt when a trauma occurs around the age of six years old, as this is when we are developing awareness of shame[164]. Obviously, we feel the effect of shaming more strongly when the person hurting us is someone we love, such as a parent, as we cannot allow ourselves to think it is their fault, therefore it must be ours and the shame can be enormous.

It has a deep impact if we are shamed by teachers, perhaps because the shaming occurred in front of the whole class. I have worked with many survivors who have vividly remembered a shaming statement by a teacher. The result has been profound. I worked with a teenager who constantly failed her exams even though she was brilliant in class. This was because when she was twelve she was shamed by her teacher in front of the class, the teacher said, 'You will never pass an exam,' Every time she took an exam she was triggered and unable to think. However, after one Heal For Life process she is now successfully completing her university degree in mathematics.

Our parents tend to socialise our shame so that it is reinforced by others to become acceptable behaviour to be ashamed of, and to a lesser extent so do our teachers, older siblings, community, family, and social group as well as peers as they shame us into 'correct behaviour'. Since children are more vulnerable and impressionable than adults, shaming messages received in childhood are much harder to recognise and to lose. Messages of shame are usually verbal, however think of the shaming power in a look of disdain, contempt, or disgust. Sometimes, a parent's look of disgust is enough to lead a child to a feeling of self-loathing[165].

Robin Grille, author of 'Parenting For a Peaceful World' calls shaming an anger release for parental frustration. He states, *'Shaming acts as a pressure valve to relieve parental frustration. Shaming is anger-release for the parent, it makes the shamer feel better – if only momentarily.' He poses the question: 'When made to feel unworthy, children often work extra hard to please their parents. This makes the parent think that shaming has 'worked' – but has it?'*[166].

Feeling shame can stop us from deciding to heal because we believe deep inside that we caused the abuse. This often happens, as mentioned, when it is a parent we loved that has abused us – we cannot bear to think it is their fault, therefore it is safer not to try to heal. If we heal, we will have to acknowledge that someone we loved did something very bad, and that the abuse really did happen.

If you feel ashamed of what happened to you, do try to recall what was said to you so you can recognise ***that the abuse or trauma was not your fault***. The feeling of shame is essentially an action that you are taking responsibility for and this has changed the way you feel about yourself, for example, the all too common feeling 'I am bad.'

Feeling ashamed stops us from healing because it stops us from blaming the abuser and we blame ourselves instead. I repeat: *abuse is never our fault.* There is much confusion about the difference between shame and guilt, I encourage you to use the word that reflects how you are feeling. It is important to recognise that both these feelings are most likely because *you feel responsible for something that, if you were a child, was not and cannot be, your responsibility or fault.*

There is No Shame in Being a Survivor

Why should we feel shame at having been abused? Why should we feel embarrassed and not want to claim this as part of our childhood history? We can make a decision to hand the shame and guilt back to where it belongs – not with us but with the person or people who abused us. I feel no shame about saying I am a survivor of childhood sexual abuse, and sexual abuse from many different perpetrators throughout my childhood and teenage years. It doesn't define me, though it may, perhaps, explain me a little. I know it wasn't my fault, and while I know it shouldn't have happened, it did happen. I am also not looking to blame. It has made me the person I am today. I have grown, through healing, from my childhood. I am not bad or lesser than anyone else because many men raped me in my childhood. *It was not my fault.*

Those of you who have suffered sexual abuse may feel ashamed if you were sexually aroused – that happens, it is nature, please know that that is normal. It is normal to feel sexual arousal when remembering sexual abuse.

In some ways it is even harder for men who have suffered sexual abuse: if the abuse occurred at the hands of a man there may be a deep fear that they might be homosexual, and if it was sexual abuse by a woman they are sometimes expected to consider themselves lucky! Fortunately, such attitudes are starting to change, but it is very sad that so few men feel that they can reveal their sexual abuse.

Any shame is the worst feeling.

It eats away at self worth and strangles the soul. The most natural instinct then is to try and throw it away as far as you can. But it is part of us whether we like it or not. I found the most effective way to deal with my shame was to embrace it, wrap my arms around it, talk to it and to listen to it.

If it was my own shame I found I needed to begin the process of forgiving myself. If I decided it was the other's shame I needed to give it back to them to deal with if possible.

Shame has a purpose and it will teach us if we are ready to learn.

I found it helped to see it as an enemy and as with any enemy I could try to fight it, run away from it or choose to befriend it. I chose to befriend it and I found it was a win win situation. I was enormously helped by reading Henri Nouwens book called The return of the Prodigal Son.

- Don Fairlie (a peer support volunteer at Heal For life).

Dreadful things happen to people in life, and so many of those circumstances can be said without shame – like losing a child, the death of someone close, or serious health problems. I haven't suffered from those issues: ***I have suffered from child abuse.***

If you feel you can't tell anyone 'I am a survivor of child abuse,' ask yourself 'why not?'

You never need to disclose who abused you unless you want to. It seems apparent in today's society that to have been abused is a matter to be ashamed of, as if we had let this happen to ourselves deliberately – but of course we did not, and it was not our fault. If we can start to throw off the shame of being abused, society might start throwing off their collective shame, and the issue might be addressed more effectively.

Suggestion

Do you have a shaming comment that you remember? Spend some time allowing yourself to release the fear around the comment. Consider if you are ashamed of what happened to you and decide what you can do for yourself to let go of the shame. *It wasn't your fault.* Who might you tell that you were abused? Maybe start with Lifeline or a very safe friend.

Forgiveness

If you feel shame about what happened to you, guilty that you didn't stop it, that you allowed it, or blame yourself with thoughts like, 'I was too naughty' or 'I shouldn't have kept going back,' a helpful step in your healing is to forgive yourself (this step is much easier if you are Christian, as it is a fundamental part of the Christian faith that Jesus has already forgiven you, in which case, who are you to not forgive yourself?)

It was not your fault that you were abused, and while any part of you thinks it was, your healing will be severely handicapped because you will be unable to forgive yourself for what happened.

Forgive yourself for the fact that the abuse happened to you. Forgive yourself for the things you had to do in order to survive. Forgive yourself for the ways you behaved towards others as a result of your dysfunctional upbringing and thought patterns. Lack of self-forgiveness – not forgiving ourselves – disempowers us and is a barrier to happiness. *It importantly means the abuser still has power over us.* We blame ourselves for so many things – we are accustomed to accepting blame, as many of us internalised blame for so much when we were young.

It is time to recognise that forgiving ourselves is perhaps the first and necessary step before we can forgive anyone else. We have taken on board so many negative messages, and allowed ourselves to feel like the person in the wrong. I think it is easier to heal and to change our behaviour once we have forgiven ourselves. Perhaps, at some moment we may choose to consider forgiving the abuser.

Forgiving is not forgetting, it is not accepting the behaviour, it is simply not letting the person have any power over you. It is taking your power back. The abuser couldn't care less whether you have forgiven them or not. It is only affecting you and your enjoyment of living.

It's natural that some of the thousands of thoughts we have each day will be negative, but remember that you don't need to listen or continue to believe them, particularly if they are unhelpful.

Remind yourself these are learned messages you were not born with; this is a negative message, and it is time to get rid of the negativity that is holding you back from experiencing the good things in life.

It is time to take your power back.

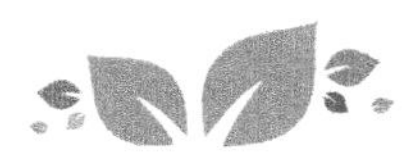

CHAPTER FIFTEEN
Suggestions and Strategies for How to Keep Healing

Healing is an ongoing journey. Each of us can choose how much time and energy we want to give to improving and changing ourselves. The more time we give to our healing, the more effective the healing will be: it is as simple as that.

Although I have given you some suggestions throughout the book let me now suggest you consider working on five key areas every day to optimise your healing. All of the suggestions earlier in the book can also be put under one of these headings.

The five areas are:

1. *Movement*
2. *Connection – with inner self and others*
3. *Integration of the brain*
4. *Self-love*
5. *Spirituality*

1. MOVEMENT

Connecting with your Body Through Movement

You will start to feel safer when you feel in touch with your body. You can start the really core work of healing from trauma only when you know what feeling safe and being in your body, truly means. Movement not only helps us to connect to the body, but it also helps connect us through our cerebellum to help us to regulate our emotions[167].

We need to build a relationship with our body if we want to be aware of our internal state, and movement is the obvious way to do this. The more dissociative you are, the more connecting with your body will help you to feel that your body is part of you, and the less you will disassociate. Movement helps towards body and mind integration. Your body experienced the trauma and it also needs to be given the chance to release the tension that it has stored from the experience.

If you are unwilling to move your body or if you find there are some parts of your body you do not want to move or which often feel stiff, it might be that they are connected with a specific trauma. If you move that part of your body it can perhaps help you remember the trauma and so free yourself from the memory, as well as free that part of your body.

The object of doing movement is to become aware of your body and recognise different feelings in your body, particularly the feeling of being safe. You can only really work successfully on being in your parasympathetic state when you can feel yourself in your body. Movement can also be another very good way to connect to your emotions. The more you are connected to your body the more you may be able to feel your emotions.

First Small Steps

This may be as small as feeling the sensation of pouring running water over your hands, or using a tension ball or holding your hand against your body and ensuring you can feel your hand making contact with your body.

Another idea is to play some music and slowly move each part of your body starting with your head and then include your neck, then move from the waist up and then from the hips up, just keeping your legs and feet still, all the rest of your body moving, then start moving your legs and finally your feet. When you have reached your feet, and moved around the room as much as you feel able to do, start moving back upwards and slowly still each part of your body as you move upwards until only your head is moving. Then, still your whole body and be aware of the feeling of total stillness. You can do this exercise without music if you find that easier.

Other ideas are:

- *Be aware of your body* as you are doing ordinary activities such as hanging the washing on the line.
- *Feel what happens in your body* when you feel unsafe, when you are triggered.

When you feel ready to move on to larger steps, you can try:

- *Walking*

  Walking mindfully, being aware of the feeling of walking, of what you are walking past, the smells, the noises.
- *Rocking*

  Rocking is very soothing, and you can use a rocking chair or just sit and gently rock yourself backwards and forwards for as long as you like.
- *Dancing*

  If there is a Gabrielle Roth (Five Rhythms) group near you, or any sort of movement group, do try it – or ballroom dancing, jiving, or really any form of dance. The Gabrielle Roth method is brilliant for helping you learn how to use body movement to release emotions.

- *Yoga*

  Yoga combines mindfulness with physical body improvement. There are many different levels of yoga you can try.

- *Walking a Labyrinth*

  This can be a very powerful experience. We have one at Heal for Life that is a copy of the Chartres Cathedral labyrinth, and I have witnessed extraordinary emotional break throughs from people who have walked the labyrinth. Do try it. On the way in to the labyrinth, you let go of whatever you need to get rid of, and going out you take in whatever it is that you feel you need to take in.

  I am not sure why it works so well, but it does. Walking does connect you to the Cerebellum, and there will be a clear scientific explanation one day. You can walk the labyrinth just with your fingers, not as effective but a useful exercise. You can download one online.

- *Shaking it Out*

  Try shaking yourself to get rid of anything you do not want to think about, to clear your brain. Shaking is the natural way the body releases trauma.

- *Listening to Music and Free Moving at Home*

  If you listen to music, while moving your body this will help connect you to your emotions as this helps engage the right brain (the emotional brain). Research has shown that people who exercise are less likely to suffer from depression and people with depression can improve their health with exercise[168].

The invitation is to choose to do some form of exercise or movement every day. Even five minutes will make a difference. It is a shame that the more depressed we become, the less we are willing to move. Therefore, it is incredibly important you fight that wish to just do nothing!

2. CONNECTION

Connection with Others

Our brain only changes through connection with others[169]. Although, using a mirror we can help ourselves, however there is no substitute for connection and communication with other people. Connection with others can be very hard because for many survivors' isolation feels safe. The brain knows it is in control and there will be no danger. However, isolation generally means minimal healing. Try saying to yourself as a starting point, I *can* connect with others. I *can* do it safely. It is all about overcoming the internal messages.

Please consider what *small first steps* you might take each day to break down the barriers to free yourself from isolation – to change the fear of meeting people; to lose the need to control the meeting of others.

Ways to connect might include:

- *Making the effort to talk to anyone in the shops or in the community*

  Just a hello is a start. People love a friendly connection. I have found if I smile at someone they smile at me and I feel good inside.

- *Eye contact when talking with a stranger or to anyone you meet during your day*

For some of you, eye contact will feel extremely dangerous and threatening as your sympathetic nervous system may be on high alert. Working on making eye contact will help you to lower your anxiety, although it may not feel very safe at first.

- *Connect through a like-minded Facebook page (like Heal for Life)*

  While this is not a person, at least you are starting to connect and consider yourself worthy of connection.

- *Making a phone call to someone*

  If you don't yet want to call someone you know or someone from a group you are going to, then calling Lifeline or a similar organisation is a good small step to take. It is very usual to have issues around making phone calls.

  If it helps, you can ask someone you trust to call you, making sure you have put their name and number in your phone so their name comes up when they call. No ID phone calls may be too much or not safe.

- *Research any self-help groups in your area*

  This can be done online.

When you have achieved some of the steps above then consider:

- *Joining a local club*

  In our local town of Cessnock, we have many social groups, such as a teddy bear club, a wood turners club, as well as Rotary, Probis, and many others. You can call your local council to ask for a list of community groups or research for yourself online. It takes courage, but it is healing. It also shows you that you are starting to make your healing a priority.

- *Asking at your library*

  This is a good starting place to find community groups and also is a good first step. You can go into the library to look for helpful books on healing.

- *Joining a church, synagogue, mosque, or relevant place of worship*

  If you have a faith – you might find a place of worship you like in your area.

- *Volunteering*

  This will mean you are not only helping others but you are also helping yourself and hopefully you may even make some friends.

  It can be very, very scary to reach out, but the rewards are worth it.

- *Getting involved in a survivor's organisation*

  Allowing your voice to be heard, and allowing yourself to participate, can be powerful and validating.

As you progress in connecting with others, a further big step is when you can have friends or can be part of a group where it is safe enough to be real, to be vulnerable, be your true self. This is a really wonderful space to get to.

Joining a group may be the way you may meet someone similar to yourself with whom you can connect. One of the great benefits of our healing weeks is that it offers participants the opportunity to reach out to make connections to others in the group after they leave, and they also learn that they are not alone, that no one is perfect, and most importantly that it is not necessary to be perfect to be likable.

Connection with Inner Child

When people ask me, 'How long will my healing take' I answer, 'The more time you spend each day with your inner child, the more quickly you will heal.' And whenever someone rings me in crisis I ask, 'When were you last in touch with your inner self?' The answer invariably is 'Oh, not for ages.'

I know of no other way that is more effective to heal than connecting with your inner child.

Your inner child will tell you how you are feeling, will give you insight, and knows what you need to do to keep healing. You can connect through any right brain activities. One method I use is to visualise myself going from my head down into my heart to support me to connect with my little girl.

Chapter Seven will have given you suggestions already but here are some reminders and other ideas:

- *Ask your inner child what he/she is feeling*

  Do this several times a day. Take three deep breaths and ask yourself how you feel. Then release, or at the very least acknowledge, the emotion.

- *Ask you inner child what they would like to do today*

  And then DO it.

- *Write a question to your inner child*

And let him or her write the answer.

- *Talk to your inner child*

  Comfort and acknowledge him or her, particularly when in a stressful situation.

- *Nurture your inner child*

  Hopefully you will do this every day, ideally by doing the doll exercise, and of course also hugging yourself and saying affirmations will help too.

- *Spending time with small children*

  And joining in their play – drawing, colouring in, or writing poetry with your non-dominant hand, riding a bike, playing with your own children or grand-children is also very helpful.

- *Look in the mirror as you pass one and talk to your inner child*

  Tell him or her how wonderful and special they are.

- *Try to do something that is fun!*

  At least once a week.

'When we connect with nature we also connect with our inner child.

So next time you go to sniff a flower, lie on the grass, or listen to the birds, pause a moment and ask your inner child to do it for you. Then feel the fascination and joy as your wonder child shines through.'

– ***Guy (2006)***

Whenever you feel uncertain, confused, or ill at ease, connect with your inner child and then you may be able to find what the emotion is and the probable core of the problem. Practice makes perfect.

Remember if you are having difficulty connecting, it is likely to be you, the adult, creating the blockage and it is usually because of fear. If you start getting headaches, feeling tired, sleeping all the time, reacting being angry, having panic or anxiety attacks, or are inexplicably ill, the chances are that you have not been in touch with your inner child recently. Notice and know your own warning signs.

The third area for continuing your healing is integration of the brain and body.

3. INTEGRATION

Integration is the key to good mental health. When we are more integrated we will be able to observe how we are feeling in our 'adult' ego state, this will help us to live mindfully. We will have more empathy, and we will be better balanced. The prefrontal cortex will be able to regulate us and lessen the likelihood of fear taking over. This means we will make decisions, being aware of all the implications.

First Steps to Left / Right Hemisphere Integration

- *Naming the feeling*

The beginning of integration is naming what we are feeling. Saying how we are feeling engages both parts of the brain – this is why it is essential.

- *Practising mindfulness*

  Being in the now. One simple way is to be aware of five things you can see, five things you can smell, and five things you can hear. There are lots of other mindfulness exercises online. Research has shown that mindfulness actually changes the structure of the brain for people who have suffered from trauma[170].

- *De-triggering*

  Remember while you are triggered you are being controlled by your right brain, and there is minimal connection to your thinking brain. That is why naming the fear is essential. Each time you detrigger you are moving towards brain integration (healing).

- *Moving opposite ways with your body*

  Physical exercises that cross the midline of your body supports integration. Touch your left shoulder with your right arm; touch your left knee with your right arm and then any other parts of the left side of your body with a right part of the body. Do the same with your left arm. Touch the right elbow to the left knee, then the left elbow to the right knee. Place the left thumb and right forefinger together while the left forefinger touches the right thumb.

- *Learning to juggle*

  Involves co-ordination of the hands and eyes.

- *Visualisation and activity*

You might visualise how you are going to make an object, then make it. It's the visualising (a right brain activity) followed by an action (a left brain activity) that aids integration.

- *Making an inside / outside box*

  This is very helpful in many ways. Find a box with a lid, a shoe box will work well. Then decorate the outside with how you show yourself to the outside world. Decorate the inside with how you really feel about yourself. You can use colours, small objects, things from outside, anything at all. This is a good exercise to do once a year.

- *Jigsaw puzzles, chess and checkers*

  Any games where you need to picture something while planning what you are going to do next are excellent for integration.

- *Coloured pens exercise*

  Using coloured pens write on a piece of paper in a different colour from the actual colour you are using. This involves your right brain seeing the colour and your left brain having to write a different colour down.

- *Learn a musical instrument*

  The left brain has to work out how to play while the right brain enjoys the sound you make.

- *Using electric toothbrush on your tongue*

  Do for ten seconds on each side of your tongue.

- *Walking being aware of ensuring both sides of your body are moving equally*

This will help you become aware of how your body is integrating. It amazed me how differently my left and right sides of my body moved!

4. SELF LOVE

I think the key objective of healing is to fully love ourselves. Powerlessness leads to lack of self-worth, which is equal to lack of self-love. The question is; what can you do to help yourself love yourself? Self-love is putting yourself and your needs first, as only then can we effectively meet other's needs. Putting all of our energy into our children for instance is not self-loving and can lead to disaster as the children will eventually grow up and leave us alone to lead their own lives without us (we will only have ourselves)

Utilising all the resources mentioned so far in this chapter is self-loving; it is caring about yourself and your own welfare. Connection with the inner child as we have discussed is particularly critical to self-love.

What else can you do to foster self-love?

See The Positives About Yourself

It doesn't matter if you don't actually feel these things right now, but write down some positive qualities that other people might see in you. Ask a friend to tell you what he or she feels is good about you. You can train your brain to see yourself as others do.

Allow yourself to invest, perhaps five minutes each night before you sleep, because *you matter,* and your healing is important.

Here are some examples of things you might write about yourself:

- I am a genuinely good person
- I make a valuable contribution
- I try hard
- I am an excellent worker
- I am friendly
- I love my children
- I care about people
- I am kind

It may feel uncomfortable to write these things down, do try to give it a go. Your perspective will start to shift once you have been doing this for a while. If you feel empowered to write more positive things about yourself as you remember them, that's great – it's also helpful to repeat these affirmations to yourself as part of your reflective nightly routine. Even better if you do it in front of a mirror or have the courage to say it to a friend. This strategy helps you to support yourself rather than having to rely on external validation from loved ones and friends. It also helps to build resilience.

It's important for us to remind ourselves regularly about what makes us a good person, and to be able to not have to rely on others to build us up. Some people may consider it to be egotistical to think nice things about one's self, but in my opinion, it is showing selflove, and very important to healing.

Deal with unhelpful and negative thoughts

A mindfulness mediation or similar activity may help. Concentrate on your thoughts, and see what you are subconsciously telling yourself that is negative. You might be saying to yourself 'No one cares about me,' 'I'm hopeless,' 'I don't matter,' 'I'm no good at 'X',' 'I can't do anything right,' 'How can anyone love me?' 'I'm worthless,' 'I always mess things up,' etc. All of these thoughts are negative and unhelpful. To deal with these negative thoughts, the suggestion is to hand write the negative thought, and then write three to seven reasons why it is not true.

Here are two examples:

- ***'No one cares about me'***
- *My family and friends love me; I have friends and work mates who care about me; My contribution is valid and valued; My partner loves me*
- ***'I am hopeless'***
- *I do an excellent job at work; I matter to my family, friends and colleagues; I am a genuinely good person; I am excellent at my job and my ancillary roles; I make a valuable contribution; My family and friends are proud of me*

This strategy helps you to dispel unhelpful, negative thoughts and stop a downward spiral of negativity in general.

Learning Not to Take Others Behaviour Towards Me Personally

If you find that you take other's behaviour towards you personally, this suggestion may help you to recognise that their behaviour is *about them*, not *about you*.

For example, if someone yells at you, the possible reasons could be:

- You might have done something wrong (still no excuse for yelling!)
- They are having a bad day and taking it out on you
- They have misunderstood something and the mistake is theirs but they don't realise it
- They've just been yelled at and are reacting to that by yelling at you
- They might feel insecure and this is the only way they know how to deal with it
- They might be having family problems at home that are making them angry
- They might be dealing with grief or health problems that make them angry
- They are tired and stressed and impatient
- They are triggered

You can respectfully say, calmly, 'I understand you are under pressure, or tired, or feeling stressed out right now, however it's not okay to speak to me that way.' Or you can choose to walk away and ignore the comment. This sets boundaries and lets the other person know where your boundaries lie.

Try to learn not to take things that other people say or do to heart, and don't let others affect the way you feel about yourself. Instead, try to mentally take a step back and think of all the possible reasons why they may have acted that way. You may never find out why they behaved the way they did, but it's likely to be more about them than it is about you, and therefore try not to take it personally. *No one can make you feel anything unless you let them.* If someone shouts at me I can choose to just think 'oh they are in a bad mood' or I can choose to react and be angry back which may have terrible repercussions and will likely leave me feeling in a very bad mood.

Ask yourself which reaction will make you feel better. How do you feel after you have been angry with someone and how do you feel when you don't react but stay in a calm loving space? I prefer to stay in a loving space!

- *Make a poster using a photo of yourself as a small child*

  Then, underneath write loving thoughts such as 'I am 100% worthy'; 'I am 100% blameless,' then decorate the poster in a way that looks nice to you, and to honour yourself, and look at the poster every day and read the affirmations you have written.

- *Create shelf space and find things that you love*

  Find things that are beautiful to you, and put them on the shelf. You can collect beautiful objects from op shops or on the beach (or anywhere) but only have things you love to look at and have them somewhere where you will see them often.

- *Make an affirmation box*

  Fill it with loving things about yourself.

- *Try to look in the mirror and say, 'I am lovable'*

It may take ages even to look in the mirror – when you can do this, you are well on the way to healing. If you don't like the look of your face, start by looking at your body, or if you love your body but not your face, look at your body first.

- *Do something loving just for yourself*

  A massage, go shopping, have a bath, have a long walk – whatever feels good to you.

- *Observe when you use negative strokes*

  Notice when you say negative things about yourself to others, and try to change this habit.

  Negative strokes are when you say something bad about yourself, so the other person will say nice things to you.

- *Work towards an internal locus of control*

  This means remembering the Heal For Life Aspirations that no one can make you feel anything, you are in charge of your life, how you feel each day is your choice. Do not look to others to give you a sense of self-worth.

- *Embrace your gender*

  Whatever your gender may be. Be proud of your gender. Don't hide your gender. Do something exciting with your hair, change the colour, the cut. Be proud of your gender identity.

- *Embrace your body shape*

  It is a choice to diet, or to eat more, or to change your body, however please do not fall into the trap of loathing your body and then also feeling guilty about not changing it. One step at a time. Now may not be the time to change your body, make the CHOICE that you are not going to diet and that you will love you as you are, for now. If you choose to diet as part of self-love, be kind to yourself about your progress.

When you're in the shower feel and love your body.

- *Find an activity that is special to you and validates you*

  One of our community members collected old prints from children's books and made them into pictures and sold them at markets. The completion of the task was validating and people purchasing the pictures served as external validation, too.

  Everyone has a talent at something. What is yours? Mine is cooking, and I get great joy out of cooking and eating so I do not short-change myself – I always have a lovely meal, even when on my own, and make whatever I am eating look good as well as taste delicious.

- *Create a vision board*

  Put on it what you want to achieve, own, or aspire to, as it will give you something to work towards. What you put on your vision board is entirely your own choice.

5. SPIRITUALITY

Spirituality is not about religion there is a big difference between the two. Religion is organised with a set of beliefs and practises that go with that particular religion. Religions often imposes on us obligations as to what we *should* do in order to heal – such as 'Pray more'. 'Ask God to heal you'. You are not a good Muslim, Christian, Jew or Buddhist if you cannot hand over your abuse to God, or in the case of some religions if you cannot heal by raising your self awareness to rise above your pain.

For me my sense of Other, sense of God, is that this great power of love is there to give me the courage to heal, so that my own self-awareness and self-love can be raised by the journey of healing.

I like the thought of a God who bore witness to my pain and wants me to remember so I can experience so much more love. For me God is love.

Spirituality for me is about finding that Love which is outside of ourselves. Spirituality can be described as a sense of peace and purpose. Spirituality looks to answer the question; 'What am I here to do?' Spirituality can be defined as exploring the meaning of life. It is beyond the physical or material world. Spirituality gives us an understanding that we are an essential part of a bigger picture. It gives meaning to life and to living.

To explore you own spirituality you might consider looking at religious and spiritual images online and see what you respond to and what you feel negative towards.

Look at what was imposed on you as a child, and explore if that is your own beliefs and truth. In connecting with our spirituality, we usually come to count our blessings. An essential part of growing our sense of purpose is to recognise what in life we are grateful for.

As a part of our daily life, gratitude is very rewarding.

Being grateful helps me move forward in life[171].

Gratitude means I am thankful for what I have and who I am. It means I won't allow negative thoughts run my life. I choose to be grateful several times a day for who I am. It stops me allowing myself to worry or feel anxious.

Now to ensure you are caring and helping yourself to heal I suggest you reflect on your progress each day.

Reflection

I suggest you decide an amount of time to spend on each area every day, and that you keep a journal to record what you do each day and that in the journal you also note how you have been feeling during the day, and how you are travelling. The journal, and your overall review of how you have managed during the day, is your *reflection* and summary of your progress.

Let me give you some more ideas for ways on reflecting. My suggestion is that you consider doing this first thing in the morning and last thing at night.

In the morning you might like to have a few headings to keep your mind focused, and to give consistency:

- *What I am grateful for today?*

This can be about something small or large, try to find something you can be grateful for (this is much more useful and positive than starting the day with anxiety and worry).

- *What I choose to do today*

  Reflect on what you are intending to do today and make sure this is what you want to do. Argue with yourself if you are doing something because you HAVE to.

There is nothing in this world any of us *have to do*. Let me explain. If I don't do something there maybe consequences that I need to consider before making a choice. If I choose to not pick up my granddaughter from school after having previously committed to do this, then I need to consider 'in that event, what will happen?' My daughter is likely to feel hurt and angry, I can choose to have my daughter feel angry and not pick up my grandchild, or I can consider that I love my daughter and if she is happy, I am happy, then I may choose to pick up my granddaughter – by reflecting on it, the task of picking up my granddaughter becomes a *choice* rather than an obligation.

Each morning I choose what I will do and I am much happier as a consequence.

Other questions you might choose to ask yourself:

- What would make today great?
- What am I feeling?
- How am I going to nurture myself today?
- What do I want to achieve today?

I suggest you decide on different questions or headings for yourself. It can be a good idea to also have a section for each of the five activities, or have a section for however many of the areas interest you. Shape your daily program around what you want to do, and perhaps write in your journal what you are going to do under each heading each morning.

In the evening, take ten minutes reflecting on what you have achieved during the day.

Some questions or headings to consider:

- What did I feel during the day?
- What did I learn about myself today?
- What do I want to let go of?
- What was the best moment of the day?
- How did I feel?
- What was the worst moment of the day?
- How did I feel?
- When did I nurture myself today?
- How could I have made today better?
- Did I feel safe all day?
- Did I achieve what I intended under each of the four areas?

Using a journal to note the answers is a great help. Choose the questions you want to ask yourself and make them the same every day. Notice how you feel when you write the answers.

Healing happens when we give time to ourselves to heal. I encourage you to love yourself enough to decide to give yourself the time you deserve in order to effectively heal. If you give yourself this time in addition to allowing yourself time for de-triggering and processing with a therapist (or on your own), the rewards will be enormous. It's your choice, it's your life. Do you want it to be influenced by those who hurt you when you were little? Or do you want to claim your life for yourself?

In case any of these apply to you I would now like to outline the most common problems people approach me with. This may be a helpful reference for you when in need.

A Few Common Problems You May Experience

Panic attacks

Panic attacks happen when our amygdala is overwhelmed by a memory and we experience a childhood trauma as if it were happening right now. This is because the amygdala has no sense of time or chronology – everything from the amygdala is experienced as a 'now' event. For example, in a flashback or panic attack, you're having the same sensations and emotions that you had at the time of the trauma. Therefore, you are feeling as though you're experiencing the trauma again because the nervous system and the body can't tell the difference.

This is probably the best tool in the whole book so I am going to repeat it here, I suggest you put the detriggering format on your fridge.

De-trigger

Look at someone, or look in a mirror, and say 'I feel frightened, terrified, scared' (however best describes the feeling for you) – this will de-activate the amygdala. Then comfort yourself, reminding yourself that it happened in your childhood, that it isn't happening right now, and that there is nothing to be frightened of right now. This will calm the sympathetic nervous system. Then, you can later choose to work on what you remembered during the panic attack with your therapist, by yourself, or with a safe person.

Feeling Overwhelmed By Emotion

Our ability to self-regulate differs depending on our attachment style. Have you ever had the problem of crying for days without being able to stop? In this case, engaging the left thinking brain to bring back some control and to lower the sympathetic nervous system is very helpful. You can write questions or ask yourself out loud, 'Why am I crying?' or 'Why am I feeling so sad?' Whatever question is relevant. Then write the answer using the non-dominant hand. With the dominant hand, you can write comforting things to yourself like, 'Dreadful things happened in my past but they are not happening now.' If answers come up, respond to them – this will utilise the left side or your adult self to self-comfort and to contain the emotions you are feeling. You may find yourself arguing, 'But I can't stop crying,' and your logical voice might reply,

'You can if you choose to. Do you want to?', and so on. Concentrating on the questions will help engage the left brain and slow the emotion. Talking is even more effective. Talk to yourself in the mirror. Writing or talking and asking questions of yourself will all engage the left brain and help you regulate the emotion. The worst thing you can do is just cry, it will not help you or heal you unless your adult self is acknowledging what you are crying about, and offering comfort.

A Very Strong Emotion That Will Not Go Away

You may believe that a very strong emotion you are having relates to something in the now, but remember that a large majority of emotional reaction comes from childhood, when you are experiencing a strong reaction, ask yourself 'When did I have that same feeling in childhood?' If you can do the process that I explained in Chapter Eight, connecting with your inner child to explore more about when you first experienced that feeling, this will help enable you to release the feeling.

As an example, if you are feeling abandoned and upset because your boyfriend has to go out for the evening without you, you might choose to remember when you *first* felt that feeling of being abandoned, you might recall that you felt abandoned when your dad died when you were three. Releasing how scary that was and how sad you were, will then enable you to recognise the emotion is from that childhood time and that your boyfriend has not abandoned you, it is not the end of the world because he cannot be with you for the evening. I know I have included this before, however I am deliberately repeating myself as this is SO important.

Addictions

Any of us can go on covering our pain for as long as we like or need to, but alcohol, drugs and other addictions are short-term, destructive solutions. Every time you want a drink, sit down and write with your dominant hand to your inner self, 'What am I feeling?' or perhaps, 'What feeling am I avoiding?' Sometimes, we drink to overcome feelings of worthlessness and shame, most often because of fear or because we are triggered. Sometimes we drink because we feel it is the only way we can feel OK about ourselves. Instead of drinking, try to do something loving for yourself instead.

As you release your childhood pain you will overcome your addictions, and have no further need of protection and self-annihilation. However, be kind to yourself, as healing addictions takes time and you are likely to fall backwards – sometimes until you reach that place in healing when you love yourself enough to stop.

Overwhelmed By Life Events

A feeling of everything being too much, that you can't cope. This is right-brain activity; so again I suggest you bring in some left-brain activity. Sit down and make a list of all you are worried or anxious about. You may be surprised at how short the list is (well, that is what usually happens with me) then you can analyse which item on the list you will tackle first. Overwhelm seems to be very common with us survivors, I believe it is due to the lack of self-regulatory capacity from experiencing a dysfunctional childhood. In addition to this, talking to yourself in the mirror; again, asking yourself questions out loud will help engage your left brain.

Restless Legs (and Other Body Parts)

Try to make yourself aware of the restless movement and ask yourself how you are feeling, if your attachment style is dismissing you may need to write the question and answer with your non-dominant hand. Say aloud, 'I feel frightened / scared / terrified / unsafe' to yourself in a mirror or to another person, allowing yourself to feel without judgement what you are feeling internally – this will bring your social engagement system back online, meaning you are out of fear, allowing your body to start to regulate and calm down. Restless leg syndrome, in particular, is the body trying to minimise the effects of stress hormones[172].

Restless legs syndrome occurs when we cannot allow ourselves to feel, Usually, restless legs will cease when we are in touch with our feelings. All of the areas of recognising feelings mentioned before will help.

How To Resolve Conflict

Most people dislike conflict, and I have noticed that survivors of trauma are even more likely to hate conflict, as they are frightened of it. Paradoxically, some survivors feel safer in conflict and will create it in order to feel safe. Is that you? Survivors typically don't want to be disliked, and don't want to cause more problems. How do you feel about conflict?

The problem is that avoiding conflict, if the conflict is with someone you have to see often, or who you care about, is a really poor option. Conflict arises when two people have differing opinions, and both people have emotional issues around the subject (without emotion involved there would be no conflict.) The problem is that the emotion that arises and causes conflict usually has absolutely nothing to do with the person or the issue we are confronted with in the now, and everything to do with something from our past. Remember: a large percentage of our emotional reactions come from our childhood experiences.

Here I would like to suggest a technique to consider when you are wanting to resolve conflict with someone you care about. It certainly works at Heal For Life where we are all survivors and conflict can easily occur.

The first vital step is, when you are in conflict with someone, to stop and consider what this might be reminding you of in your past.

As an example:

Jenny went walking every day with her local walking group. One of the men, Peter, accused her of being 'unhealed' and 'difficult' and then 'talked over her' and 'didn't listen when she tried to answer back' (Jenny's interpretation of events).

Jenny was deeply upset and went to the facilitator of the walk, and Jenny felt that the facilitator was unsupportive of her – this made Jenny really angry, she then talked to her partner, and she perceived him to be unsupportive as well. After this, Jenny felt more and more angry towards Peter. She came to ask me what she could do about this 'arrogant man' – as Jenny spoke she was visibly upset over the incident, so I asked her, 'Who does Peter remind you of?' Jenny instantly answered that he reminded her of her father. So, I asked, 'How did your father behave towards you?' and she said that she felt that her father never listened to or supported her. Then she started crying. It was clear that the emotion she was feeling was nothing to do with Peter, but rather had everything to do with her father. I helped her express her fear and anger towards her father, and after this she was able to realise that Peter didn't matter at all, and that she could just ignore him and walk with someone else. All her emotions towards Peter were actually emotions she had never been able to express about her father. Furthermore, the perceived lack of support from the facilitator and then her partner had intensified her feelings against poor Peter.

The problem was hers to solve and the anger she was feeling had nothing to do with Peter, even though his remarks were unkind and thoughtless. Again, it is helpful to remember that the vast majority of emotions we feel are from our past.

If there is no connection to our past, we can ignore anyone's poor behavior or tell them, without emotion, that their behavior is not acceptable to us – but if there is emotion, then it helps to consider that it most likely will have come from a similar experience in our childhood.

In practicing this, you can find excellent healing opportunities – look at the conflict, examine the emotions, and then ask yourself 'when did I first feel this way?'

You search. And search. You don't give up. And then you stumble upon a light.

It's weak at first but as you get closer and closer it gets brighter and brighter.

At first, you're hesitant to touch it, or go near it.

But it envelops you without giving you a chance to back away.

And it floods you with a love you never felt before.

The kind of love you've been starving for.

The love that comes from within, for yourself.

The love you've always deserved.

It's hard to swallow, hard to take in after living on

an empty stomach for so many years.

But slowly, you take it in.

Slowly you feel something changing in you.

You start to think of yourself differently.

You stop blaming yourself for your tragic life.

You start forgiving yourself.

You start seeing your blessings.

You start feeling grateful for little things.

You start to see the Hand of God that has been reaching out to you,

Just waiting patiently for you to take it so that

He can lead you to your healing and your salvation,

You take it. You start taking baby steps with Him.

And you realize that healing is a journey.

And you realise that miracles do exist (because you are a living miracle).

You realise you found the hope you've been searching for.

I am Denise and this is MY healing journey.

- Heal For Life Guest.

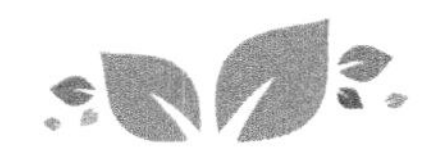

CHAPTER SIXTEEN
The Heal For Life Healing Program

Don't bother asking me
How it came to be
That I was on a mountain top
So high I thought that
I could see the sea

Gathered there with strangers
On this scenic site
A site to become sacred
And in our hearts
For evermore
We had a common thread
That held us there for a week
You see we were all
survivors
Of a childhood holocaust

Some may say we were self-indulgent
Others may laugh
It's all codswallop
And just emotional hoo-ha
One by one we took our turn
To speak forgotten truths
I listened as I waited for my turn
A slight acknowledgment of the facts
Said by one and all
No gory details for us to hear
Just simply said and done.
Later on, a few days in

We played like children
Fancy dress and all
We sang around a camp fire
What a joyous day.
And after a meal
It just came out
I spewed my horrid past
Of dark stormy days I preferred it hide.
For once the gasps I heard
Were not the frightened cries
Of someone scared of me
But gasps of love and empathy
For the boy in me.
No false tears were shed
And I was amazed
At the compassion shown
By this band of strangers
Who carried their hurt along with me.
So now it's almost over
I feel sad but glad
That I met this band of strangers
Who like this mountain top
I hold high up in my heart.

- Dale Lynch. 'This Group of Strangers'. From West Australia. A peer support volunteer.

The program is a five-day residential program to allow the guest to go deeply and safely into their trauma knowing there is time to integrate anything that is learnt about childhood trauma before going back into the outside world.

Heal For Life was founded to provide a place where survivors could safely feel their emotions without time limitations, judgment or need for explanation; where validation would be provided because *all* participants both as workers and guests would be survivors of abuse. It was also founded on the belief that the person best able to know what they need to do in order to heal, is the survivor themselves.

Each guest is given unconditional love and respect; it is our honour to support the guests.

We recognise the courage each guest has shown in deciding to heal. We also recognise the importance of the relationship between our team and guests: taking into account of how that will impact on one another.

Peer Support at Heal For Life

What is unique is that our therapeutic approach is carried out in a residential setting *by* survivors *for* survivors of childhood trauma.

Peer support led programs *have been evidenced to be essential to effectively reach vulnerable communities*[238].

The HFL framework is peer support driven, meaning the team working to deliver the program, are all former participants of the program and have all personally experienced childhood trauma and have now trained in Trauma Healing so they can support our guests. They bring their own lived experience of trauma to the role making their support, authentic and validating. It provides the guest with the opportunity to see the possibility of not only healing from trauma, but thriving in the world. It also gives encouragement to our guests, knowing that each person supporting them has already walked a similar path towards healing. This removes a sense of superiority and separation between guest and worker.

Research into the effectiveness of our model was carried out and stated that the facilitators own healing as a result of their prior engagement as a participant of the program provided a working framework for participants on the program to see the possibility of healing from childhood abuse and trauma. Moreover, the program facilitated a different way to live after childhood trauma through the active role modelling of the facilitator. This model provides participants with the possibility of hope.

The residential peer support approach was seen to lead to the promotion of self-empowerment in guests, as the experts in their own healing. Empowerment and safety have been found time and time again to be central approaches used in rape-crisis centres[239].

Research by McCormack and Katalinic (2016) concluded that one of the great advantages of our program is that it suggests that psychological growth is possible. It instils hope for both participants and facilitators through our peer support trauma program[240].

In order for that growth to occur, and continue to grow, the supervision and support of peer support workers is critical. All peer support volunteers and workers have access to counselling and psychological support as part of Heal For Life's commitment to the safety and wellbeing of our staff.

The team on each program consists of a facilitator with tertiary level qualifications, and a minimum of three other people often with appropriate external qualifications in counselling, psychotherapy or psychology. All team members are also trained in Heal For Life's internal training program.

Heal For Life's internal training for peer support workers is an intensive program that has developed over 20 years of delivering peer support based programs. We are dedicated to achieving quality outcomes for clients and are regularly audited by the Quality Improvement Performance Council to ensure the highest standards of safety and professional care are maintained. It is very important to us that even though we are survivors we ensure that we provide the best possible safe and professional care to our guests. Every six weeks we run training for our team and any ex-guests to encourage ongoing learning and healing.

Our consistent achievements in this area have made Heal For Life a preferred service provider for government and non-government organisations including FACS, Victim Support Services and Anglicare.

The Heal For Life model also recognises the important contribution of Psychoanalytic, Rogerian, General Systems Therapy(GST), Gestalt, and Emotion Focused Therapy(EFT). These and other therapies have all contributed to aspects of our model. However, the core of our model is the belief that release from fear created by the core trauma is of prime importance and an imperative step for effective healing to enable longterm neurobiological changes. Heal For Life participants adopt the knowledge that the identification of a trigger is a gift, as once a trigger is identified it can be processed and released. This ensures that a trigger no longer has an impact on our mental and emotional wellbeing.

Heal For Life considers there is a critical place for medication as it can help to establish neural network balance. The ultimate aim of the work is to reduce, in both workers and guests, reliance on medication.

While recognising that trauma is a serious mental health problem. 80% of Heal For Life guests have been diagnosed with a mental illness[241]. HFL believes in the ability of every person to heal to a greater or lesser extent (dependent on effort) from mental illness caused by childhood trauma.

Importantly, we wanted to create a place where supervised well trained professionals, who are themselves survivors of child abuse can provide safe effective treatment.

Heal For Life knows the importance of good governance and external accreditation. On the board of directors are representatives in the area of law, finance and mental health as well as business leaders. Heal For Life welcomes experts as directors, who are not survivors. Heal For Life also always ensures that we have the highest level of external accreditation. We are proud that we have for the last nine years met the high external standards necessary to withstand external criticisms of peer support programs. Fortunately, much of the controversy of 'false memories' has died down, due to the evidence science has provided to inform the debate. At

Heal For Life we recognise each person's truth is their truth; it may not necessarily be the truth in the eyes of the law. We are about healing not advocacy.

When asked the question 'What if my memories are false?' our response would be something like 'the most important thing is to process what feels true to you, it's your healing journey no one else's, you don't have to go and declare them to anyone unless you chose to'.

Many survivors distrust their memories. While it is true that memories can be unreliable, what is important for the journey of healing is that they are validated by the individual. Heal For Life believes strongly that individual validation is the most critical component of healing. We actively discourage guests from sharing the history of their trauma with each other. It is not healing to do so. The team are there to perform that validating role. It is not important what another person thinks of our trauma history. What is important is that we show love and acceptance to our own experiences. Our policy to not share trauma stories prevents damaging comparisons and self-judgement which can prevent healing. It prevents individuals from taking on the trauma of other people or from becoming retraumatised by the stories of others, events which have been evidenced to cause major problems in inpatient mental health facilities[242].

Our programs currently run in Australia, the Philippines, and England. Hopefully, other programs will have started in other countries by the time you read this book. You can check our website or Facebook page for all up to date information.

The Heal For Life model brings together the intuitive knowledge of survivors, research from Heal For Life's own experience, combined with the latest research from neuroscience.

Philosophy of Healing

We Believe:

- Every person has the innate ability to heal from childhood trauma and abuse.
- Those of us who have suffered child abuse or childhood trauma are the most able to understand and support others to heal.
- It is essential we utilise the latest neuroscience research, combined with our own anecdotal and intuitive knowledge. This ensures only those who have participated in the program and are actively healing, can support our guests.

Safety is imperative, in order to heal a person has to feel and be safe.

- It is essential for each person to be responsible for their own healing journey, as each person knows best what they need to do in order to heal.
- Healing is holistic and integrative in nature (involving body, mind and spirit)
- Discovering and feeling self- love is essential.
- All people, regardless of race, religion, gender, culture or sexual preference have the right to heal.

Objectives of HFL Healing Programs

By the end of the Healing Week, we hope our guests will be able to:

- Recognise the importance of feeling safe.
- Find and establish a safe place, either in reality or in their imagination.
- Be able to de-trigger and know the signs of when they are triggered

Establish a connection with their 'inner child' and recognise the importance of this relationship for their own healing.

- Love, re-parent and re-empower their wounded 'inner child'.
- Demonstrate by the way they speak and act that they are beginning to love themselves.
- Actively engage in, and take responsibility for, their own journey of healing.
- Actively counteract feelings of shame or guilt by fully appreciating that their childhood abuse was not their fault.
- Use knowledge of the effects of trauma on the brain to be able to explain how the changes in their own developing brain have affected their emotional and behavioural patterns.
- Use knowledge of their attachment style in childhood to understand and begin to change their current relationships with others.

Demonstrate developing skills in the use of new tools that can help when in crisis or when entering a challenging situation.

- Demonstrate increasing self-responsibility in daily living that shows respect for the interconnectedness between physical, emotional, spiritual and mental health.
- Apply the principles of Transactional Analysis to improve relationship with self and to counteract negative parental messages learned in childhood.
- Continue to practice setting appropriate boundaries with self and others.
- Feel confident to apply what they have learned during the healing week to their situation when they get home or back their day-to-day living.
- Laugh more often and find more joy in living.

HFL Mission and Vision

Mission

Empowering people to heal from childhood trauma and child abuse.

Vision

- To be a centre of excellence for healing from childhood trauma, depression and anxiety.
- To be a valuable resource for survivors and their families, available through all media forms.
- To assist survivors of child abuse without discrimination by age, gender, sexuality, physical ability, spiritual beliefs or cultural background.
- To have all healing programs run by survivors of child abuse.

- To have survivor-facilitators of the highest professional standards, supported by committed and loving trained peer support workers.
- To be a community living by Christian principles (regardless of person faith or beliefs) committed to loving and caring for each other as well as the guests who choose to come.
- To have a nationally-accredited training course for survivors, ensuring the Heal For Life Foundation philosophies can influence the way survivors of child abuse and childhood trauma are healed.
- To encourage change in the way parenting and child-rearing is approached when supporting children who have suffered from trauma.
- To promote a better understanding of the effects of childhood trauma and abuse, encouraging people to see the connection between diagnosis such as depression and anxiety, and how they relate to their childhood.
- To facilitate the program within all cultural communities with cultural humility.

Survivor Experiences at Heal For Life

I thought you might find it helpful to read what other survivors have to say about the program. You will find after each healing week we post on our website comments from some of the guests.

Mayumarri, also known as Heal for Life has given me a new lease on life. I have been attending healing weeks since 2011 and I am now happier and more well-adjusted than I have been in decades.

The Heal for Life program has worked for me for several reasons.

Mayumarri is a beautiful place to stay with bush, wildlife and an awesome lake to swim in. I have always felt extremely safe on the property and able to be myself. I have learnt so much about my inner child and my triggers and have been able to release many years of repressed anger and pent up emotions. Being free to express myself in a safe and fully supported way has been so important to me.

I also found that the scientific information I was provided about how trauma in early childhood affects brain development, was amazingly empowering.

My healing journey is moving forward. I can honestly say that coming to Mayumarri has been life changing. With the tools that I have learnt from Heal for Life I have been able to overcome my past, heal my pain and truly live. I now love my life and I am excited to live it.

Thank you, Heal for Life.'

- Kate Welch

When I first came onto the property I felt safe, like I was coming home, yet I had never been before. I was encouraged to be silent for the first part of the week, this was something very strange for me, I embraced the concepts of the healing week, but I watched rather than fully participated.

I went through the motions of learning and understanding, I began to write and journal how I was feeling.

The concept of meeting my inner child was very foreign to me, I couldn't look at a baby let alone find one that represented an image of the little me with hazel eyes and love it.

I went back to Heal for Life as I wanted to learn more, understand more and I realised that I had no boundaries in my life- well it took me 12 months of experimenting and implementing new boundaries that I am still working on building today in all aspects of my life.

I tend to not show my true self to the world, cover it up with a smile, positive outlook and want everything to be functioning in a normal way. I had developed anxiety and depression from carrying all this weight around with me all my married life, as I married a man who wanted to control me, physically and verbally abuse me. I had gained 5 stone while having my children, and dealing with the decline & death of my parents.

Several times in my life I remember just freezing and accepting whatever happened to me, this was my way of surviving , once I had uncovered a trauma created from being raped as a little girl, things began to make sense, why I acted this way & that. Why I always covered up how I really felt.

By attending Heal for Life where I am free to be my real self- no cover ups, just what you see, I am healing slowly, by pealing back the layers of the onion that I have enclosed my true inner child.

I am starting to feel good in my own skin, I am being authentic and true to myself. I am speaking my truth; it has been a challenging journey and one that has caused some difficult decisions to be made. Some friends have chosen not to continue to be my friend, which is sad but I am the only person who can put myself first and always look after me.

I now know that my safe place is outside, being one with nature, listening to the birds & other sounds, just being still like being in a meditation.

I love stretching and doing a simple form of yoga that allows my body to perform at its optimum. To move with ease and be able to run when I need too, walk and just appreciate the wonderful array of calm & peaceful wildlife that abounds.

Feeding my body with nutritious food has also become an essential part of my life, one that has awakened a great need to be self sufficient and self reliant. It is like my physical body is catching up with my emotional, spiritual and essence of who I was born to be, to realize and become my full potential, to be comfortable in my own skin.'

- Michelle Wilkinson

Below is a letter sent to our coordinator Penny Garvey in West Australia after a sponsored kids camp there.

Dear Penny

Thank you for choosing my son to be a part of the healing week earlier this year.

I wanted to take this opportunity to express to you and to your team how grateful I am for the love and support you have shown my son through his journey. Words alone cannot describe the impact Heal For Life has had on my family, I truly believe that you saved my son's life and altered his future in a way that I couldn't.

Before attending the healing week my son had gone through a period of suicidal thoughts stemming from the trauma of broken trust and abandonment from his father which led to his struggle with major anxiety and horrific illness when facing even the smallest of daily stresses. The boy I dropped off was vastly different from the boy I picked up seven days later. It's almost unimaginable how dramatic an effect can take place in such a short time. And it saddens me to think where my son would be today if he had not been given this opportunity to attend the healing week at the young age of eleven. I'm not sure he would have made it to adulthood.

Imagine the number of teenage and child suicides that could be prevented if suffering children had the same opportunity that he had, attending a healing week at the first sign of trauma. Restoring someone's mind and spirit and equipping them with tools and confidence. To find their voice and follow their journey knowing they are Ok and loved and special is truly powerful.

I hope you find more sponsors for your wonderful work.

- C. Hutchinson

I feel happiness, I feel joy,
I now have tools which I can employ,
I've found calm and discovered peace,
I can actually feel my endorphins increase,
I've learnt to laugh, I love to sing,
I want to experience everything,
I now can run, inside I fly,
I'm ready to wave depression good-bye,
In my mind my dreams can soar,
Others can't scare me anymore,
Something's changed inside of me,
Something only, I can see,

New colours gleam, my world has grown,
It's a new way of being that I've been shown,
My body feels so free and light,
I have contentment within my sight,
I am no longer running scared,
I'm open to things I wouldn't have dared,
But best of all I've found real love,
Love from inside, outside and above,
I don't have to live in shame,
I feel brand new but look the same,
I love most people and they love me,
I'm now happy just to be,
My eyes are open and I'm so glad,
'cos I've learnt that I'm not all bad,
I was born complete and whole,
A beautiful being, a pure soul,
But that got lost so early for me,
I had no idea that I could be free,
No-one told me that I could,
Look within and find some good,
I've felt tainted for so long,
The world has always felt so wrong,
But I've taken my power back,
By giving myself all that I lack,
I've made a decision to learn to trust,
That inside I know what's right and just,
I have so much yet to give,
So much life I've yet to live,
With love and faith and courage too,
That's now something I can do,
I love myself, I've made that choice,
I've found my truth, my inner voice,
I've discovered what I had all along,

Who ever thought I could be so strong,
I can feel free to wash and be clean,
I'm uncontaminated despite where I've been,
I deserve to be here, I don't want to die,
I'm allowed to laugh as well as to cry,
I'm allowed to eat a healthy range,
Though nurturing does still feel strange,
I'm allowed to be weary and rest my head,
On a nice soft pillow in a warm safe bed,
I can close my eyes and go to sleep,
because my worries til morning will keep,
In the new day I can jump out of bed,
And welcome the challenge of the day ahead.
I can't forget so I shall embrace,
The sadness I carry with acceptance and grace,
I'm here now so I'll approach each day,
With flourish, and hope, that I'll be okay.
I will never forget my past,
But now in the present I'm alive at last.

- From a Heal For Life Guest.

Helen who writes below runs a business helping survivors de-clutter, yet another dysfunctional consequence of trauma.

Heal for Life has been a life saver for me. I experienced masses of emotional abandonment, neglect and trauma as a child, with very little emotional love shown to me. To make matters worse I had been sexually abused on various occasions and impacted by SRA as well. My parents were both hoarders, albeit tidy hoarders, which probably spoke more of their own traumatised upbringing. I had such struggles releasing items from my home, always managing to find a pos-

sible need for them or a comfort from them. I turned to performance, perfection and control as some of many coping mechanisms, hoping it looked like my life was together. Ha ha!

During multiple healing weeks over 11 years, in the safe environment of Heal for Life, I was able to let go of and forgive, smash out at the anger pit or yell out across the valley, much of what had kept me trapped in 'child' for way too many years. Performance and perfection tendencies declined over time thankfully, as did my controlling behaviour. Learning how to recognise when I was triggered in everyday life and how then to deal with those triggers has been invaluable.

I was able to release items back home I never really needed or liked and went on to live a clutter free life, surrounding myself with items that brightened my day and made me feel special. Deep down I knew I was a woman of beauty, grace and worth in my heart, finally. How I help women declutter their homes and lives has changed over the years. Most of my clients now receive brochures about Heal for Life, as childhood trauma and/or abuse generally pop up somewhere in the conversation, illustrating beautifully the correlation between trauma and clutter.

Heal for Life is the place I wished I'd known about much earlier in life. However, I am so grateful that I now function more normally thanks to the healing I received at Heal For Life (and the good Lord), and through it all have preserved our marriage of 21 years with my beautiful husband (also a survivor!) Miracles DO happen at Heal For Life!

- Helen Maguire

Additional Heal For Life Services

There are other services we also offer to help survivors more comprehensively. We run healing programs for families, private retreats for those who are not ready or for privacy reasons do not wish to be with a group. We cater for all needs and requests as we have three centres on our property we can use.

Trauma Informed Healing for Psychologists, Psychiatrists, Counsellors and Psychotherapists

Trauma Informed Healing is a two-day training program that teaches therapists to work effectively and safely with survivors of childhood trauma. Therapists learn to attune to survivor needs, develop skills to remove trauma triggers, and help clients achieve permanent healing from trauma. Training is based on teaching the Heal For Life model of trauma processing and healing.

Offered in all countries where we offer healing programs. Only available for experienced therapists.

Maximum of six participants.

Trauma Informed Practice for workers in health and social services.

This training is for anyone who works with survivors of trauma and wants to learn more effective ways of working with this cohort. Participants learn about impact of trauma on the brain, how it affects behaviour and provide resources to improve client engagement and outcomes. It also supports the professional relationship to prevent burnout and vicarious trauma. This can be a one day or two day training and has been delivered to schools, hospitals, and many relevant organisations such as Women's Refuges.

Trauma Informed Workplace Training for Business Leaders

This training is for business leaders who wish to create a trauma informed culture in their workplaces to improve the wellbeing and relationships of their teams, ultimately leading to better performance, more creativity and a more harmonious work environment. This can be a half or full day training and can be adapted for all seniority levels.

Peer Support Training

Certificate in Trauma Theory

For survivors of childhood trauma so they can be peer support workers (or simply extend their knowledge to continue their healing journey). This is offered to anyone who has attended a healing week and wants to learn more about themselves, trauma and its impact, and ways to change themselves. It consists of seven modules taken over a year and provides a deep, experiential dive into the concepts and theories covered in a healing week. This is offered in seven parts both by distance and onsite.

Each module takes two days.

Certificate in Peer Support Healing

For survivors of childhood trauma who wish to work as peer support volunteers on a Heal For Life healing week or in private practice.

This is for anyone who is a survivor of childhood trauma and having undertaken a healing week wants to give back and help others to heal. It is by invitation only, it requires the individual to be dedicated to their own healing and demonstrate the ability to learn more. Past guests who are invited to participate usually will have relevant qualification and/or experience. It is an intensive, experiential five day program after which it is expected that the participants will also undertake the modules mentioned above.

We want and enjoy training people who are passionate about adopting principles of our programs into their own communities. We are working extensively with remote communities in the Kimberley West Australia to start to address and repair the deep pain caused by societal trauma.

The invitation is there to attend one of our programs if it feels right for you. And to join our healing community on Facebook, as being in touch with other survivors is incredibly supportive.

I also want to encourage for you to use your voice to be heard. Tell anyone and everyone about trauma. We can all speak out and demand better services, and recognition that our pain is as important as any other pain. The world will listen and the world will change and the world will be a better place for our healing and our voices.

Below is a very short list from the many wonderful books available that I have found helpful or have been mentioned in this book.

- Atkinson, S. (2014). Struggling to Forgive. Chicago: Lion Hudson.
- Capacchione, L. (1991). Recovery of your inner child. New York: Simon & Schuster.
- Cozolino, L. (2002). The Neuroscience of Psychotherapy. New York: Norton.
- Grille, R. (2014). Parenting for a Peaceful World. New York: New Society Publishers.
- Hall, L. (2018). Our Little Secret : One Woman's True Story of Healing from Childhood Trauma. Lorraine Hall.

- Ledoux, J. (2015). The Emotional Brain. New York: Simon & Schuster Audio.
- Levine, P. (1997). Waking the Tiger. Berkeley, California: North Atlantic Books.
- Peck, S. (1990). The Different Drum : Communitymaking and Peace. London, United Kingdom: Arrow Books Ltd.
- Siegel, D. (2015). The Developing Mind: How *Relationships and the Brain Interact to Shape Who We Are* (2nd ed.). New York, United States: Guilford Publications.
- Van der Kolk, B. (2015). The Body Keeps the Score. United Kingdom: Penguin Books.

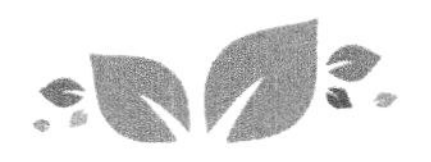

APPENDIX
Additional Information on the Brain

I hope this appendix will make you interested in the brain and that you will further this with your own research and reading. All of the information here is deliberately simplified to make it accessible. The brain is brilliant and extraordinarily complex, and no one part of the brain is totally responsible for any single action.

The brain has an extraordinary ability to change and adapt to life's circumstances, this is called neural plasticity.

Neuroplasticity

Neuroplasticity refers to the ability of neurons to change the way they behave and relate to one another, as the brain adapts to the environment over a lifetime (Cozolino, 2003).

Each of us has a quite unique brain developed to cope with our individual circumstances.

Neuroplasticity was first discovered after research on the effect of meditation on Buddhist monks; it was noticed in brain scans that the Buddhist monks brains were consistently different from other brain scans, showing that the adult activity of meditation had actually changed their brain's physical structure[173].

This was an extraordinary discovery because it means that we can change our thoughts, behaviours, and attitudes despite what happened to us in childhood, and despite how bad you might be feeling today, your brain can change and you can make the choice to be different.

Our entire social welfare system, as well as our understanding of human nature, will be, or should be, deeply impacted by this discovery. Previously, it was a commonly held belief that a person could be born 'bad' or 'incapable', much like someone with an incurable illness. Welfare systems felt they had to manage and support such people throughout their lives, rather than help them overcome their problems. Our welfare system in Australia, and indeed throughout the world, is predicated on the understanding that people cannot help themselves, and that the welfare system has to support them.

Brain plasticity, however, means this is simply not true, and that in fact we are all born with the capacity to succeed, to make something of our lives, to be successful. The hurdle here is that the brain develops based on external input, which means that we develop our self-beliefs depending on our environment. As an extreme example, this plasticity means that no one is inherently a psychopath, rather science is proving it is a combination of early life trauma and genetics which impact on an individual's behaviour[174].

Children who are born with brain deformities can be supported by neurologists with a specialisation in brain deformities. The route to healing will be dependent upon which part of the brain has suffered damage, and will be different from what I discuss in this book, as I focus specifically on the damage caused by stress hormones released as a result of experiencing trauma.

Epigenetics

One of the most exciting new areas of study relates to epigenetics. They are the 'software of the brain' whereas genes could be called the hardware. Epigenetics can best be understood as heritable changes in gene expression. Epigenetics control how the genes relate and react. The gene is what we inherit, however how our environment affects our genes is called epigenetics. These two influences combined (genetic predisposition and epigenetic mechanisms) coupled with specific characteristics of stress itself (intensity, duration and nature) are all factors that need to be taken into account to determine the likelihood of how individuals cope with trauma[175].

Our genes determine the colour of our hair, eyes, and our predisposition to the different impacts on behaviour from trauma. For instance, some of us carry a gene that predisposes us to depression as a consequence of trauma, however this gene is only activated via epigenetics if we suffer from trauma. It is unlikely to activate unless we experience trauma[176].

It was formerly accepted that humans were born with a certain number of genes and DNA and that this was fixed – that was it, and that dictated our destiny. It has been discovered, however, that although we are born with a certain number of genes, these can be turned on or turned off dependent on external stimuli. Epigenetic processes are dynamic in nature, meaning appropriate interventions, such as therapy can counteract or reverse the negative effects of trauma, therefore building resilience through changes in gene activity[177].

A newborn is not a blank slate. The infant's brain after birth is about a quarter of a fully grown adults brain[178]. Twins separated at birth will still have many similar ways of moving and speaking, and usually can be identified as siblings by looking at their mannerisms alone, and all of this is passed through epigenetics. We also pass on intergenerational trauma through epigenetics and we pass down any changes in our genes that have occurred to us through our lives, to our children. Epigenetics provide an answer as to how we can change what we initially inherited through our genes from our parents, and how we can change what we pass on to our own children – healing from trauma positively impacts our epigenetics, reducing the likelihood of our pain being passed down to our offspring. We cannot control our genes, which we inherit, however we can modulate our epigenetics or change our epigenetics through healing, therefore nullifying any negative characteristics we have inherited[179].

Genes and epigenetics help shape our brains. They contribute to our temperament, our personalities, and to what makes us unique[180].

Let us now look at what is known about the brain as an overview.

The Brain

The brain is an amazing organ. As mentioned, it is designed to adapt and grow depending on life experiences. Amazingly, 70% of the human brain develops after birth, and doubles in size in the first year of life[181].

This single organ controls all body activities, ranging from heart rate and sexual function to emotion, learning and memory functions. It shapes our thoughts, words and actions [182].

The brain is the major component of the central nervous system. It weighs about 1,300 grams and is contained in the skull. The brain consumes about 20% of the body's total oxygen intake. The brain is vertically divided in two parts, the right and left hemispheres[183].

Babies are born prematurely compared with other primates[184]. It is thought that, due to the small size of the woman's birth canal, the head cannot develop sufficiently to accommodate a larger brain. Consequently, much of our survival mechanisms are learned after birth, mostly from our primary carers. For optimal survival, we learn how to adapt to the surroundings into which we are born. This means our brains grow and develop depending upon what we learn from our primary carers, often our mother and/or father, or a significant other, and the greatest impact on the developing brain is from our earliest years. This means the environment we grow up in has a huge impact on us throughout our lives, or at least until we heal[185].

Cells in the nervous system are called nerve cells, or neurons. It is these neurons that create the ability to change the way we think and act. Let me explain a bit more about neurons.

Neurons

Neurons are the core components of the brain and spinal cord. Neurons carry messages through what are called 'electro-chemical' processes. There are, approximately, 100 billion neurons in the human brain, each forming synapses (junctions) with hundreds or thousands of other neurons. It is the way these neurons connect with each other that gives the brain its plasticity.

The child's brain has twice as many synapses (connections between neurons) as the adult brain – this is why children can learn so quickly. However, the brain processes more efficiently as we get older [186].

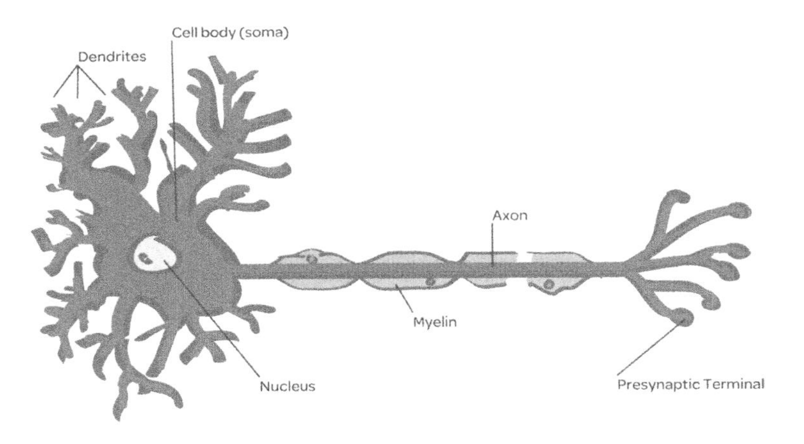

The brain weighs the most at the age of twenty; thereafter, you lose about a gram of brain mass per year. Only about one half of the neurons generated during childhood development survive to function in adult life. If, during critical periods, the brain does not receive what it needs – either sensory, movement or emotional input – it will not develop to its full potential. The unused connections die. Those that remain become stronger and less subject to change.

Injury, sensory, or social deprivation will affect each of us differently, depending on our age[187] An experiment with kittens was conducted, where the kittens had one healthy eyelid closed at birth; when they were opened at the age of six months they were unable to see – the unused optical neurons had died. However, the same experiment carried out on an adult cat showed no deterioration[188].

This experiment illustrates that the connection of some neural pathways, if not developed in early childhood, may never be fully realised. This means that enriched environments – living in an environment where there is a lot of varied stimulation in childhood – leads to diverse neural pathways. There are many different neurons each with different functions.

There are different categories of neurons

- Sensory (or afferent) neurons: send information from sensory receptors (e.g., in skin, eyes, nose, tongue, ears) TOWARD the central nervous system.
- Motor (or efferent) neurons: send information AWAY from the central nervous system to muscles or glands.
- Interneurons: send information between sensory neurons and motor neurons. Most interneurons are located in the central nervous system.
- Mirror neurons enable us to mirror the brain of the person with whom we are interacting, whether listening or speaking. For example, if I talk to you from my left (thinking, logical) brain, you will respond logically. If I interact with you from my right (emotional) brain, you will respond emotionally. We mirror the behaviour of people around us. Your left brain activates my left brain[189].

- Optical neurons As discussed when I was describing how to de-trigger, the strongest neurons are the optical neurons.

Let us now relook at the different parts of the brain most affected by trauma. Of course, all of your brain will be affected in some way. The first areas I will outline in detail are the brain's two hemispheres (brains). The way we utilise and connect the two hemispheres of the brain is very much affected by trauma.

Right and Left Hand Sides of Brain

The brain has two hemispheres (sides) that are largely responsible for different functions. The right side of the brain controls the left side of the body, and the left side of the brain controls the right side of the body. In many animals, the hemispheres are identical to help survival, e.g. dolphins. When it's time to rest, a *dolphin* will shut down only one *hemisphere* of its brain, and close the opposite eye (the left eye will be closed when the right half of the brain sleeps, and vice versa) so that they can always be alert to danger[190].

Many birds also sleep one hemisphere at a time. This is to ensure that they are always awake to danger. In primates such as humans, however, the hemispheres perform different functions and usually work together in a complex and complementary manner. So that we use our emotions(right brain) and logic(left brain) while making decisions

Table (1) summarises the functions of the brain hemispheres. The most important points to remember in relation to healing is that the right brain is ***unconscious and non-verbal***, while the left brain is ***conscious and verbal*** – this is very important. The right brain lights up during trauma whereas the left brain is more shut down[191].

The right and left are two halves of one brain – they are two quite separate systems, each with unique structure and systems, this has been a recent paradigm shift in understanding[192].

Functions of the Brain Hemispheres

RIGHT HEMISPHERE	LEFT HEMISPHERE
Controls left body	Controls right body
Non-verbal	Verbal / language
Feelings	Thoughts
Unconscious	Conscious
Holistic thought	Analytic thought
Intuitive	Logical
Abstract	Linear

Creative	Rational
Art / music	Science and maths
Past and present	Present and future
Simultaneous, implicit memory	Sequential, explicit memory

193

As discussed throughout this book our brains are structured to enable us to make good decisions based on input from the logical (left brain) and the emotive (right brain) in response to a problem. However, when people suffer trauma, the link between the right and the left hemispheres of the brain, a structure of the brain called the corpus callosum, is usually smaller[194]. This means the two halves of the brain do not easily make decisions together. Therefore behaviour is likely to be based on emotional input only (right brain dominant), or over intellectualisation(left brain dominant), or it may 'flip-flop' between the two hemispheres. Those who have suffered trauma will often find it hard to utilise both sides of the brain together.

All that we learn in the first months of life is stored as unconscious memory because the right hemisphere is unconscious. In the first eighteen months of life, a child is learning emotional regulation (control) and attachments (to other people)[195]. As our left brain becomes more active, we become able to remember incidents from our childhood as the left hemisphere is conscious. As the left hemisphere develops, our speech also begins to develop. The area of the brain responsible for speech production was first identified by Paul Broca and is therefore known as 'Broca's Area'. The Broca's area is only in the left hemisphere.

For most tasks in a brain that functions typically, both hemispheres work very effectively in conjunction with each other[196].

For many years the left hemisphere was thought to be dominant over the right hemisphere, and therapies such as Cognitive Behaviour Therapy (CBT) and Narrative therapy utilised the left-thinking hemisphere. However, more recent research emphasises the ultimate dominance of the right hemisphere in our life decisions. Although, both sides of the brain are involved in emotion, Cozolino (2002) suggests that the right hemisphere's role is to express negative and defensive emotions, which Cozolino (2002) terms 'executive veto', meaning that the right hemisphere ultimately has control over the left hemisphere of the brain[197].

'The cognitive revolution, like radical neuro-behaviourism, intentionally sought to put emotions out of sight and out of mind. Now cognitive science must relearn that ancient emotional systems have a power that is quite independent of neo-cortical cognitive processes'. (Panksepp, 2008)

'The right hemisphere is centrally involved in non-verbal, emotional communications and forces the activation of reaction to danger'. (Schore, 2009)

The right brain is where trauma is stored as implicit, unconscious, sensory-based memory. *Therefore, people heal from trauma by accessing their right, unconscious hemisphere where the trauma is held.*

Trauma cannot be healed via the left hemisphere of the brain because trauma is held in the right brain. This can lead to a person feeling inadequate when left brain therapy is used too early in the healing process. However hard the person tries, they will not be able to change their thought and belief systems: the right brain will veto the change in belief, and will not allow the left brain to change. Therapies such as narrative or cognitive therapies, can be incredibly helpful later on to help us *retrain* our thoughts but I do not believe will actually heal our core trauma.

Interestingly, the right brain can control both sides of the body (necessary for the body in times of danger), whereas the left brain controls only the right side of the body. The left brain cannot cope with stress – we switch to the right brain in stressful situations even though we may be unaware that we have done so. As suggested by Siegel(2006) Healing creates integration between the two brain hemispheres, when areas are separated and allowed to specialise in their original functions and then link back to together, the systems is integrated[198].

As this integration occurs the corpus callosum may increase in size as has been seen in brain scans.

Corpus Callosum

The two hemispheres are connected with bands of tissue called the corpus callosum. The corpus callosum could be described as the brain's super highway, containing 200 million connecting neurons. It was recognised that the corpus callosum can be underdeveloped as a result of trauma[199].

One impact of an underdeveloped corpus callosum is a decreased ability to understand and perceive what others are thinking[200]. Some individuals are born with this social difficulty, and can often be diagnosed with Autism Spectrum Disorder.

As mentioned a problem that applies to many of us is the tendency to *not* use both hemispheres together for effective decision-making.

Let me now briefly describe the other parts of the brain which are helpful to understanding the impact of trauma on the developing brain. This is a *simplified* description as the brain is amazingly complex and many parts of the brain are involved in any single activity.

The Brain Stem

The brain stem is the oldest and smallest region in the evolving human brain. It is similar to the brain possessed by the hardy reptiles that preceded mammals, roughly 200 million years ago, and it regulates automatic behaviours like sleeping, breathing, blood pressure, heart rate, blinking, and swallowing. Lacking language, as it is pre-verbal; *its impulses are instinctual, repetitive and rhythmic.* It's concerned with fundamental needs such as survival, physical maintenance, and hoarding, dominance, preening, and mating[201].

It is at the base of your skull, emerging from your spinal column. It controls chemical balance and the rhythms of the body.

Non-conscious actions of the brain stem are controlled by our limbic system. We need to know about the brain stem because many of the actions of the brain stem are activated by stress hormones released at the time of trauma [201].

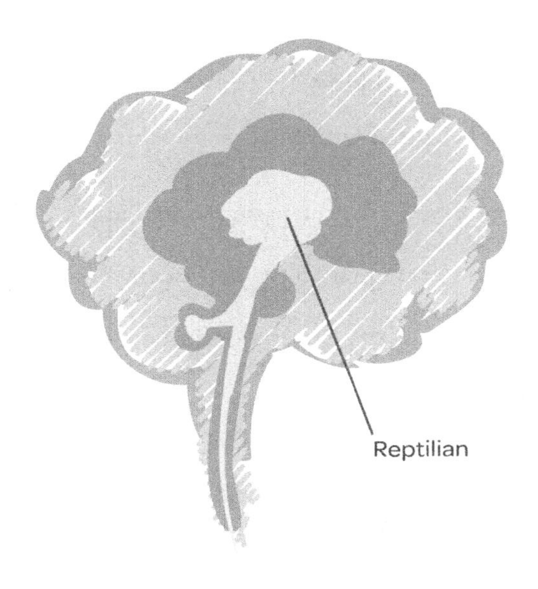

The Limbic System – The Emotional Brain

The limbic system gives us the ability to experience and express emotions and also maintains the immune system and the body's capacity for self-healing. To ensure survival it governs the fight, flight, or freeze mechanism necessary as a reaction to danger. It is involved in bonding needs, and manages maternal functions such as nursing, including emotions linked to attachment. It perceives and interprets the world from an external and environmental input. It is the area responsible for sexual activities such as, procreation, affection, and sexual behaviours. It is the connection and affection between two people that is part of the limbic system's function. This part of the brain is highly affected by early childhood experiences[202].

Hippocampus Particularly in Left Hemisphere

The Hippo Campus is a part of the limbic system and plays a central role in our *consciously* accessed memory, known as explicit (conscious) memory.

The left hemisphere hippocampus is responsible for the encoding and storage of explicit memory and increases in size with learning. The hippocampus is responsible for recalling the order of events in which they happened. The hippocampus starts to develop after the age of around two years old[203].

The hippocampus is where short-term memory is converted into long-term memory and then often stored elsewhere in the brain. It stores declarative memory – that is, facts and figures like learning lines of poetry and spatial memory.

It also controls the ability to read maps, to know the route through a city. How many of you have problems with spatial memory?

The hippocampus also allows the child to develop a sense of time and ability to differentiate sequence of events. It stores events in chronological order. At times of high stress/trauma, stress hormones damage the hippocampus and stress overload impairs the working of the hippocampus and its ability to store explicit (conscious) memory. This means children who have suffered trauma, are less able to learn or remember, particularly in relation to declarative and spatial memory as described above.

The time when the damage – as a result of trauma to the hippocampus is greatest – is between the ages of three and five years (most significant at four years of age, least significant at eight years of age) and 11 to 14 years[204].The extent of damage is dependent on the nature of the trauma. Trauma reduces the volume of the hippocampus. The impact on volume is determined by the severity of abuse. Reduced hippocampus is associated with Post Traumatic Stress Disorder (PTSD), our most common diagnosis, and Dissociative Identity disorder (DID). DID is associated with chronic trauma and abuse, usually by a primary caregiver, before the age of nine.

'This damage to the hippocampus affects us as adults, as new learning and memory are harder for people suffering from PTSD'. (Bremner, 2002)

'Severe childhood trauma reduces the size of the hippocampus'.(Bremner & Randall, 1997).

Stress prevents the hippocampus from functioning and prevents the storage of explicit memory of an event created in a stressful moment. Further to this, when our hippocampus is impaired it affects our vision, hearing and touch[205]. Many people have reported to me that they can see and hear more clearly after healing, and many people also find they are more sensitive to touch after healing.

'The hippocampus places the individual in the context of space and time and what is happening in relationship to the future and the past, relating present information to other experiences and memories that we have collected'. (Nadel & Bohbot, 2001)

Dissociation and the hippocampus are related. Decrease in size of the hippocampus relates to increase in dissociation. The hippocampus tells us who we are. A breakdown within this area of the brain leads to a disintegration of what we term the 'self'[206].

Without full use of the hippocampus we lose context for our memories, which can lead us to have gaps in our memories.

People with DID tend to have the smallest hippocampi. They are also usually individuals with the greatest difficulty in finding their way anywhere. As mentioned above, the hippocampus is associated with the ability to read maps[207].

Amygdala

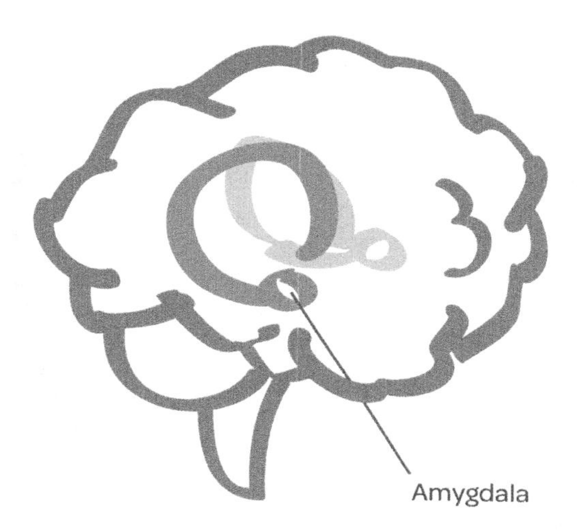

The amygdala sits at the head of the hippocampus, and is also part of the limbic system. Small, and walnut-shaped, the amygdala hangs off the front of the hippocampus at the top of the brain stem[208].

The amygdala functions to warn us of danger by feeling fear, and it holds the memory of any perceived previous life threatening situation to ensure that we react to avoid harm. This has huge implications for us as when the amygdala is reminded of a trauma that we suffered from(when we are triggered) we will react before we can think, and we will have no control over this reaction. This means that, as we cannot control our fearful reaction, there is no way we can consciously stop ourselves reacting

It is the central neural hub of all that we experience emotionally. As the amygdala's job is to protect us from any life threatening danger, it must also have power over the rest of the brain to ensure survival. For this reason, all information received through our senses – touch, sight, hearing, taste, and smell – are scanned by the amygdala for danger *before* the sensation is processed by our thinking brain, the amygdala works ahead of the conscious, thinking brain by about a fifth of a second.

The amygdala is fully functioning well before birth. The baby needs to learn, even before it is born, who is possibly life threatening or unsafe.

Electrical stimulation of the amygdala leads to feelings of déjà vu, anxiety, and memory-like hallucinations. Equally, destruction of the amygdala will eliminate anxiety reactions altogether. It is a key component in the neural networks involved with fear, attachment, early memory, and emotional experience throughout life[209]. With this in mind, people with Schizophrenia tend to have reduced amygdala volume and patients with lesions in the amygdala have an impaired fear response[210].

The amygdala is an organ of appraisal, and contributes emotional balance to experiences. It is the core of the networks of both attachment and emotional regulation.

The fear response, however, can be inhibited by constant and gradual exposure to the trigger; this is what happens in de-sensitization therapy. If no danger occurs after activation, the amygdala gradually stops reacting as though the specific stimulus is dangerous. Constant exposure to the thing that is feared helps us to understand that it is just a trigger, and that it need not be feared. However, many survivors find this a very difficult and unpleasant process as the process of desensitisation can be re-traumatising because re-visiting the trauma again and again, can leave the survivor in a heightened anxious state as the fear is not fully released so the amygdala is still on high alert[211].

Electrical stimulation of the Amygdala in humans increases adrenaline release, which is what gives us the energy we need in response to trauma. It is thought that our over-stimulated responses to reminders of our original trauma are mediated by the amygdala, and it is believed that trauma memory is held in the amygdala[212]. However, this is slightly simplified for ease of understanding as scientists now increasingly recognise that trauma may also be held elsewhere in the body.

The impact of trauma on the size of the amygdala seems to be dependent on the type of trauma. Neglect and physical abuse appear to increase the size, whereas overwhelming early trauma leads to a shrinking of the amygdala.

When the medial prefrontal cortical areas of the brain (the thinking part of the brain) fail to suppress the activation of the amygdala, as can happen to people with PTSD, we get an exaggerated reaction to anything that reminds us of the trauma. An example of this is when someone who has been sexually abused may have difficulty with intimate touch, however much the adult self may long for such contact the amygdala reacts and he or she becomes afraid and unable to continue.

The more the amygdala is aroused, the less the person is able to think, as the amygdala inhibits the cortexes (the thinking brain) from functioning. Therefore, the more fear is felt, the ability to think (and reason) is increasingly diminished. The location of the amygdala to the brain stem means there can be an immediate reaction to trauma. The amygdala provides automatic rapid and unconscious reaction by sensory, visceral and motor cues.

Retention of information can be significantly increased when it's presented in an emotionally charged context. This is why when someone speaks passionately or with emotion we will remember it, whereas when someone speaks without emotion we will be less likely to recall their words[213].

Cerebellum

The Cerebellum (Latin for 'little brain'):

The cerebellum houses 50% of the neurons found in the brain, despite the fact that it occupies only 10% of the total area of the brain. In 1504, Leonardo da Vinci made wax castings of the brain and coined the term 'cerebellum' which is Latin for 'little brain'[214].

The cerebellum has unique plasticity and is our brain's equivalent of a finger-print. It is different in each person, noticeably different even in identical twins. It is smaller in people with ADHD, and certain mood disorders. It has a branch structure, and over 2,000 years ago was called the tree of life[215].

The unique structure of the cerebellum has made study of it very difficult. It is clearly very important to the functioning of our brain. The traditional view on the role of the cerebellum was that it was primarily responsible for balance and motor control, but that the control of our cognitive functions, including social intelligence and linguistics, were seated in the cerebral cortex. This view is radically changing. The cerebellum is now believed to play a central role in regulating our emotional, psychological, and sensory interactions with the world around us[216].

The cerebellar vermis is the centre, and most active part, of the cerebellum and is very interesting in relation to trauma. It is considered the bridge to understanding REM sleep, EMDR, drug abuse, and ADHD.

Movement stimulates the cerebellar vermis, which is why walking such as using a labyrinth can be incredibly helpful for connection to what one is feeling. Also, it is thought that the *cerebellar vermis reduces irritability when stimulated, by rocking.*

Utilising movement in healing is likely to be of great assistance.

The cerebellum is considered to be involved in the integration of the right and left brain, and its functioning may be affected by trauma. According to Bessel Van Der Kolk (2015), trauma affects the development of the cerebellum[217].

Cerebral Cortex

Also known as grey matter, the cerebral cortex is the wrinkled, outer layer of the brain. It constitutes about 85% of the human brain's total mass. It contains more than eight billion cells. The cerebral cortex is thought to be responsible for higher-level cognitive functioning, such as language, learning, memory, and complex. It is divided equally between the right and left hemispheres of the brain[218].

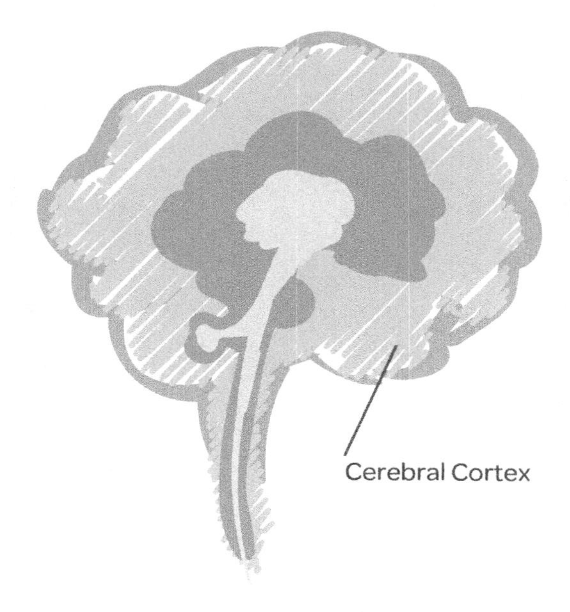

The roof of the cerebral cortex forms the part of the mammalian brain that has evolved most recently, and makes possible higher brain functions, such as learning. The fact that you can read and understand this means your cerebral cortex is functioning. Found in all mammals, it is most developed among humans.

The cerebral cortex is responsible for our ability to make decisions and judgments. When we are suffering from trauma this part of the brain does not function effectively. Those with severe developmental trauma will use this part of the brain ineffectively until they begin a process of recovery that allows the Cerebral Cortex to develop more efficient neural pathways. Also, when we are in trauma or triggered, we cannot think, we automatically react because the pre frontal cortex (part of the cerebral cortex) is cut off by hormones as our brain focuses on immediate survival.

'Scans show that during distress, there is no activity in the frontal cortex'. (Cozolino, 2002)

Prefrontal Cortex

The prefrontal cortex allows for planning, creative thinking, and the capacity to observe internal emotional states in other people (and to have choices regarding those internal, subjective states.) It is believed to regulate the higher emotions of empathy, compassion and love.

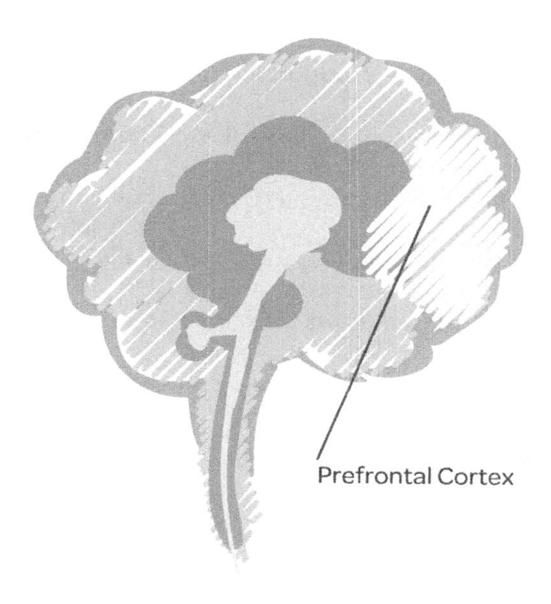

The prefrontal cortex develops at four to five years of age, and connects with every part of the brain. It changes episodic memory to autobiographical memory (strings a series of episodes together). It gives a sense of self, relates the self to memory and stores a group of memories together that have the same meaning[220]. This is the part of the cerebral cortex that is not engaged when we are experiencing, or being reminded of, a trauma(triggered).

Another area of the brain which is cut off by stress hormones during trauma or when triggered is Broca's Area – a part of the Cerebral Cortex.

The Broca's Area

The area of the brain principally responsible for speech production, Broca's Area, shuts down as a response to the release of stress hormones. This phenomenon seems to account for the 'speechless terror' that traumatised individuals face when attempting to verbalise what they are experiencing[219]. It is why speaking while feeling an emotion from the past helps brain integration as well as lowering the sympathetic nervous system so calming oneself.

The Right Superior Temporal Gyrus

A common coping mechanism for survivors of trauma is the development of a strong intuition. This part of the brain of a trauma survivor is usually larger than average, and is also responsible for headaches. The larger superior temporal region means most survivors of trauma will be very good at determining what another person is thinking or feeling, even when they may not be openly expressing this emotion. Unfortunately, some of the inability of a trauma survivor to learn effectively at school is because their superior temporal lobe is too busy determining what the teacher is feeling, rather than listening to what the teacher is saying[221].

Hormones and Neurotransmitters

Hormones are chemical substances that act like messengers from one part of the body to another. They are made in one part of the body and travel to other parts where they help control how cells and organs do their work. As an example , thanks to the activation by hormones of our sympathetic nervous system, the 'fight or flight' system takes over when we're scared.. The hormones that are released when the amygdala becomes aware of danger, shifts the focus of the body and the brain from long-term to short term survival. In conditions of ongoing chronic stress, damage can be caused to the body and brain through continued, sustained high levels of stress hormones [222]. There are three important stress hormones to be aware of. These are: *adrenaline*, *norepinephrine*, and *cortisol*.

Adrenaline

Adrenaline is often known as the fight or flight hormone, adrenaline is produced by the adrenal glands after receiving a message from the brain that there is a stressful or unsafe situation or a reminder of past trauma.

Adrenaline, along with norepinephrine (described below), is mostly responsible for the *immediate* reactions we feel when feeling unsafe or stressed. It comes into action immediately, your heart races and you feel a surge of energy. This is the body's way of being to run from the stressful situation. It also focuses your attention.

Norepinephrine

Norepinephrine is a hormone similar to adrenaline, and it is released from the adrenal glands and also from the brain. The primary role of norepinephrine, like adrenaline, is arousal, this allows us to meet danger. You become more alert, more aware, and more focused. It helps to shift blood flow away from areas where it might not be as crucial, like the skin, which makes it responsible for sweaty palms, and why we can have problems with control of our body temperature as the hormone directs the blood flow to areas such as muscles making it easier to flee from danger. It triggers the release of glucose (sugar) into the blood.

Increased levels of norepinephrine prepare us for fight or flight but still higher levels lead to anxiety, arousal, irritability, and a heightened startle response. How many of us jump when a door slams or a balloon bursts? **Low levels of this hormone have been shown to play a role in ADHD, depression, and low blood pressure[223].**

It is not known why we have two hormones that are similar in nature – perhaps we have both hormones as a backup system. It may be that if our adrenal glands are compromised we can still activate ourselves to react to stress and danger. These two hormones can continue to be released until you return to a calm state. If you have been triggered, this can take a considerable period of time.

Cortisol

Cortisol is another stress hormone – a steroid hormone – that is produced by the adrenal glands. It takes a little more time (minutes, rather than seconds) for us to feel the effects of cortisol in the face of stress, because the release of this hormone takes a multi-step process involving two additional minor hormones.

First, the amygdala has to recognise a threat. It then sends a message to the part of the brain called the hypothalamus, which releases corticotropin-releasing hormone (CRH). CRH then tells the pituitary gland to release adrenocorticotropic hormone (ACTH), which tells the adrenal glands to produce cortisol.

Cortisol maintains fluid balance and blood pressure. Cortisol interferes with the body's ability to combat illness and can lead to a compromised resistance to allergies and chronic illnesses. When fight or flight mechanisms are activated, cortisol stops protein synthesis that enables neurons to grow[224].

Too much cortisol can suppress the immune system, increase blood pressure, increase glucose in the blood, decrease libido, produce acne, contribute to obesity, and contribute to many other chronic conditions.

Let us now look at the hormones we want more of.

Dopamine

Dopamine is a hormone that activates the frontal lobes and contributes to hyper vigilance, paranoia, perceptual distortions, social withdrawal, and avoidance of new and potentially dangerous stimuli. Dopamine is our brains motivating hormone! And associated with our reward system- [225]

Dopamine anticipates our needs . So when we feel hungry and the anticipation of a wonderful meal, that is the work of Dopamine, once we have had a good meal and feel satisfied and happy , that is the impact of Seratonin.

Serotonin

Serotonin is sometimes known as the 'happy chemical'. Low levels of serotonin in the brain has been association with depression.

While there's a link between low levels of serotonin and depression, it's not clear whether low serotonin levels cause depression or whether depression causes a drop in serotonin levels. Serotonin is known to modulate mood, emotion, sleep and appetite. Low serotonin levels cause irritability, violence, aggression and depression.

It should be considered very important to improve serotonin levels for healing. As trauma survivors display many side effects consistent with high levels of stress hormones in the body such as anxiety, agitation, depression, aggression, psychosomatic illnesses, among other symptoms[226].This is why SSRI's are prescribed for depression, as they can relieve symptoms of depression by releasing an amount of serotonin into the blood stream. However, there are other ways we can choose to increase serotonin without relying on medication. Some of these include:

- Being outdoors
- Exposure to light (both the sun and lightboxes are great!)
- Exercise or movement (find movement practices that make YOU feel good, this doesn't need to be going to the gym if that's not what makes you feel good)
- Diet – include foods that are high in tryptophan (eggs, cherries, pineapples, salmon, tofu, turkey, nuts and seeds)[227].

Another important group of hormones to understand ourselves better are Endogenous opioids.

Endogenous Opioids

Endogenous opioids are natural painkillers and are released throughout our skin during trauma, or when we are triggered. Victims of serious injuries, such as survivors of car accidents, have been known to not feel much pain immediately after the accident due to the powerful effect of endogenous opioids. Endogenous opioids are also implicated in dissociative reactions including de-personalisation (the experience of feeling un-real, or losing all sense of identity) and de-realisation (when things may seem unreal), and have a profound effect on reality testing and memory processing. Endogenous opioid release is how survivors of trauma are able to self-harm and yet not feel pain[228].

When a person cuts they feel safe and warm. Endogenous opioids can become addictive.

Let's discuss a few other hormones.

Oxytocin

Oxytocin is produced as a result of social interactions. It is central to the biology of social behaviour, and it causes us to feel safe and loved. Oxytocin is also a female reproductive hormone that plays a huge role in the birth process as well as lactation, and it is oxytocin that facilitates strong uterine contractions during labour. When a baby is born by C-section, the mother doesn't receive the natural oxytocin release, and it is also reported that the use of epidural analgesia can stop the body's natural oxytocin production[229]. Those who have to, or choose to, bottle rather than breast feed have been noted to have a higher stress rates and higher heart rates due to decreased oxytocin production, as oxytocin is released with milk let-down, and is the same hormone that causes the uterus to contract and return to its original size, both during labour and when breastfeeding[230].

Oxytocin is released through a hug, a hand on the back, a hand on the heart, and when humans bond socially. It reactivates the social engagement system of the prefrontal cortex, creating a felt sense in the body of safety, trust, empathy, connection, and belonging[231].

Oxytocin allows the body to adapt, protect and heal itself in the face of challenge. It is released during mother-child interaction through warmth, touch and movement – it is the hormone of 'calm' and 'connect'. This is particularly important in the first years of life to help the child develop their much-needed Parasympathetic Nervous System[232].

Oxytocin calms the fear response as it excites the prefrontal cortex. One exciting thing about the brain is that visualising a loved or safe person has the same physical effect – considered to release oxytocin – as actually being with someone loved or safe[233].

I would like to finish by just mentioning a few facts about the adolescent brain because when working with this age group it was quite clear that healing was slower and their brain functioned quite differently.

The Adolescent Brain

The adolescent brain is different from the child or adult brain. The adolescent brain is less motivated by rewards, therefore rewards have to be greater or more thrilling.During adolescence, the brain loses unused connections, permanently trimming away what it doesn't need. What is left is more functional and efficient[234].

The adolescent brain functions differently, as the prefrontal cortex is not fully developed. As the prefrontal cortex matures, teenagers can reason more effectively, develop better control over impulses and make better judgments. In teenagers who have experienced trauma, the reactive Amygdala is often used for decision making, rather than the thinking brain.

Siegel (2012) informs us that sculpting of the brain takes place in adolescence, making this period both exciting and crucial to healthy brain development, and science is only beginning to uncover the implication[235].

This does not mean adolescents cannot make informed choices, however when presented with stressful or emotional decisions they are more likely to react, rather than respond, without fully realising the consequences for their actions. It is best to see the adolescent brain as having a well-developed accelerator, with only a partly developed brake. Although, some teenagers have the ability to balance short-term rewards with the long-term consequences for their actions, they often lack the ability to predict the consequences quite as well as adults [236].

Due to the increase in neural development, teenagers require more sleep to function efficiently, meaning in order to function properly they need to sleep in later in the mornings.

For teenagers, biological sleep patterns shift towards later times for both sleeping and awakening in the mornings. This means it is very normal for teenagers not to fall asleep before 11 o'clock at night. Teenagers require between eight and a half to nine and a quarter hours of sleep each night to function best. A recent study showed that most teenagers do not get enough sleep each night; only 15% of teenagers reported sleeping eight and half hours on school nights[237].

Knowing the differences between the adolescent brain and the adult brain may be helpful if you are under 26 years old and wondering why it seems difficult for you to heal and express your emotions. It will initially be harder for you than for older people, however you will have the benefit of not continuing to live in a dysfunctional way. Therefore, once you have released the trauma, you will make rapid progress compared to older people.

I have included this appendix on the brain with vey simplified information because I think that knowledge is empowering and essential if we are to be in charge of our own healing. I hope this appendix and indeed the whole book will encourage you to read more, learn more, and so understand more about yourself and the unfair and deep impact trauma has had on your life.

Trauma Informed Healing – taking charge of our own healing and in so doing taking charge of our lives leading us to becoming a victor not a victim. I wish you joy on your journey to healing.

ACKNOWLEDGEMENTS

Heal For Life is about collaboration and community, and much of this book is based on the training modules that we run to train people in working with survivors of child abuse. We do not supply author credits on the booklets, as our work is the result of a large number of individuals collaborating together to bring our guests the most accurate and accessible information on healing from child abuse and trauma. Our work combines an amalgamation of what others have written, out of the kindness of their hearts, for

Heal For life. Wonderful people such as June Parkin, Julia Roberts, Gloria Cartmel, and Megan Perry, have all had major input over the years and I thank them for their contributions, and hope that their material will continue to help survivors to heal through reading this book.

This book could only have happened with the loving support of my husband Rod Phillips and son Nic.

The bringing together of this book to a readable form has been a wonderful collaboration by a team of survivors, each of whom has made a significant contribution. Jessica Frisina for ensuring accuracy and inclusion of important material; Mikaela Grant for all referencing, researching and editing; Taijah Lush for questioning and ensuring the needs of survivors with complex trauma were addressed; Meg Thiering for offering many ideas on the topic of developing self love; Tristan Rosko for hours of editing.

Also Samantha Perham who created such wonderful images and formatted it all for us.

Belatedly to the rescue were also our marketing team of Jenna Williams and Tina Goncalves. The biggest thank you to them all. This book is very much a combination of great talent coming together with a shared passion.

References

Chapter Two: Defining Trauma and Self-Healing

1. Martin, D. J., Garske, J. P., & Davis, M. K. (2000). Relation of the therapeutic alliance with outcome and other variables: A meta-analytic review. *Journal of Consulting and Clinical Psychology, 68*(3), 438-450.

2. Edwards, C. (2009). *Evaulation of the Effectiveness of the Heal for Life Programme 2005 to 2009* (BA Psych(Hons) Phd). Central Coast Research Evaulation.

3. Solomon, M., & Siegel, D. (2003). *Healing Trauma : Attachment, Mind, Body and Brain* (1st ed.). New York: W.W. Norton.

4. Degruy, J. (2011). *Post Traumatic Slave Syndrome.* Portland, OR: Joy Degruy Publications Inc.

5. Heim, C., Newport, D., Mletzko, T., Miller, A., & Nemeroff, C. (2008). The link between childhood trauma and depression: Insights from HPA axis studies in humans. *Psychoneuroendocrinology, 33*(6), 693-710. doi: 10.1016/j.psyneuen.2008.03.008

6. Brown, P. D (2016). *Attachment Disturbances in Adults: Treatment for ComprehensiveR e - pair.* New York, US: W.W Norton & Co.

7. Benjet, C., Bromet, E., Karam, E. G., Kessler, R. C., McLaughlin, K. A., Ruscio, A. M., Shahly, V., Stein, D. J., Petukhova, M., Hill, E., Alonso, J., Atwoli, L., Bunting, B., Bruffaerts, R., Caldas-de-Almeida, J. M., de Girolamo, G., Florescu, S., Gureje, O., Huang, Y., Lepine, J. P., Kawakami, N., Kovess-Masfety, V., Medina-Mora, M. E., Navarro-Mateu, F., Piazza, M., Posada-Villa, J., Scott, K. M., Shalev, A., Slade, T., ten Have, M., Torres, Y., Viana, M. C., Zarkov, Z., … Koenen, K. C. (2015). The epidemiology of traumatic event exposure worldwide: results from the World Mental Health Survey Consortium. *Psychological medicine, 46*(2), 327-43.

8. Edwards, C., Mullinar, L., & Britts-Perry, M. (2009). *By Survivors, for Survivors: A Pilot Study into the Efficacy of a Peer-Operated Service for Adults Exposed to Childhood Maltreatment.* Newcastle, Australia.

9. Moskvina, V., Farmer, A., Swainson, V., O'Leary, J., Gunasinghe, C., Owen, M., ... Korszun, A. (2007). Interrelationship of childhood trauma, neuroticism, and depressive

phenotype. *Depression and Anxiety, 24*(3), 163 – 168. https://doi.org/10.1002/da.20216.

10. Read, J., Os, J., Morrison, A., & Ross, C. (2005). Childhood trauma, psychosis and schizophrenia: a literature review with theoretical and clinical implications. *Acta Psychiatrica Scandinavica, 112*(5), 330-350. doi: 10.1111/j.1600-0447.2005.00634.x

11. Ford, J. D., & Courtois, C. A. (2014). Complex PTSD, affect dysregulation, and borderline personality disorder. *Borderline personality disorder and emotion dysregulation, 1*, 9. doi:10.1186/2051-6673-1-9.

12. Ford, J. D., & Courtois, C. A. (2014). Complex PTSD, affect dysregulation, and borderline personality disorder. *Borderline personality disorder and emotion dysregulation, 1*, 9. doi:10.1186/2051-6673-1-9.

13. Ford, J. D., & Courtois, C. A. (2014). Complex PTSD, affect dysregulation, and borderline personality disorder. *Borderline personality disorder and emotion dysregulation, 1*, 9.doi:10.1186/2051-6673-1-9.

14. Kimber, M., McTavish, J. R., Couturier, J., Boven, A., Gill, S., Dimitropoulos, G., & MacMillan, H. L. (2017). Consequences of child emotional abuse, emotional neglect and exposure to intimate partner violence for eating disorders: a systematic critical review. *BMC psychology, 5*(1), 33. doi:10.1186/s40359-017-0202-3.

15. Odyssey House. (2017). *Odyssey House Annaual Report.* New South Wales: Odyssey House.

16. Royal District Nursing Service Foundation of South Australia Incorporated. (2005). *Reclaiming Myself after Child Sexual Abuse.* Glenside, South Australia: RDNS Foundation of SA.

17. Schols, M. W., de Ruiter, C., & Öry, F. G. (2013). How do public child healthcare professionals and primary school teachers identify and handle child abuse cases? A qualitative study. *BMC public health, 13*, 807. doi:10.1186/1471-2458-13-807

Chapter Three: Impact of Trauma on the Brain

18. Doidge, N. (2008). *The Brain that Changes Itself.* Hawthorn, Australia: Penguin Books Australia.

19. Ogden, P. (2015). *Sensorimotor Psychotherapy: Interventions for Trauma and Attachment.*

New York, United States of America: W.W. Norton & Company.

20. Howe, D. (2005). *Child Abuse and Neglect Attachment, Development and Intervention*(1st ed.). Basingstoke, England, United Kingdom: MacMillan Education UK.

21. Montgomery, A (2013). Neurobiology Essentials for Clinicians. W.W. Norcross

22. Ressler K. J. (2010). Amygdala activity, fear, and anxiety: modulation by stress. *Biological psychiatry*, *67*(12), 1117-9.

23. Humphrey, T. (1968). The Development of the Human Amygdala During Early Embryonic Life. *The Journal Of Comparative Neurology*, *132*(1), 135-165. doi: 10.1002/cne.901320108.

24. Humphrey, T. (1968). The Development of the Human Amygdala During Early Embryonic Life. *The Journal Of Comparative Neurology*, *132*(1), 135-165. doi: 10.1002/cne.901320108.

25. Brown, D. (2016). Attachment Disturbances in Adults: Treatment for Comprehensive Repair. New York, United States of America: AW Norton & Co.

26. Bremner J. D. (2006). Traumatic stress: effects on the brain. Dialogues in clinical neuroscience, 8(4), 445-61.

27. Siegel, D. (2012). *Mindsight: Change Your Brain and Your Life*. Carlton North, Australia: Scribe Publications.

28. Schore, A. (2013). *Affect Dysregulation and Disorders of the self*. United States of America: Norton Press.

29. Van der Kolk, B. (2015). *The Body Keeps the Score*. London: Penguin Books Ltd.

30. Australia Government: Australian Institute of Family Studies. (2016). *The Effect of Trauma on the Brain Development of Children*. Australia Government.

31. Australia Government: Australian Institute of Family Studies. (2016). *The Effect of Trauma on the Brain Development of Children*. Australia Government.

Chapter Four: Impact on the Nervous System and Hormones: What Happens to Us When We Experience Trauma

32. Porges, S. W., & Furman, S. A. (2011). The Early Development of the Autonomic Nervous System Provides a Neural Platform for Social Behavior: A Polyvagal Perspective. *Infant and child development*, *20*(1), 106-118.

33. Porges, S. W., & Furman, S. A. (2011). The Early Development of the Autonomic Nervous System Provides a Neural Platform for Social Behavior: A Polyvagal Perspective. *Infant and child development*, *20*(1), 106-118.

34. Kuhlman, K. R., Vargas, I., Geiss, E. G., & Lopez-Duran, N. L. (2015). Age of Trauma Onset and HPA Axis Dysregulation Among Trauma-Exposed Youth. *Journal of traumatic stress*, *28*(6), 572-9.

35. Combs, M., & DePrince, A. Memory and trauma: examining disruptions in implicit, explicit and autobiographical memory. *The Impact Of Early Life Trauma On Health And Disease*, 217-224. doi: 10.1017/cbo9780511777042.02.

36. Schalinski, I., Schauer, M., & Elbert, T. (2015). The shutdown dissociation scale (shut-d). *European journal of psychotraumatology*, *6*, 25652. doi:10.3402/ejpt.v6.25652

37. Zedler, S., & Faist, E. (2006). The impact of endogenous triggers on trauma-associated inflammation. *Current Opinion In Critical Care*, *12*(6), 595-601. doi: 10.1097/mcc.0b013e3280106806.

38. Porges, S. W. (2011). *The polyvagal theory: Neurophysiological foundations of emotions, attachment, communication, and self-regulation*. New York, NY: W. W. Norton.

39. Williamson, J. B., Porges, E. C., Lamb, D. G., & Porges, S. W. (2015). Maladaptive autonomic regulation in PTSD accelerates physiological aging. *Frontiers in psychology*, *5*, 1571. doi:10.3389/fpsyg.2014.01571.

40. Lee, A. A., & Owyang, C. (2017). Sugars, Sweet Taste Receptors, and Brain Responses. *Nutrients*, *9*(7), 653. doi:10.3390/nu9070653.

41. Chugani, H., Behen, M., Muzik, O., Juhász, C., Nagy, F., & Chugani, D. (2001). Local Brain Functional Activity Following Early Deprivation: A Study of Postinstitutionalized Romanian Orphans. *Neuroimage*, *14*(6), 1290-1301. doi:10.1006/nimg.2001.0917.

42. Brown, P. D (2016). *Attachment Disturbances in Adults: Treatment for Comprehensive Repair.* New York, US: W.W Norton & Co.

43. Sroufe, L. (2009). *Emotional Development.* Cambridge, GBR: Cambridge University Press.

44. Rochat, P. (2014). Early Social Cognition: The First Months of Life. Hove, United Kingdom: Taylor and Francis Ltd.

45. Delpech, J. C., Wei, L., Hao, J., Yu, X., Madore, C., Butovsky, O., & Kaffman, A. (2016). Early life stress perturbs the maturation of microglia in the developing hippocampus. *Brain, behavior, and immunity, 57,* 79-93.

46. Vohs, K. (2016). *Handbook of Self-Regulation: Research, Theory, and Applications*(3rd ed.). New York: Guilford Publications.

47. Porges, S. W., & Furman, S. A. (2011). The Early Development of the Autonomic Nervous System Provides a Neural Platform for Social Behavior: A Polyvagal Perspective. *Infant and child development, 20*(1), 106-118.

48. Cozolino, L. (2010). The Neuroscience of Psychotherapy: Healingthe Social Brain. New York, United States of America: W.W. Norton and Company.

49. Spratt, E. G., Friedenberg, S. L., Swenson, C. C., Larosa, A., De Bellis, M. D., Macias, M. M., Summer, A. P., Hulsey, T. C., Runyan, D. K., … Brady, K. T. (2012). The Effects of Early Neglect on Cognitive, Language, and Behavioral Functioning in Childhood. *Psychology (Irvine, Calif.), 3*(2), 175-182.

50. Hari, R., Henriksson, L., Malinen, S., & Parkkonen, L. (2015). Centrality of Social Interaction in Human Brain Function. *Neuron, 88*(1), 181-193. doi:10.1016/j.neuron.2015.09.022.

51. Albarracín, D., & Wyer, R. S. (2000). The cognitive impact of past behavior: influences on beliefs, attitudes, and future behavioral decisions. *Journal of personality and social psychology, 79*(1), 5-22.

52. Tierney, A. L., & Nelson, C. A. (2009). Brain Development and the Role of Experience in the Early Years. *Zero to three, 30*(2), 9-13.

53. Tierney, A. L., & Nelson, C. A. (2009). Brain Development and the Role of Experience in the Early Years. *Zero to three, 30*(2), 9-13.

54. Albarracín, D., & Wyer, R. S. (2000). The cognitive impact of past behavior: influences on beliefs, attitudes, and future behavioral decisions. *Journal of personality and social psychology, 79*(1), 5-22.

55. Vöhringer, I., Kolling, T., Graf, F., Poloczek, S., Fassbender, I., & Freitag, C. et al. (2017). The Development of Implicit Memory From Infancy to Childhood: On Average Performance Levels and Interindividual Differences. Child Development, 89(2), 370-382. doi: 10.1111/cdev.12749.

56. Perry, B.D., Pollard, R., BLAICLEY, T.L., Baker, W.L., & Vigilante, D. (2005). Childhood Trauma , the Neurobiology of Adaptation , and ' Use-dependent ' Development of the Brain : How ' States ' Become ' Traits '.

57. Harris, D. (2009). The paradox of expressing speechless terror: Ritual liminality in the creative arts therapies' treatment of posttraumatic distress. *The Arts In Psychotherapy*, *36*(2), 94-104. doi: 10.1016/j.aip.2009.01.006.

58. Harris, D. (2009). The paradox of expressing speechless terror: Ritual liminality in the creative arts therapies' treatment of posttraumatic distress. *The Arts In Psychotherapy*, *36*(2), 94-104.doi: 10.1016/j.aip.2009.01.006.

59. Centre for Substance Abuse Treatment (2014). Chapter 3 'Understanding the Impact of Trauma' from Trauma-Informed Care in Behavioural Health Services. Retrieved from https://www.ncbi.nlm.nih.gov/books/NBK207191/.

60. Combs, M., & DePrince, A. Memory and trauma: examining disruptions in implicit, explicit and autobiographical memory. *The Impact Of Early Life Trauma On Health And Disease*, 217-224. doi:1017/cbo9780511777042.025.

61. Schore, A. (2001). The Effects of Early Relational Trauma on Right Brain development, Affect Regulation, and Infant Mental Health. Infant Mental Health Journal, 22(1-2), 201-269. doi: 10.1002/1097-0355(200101/04)22:1<201::aid-imhj8>3.0.co;2-.

62. Van Der Kolk, B. (2019). The compulsion to repeat the trauma. Re-enactment, revictimization, and masochism. – PubMed – NCBI. Retrieved from https://www.ncbi.nlm.nih.gov/pubmed/2664732.

63. Ziegler, M. (2004). Psychological Stress and the Autonomic Nervous System. *Primer On The Autonomic Nervous System*, 189-190. doi: 10.1016/b978-012589762-4/50051-7

64. Porges, S. W. (1995). *Orientating in a defensive world: Mammalian modifications of our evolutionary heritage: A Poly vagal theory*. Psychophysiology, 32, 301-318: Cambridge University Press.

65. Decety J. (2010). The neurodevelopment of empathy in humans. *Developmental neuroscience*, *32*(4), 257-67.

Chapter Five: How Trauma Impact us Physically, Behaviourally and Emotionally

66. Health. (2019). Retrieved from https://www.cdc.gov/nchs/data/hus/hus11.pdf

67. Bonne, O., Brandes, D., Gilboa, A., Gomori, J. M., Shenton, M. E., Pitman, R. K., & Shalev, A. Y. (2001). Longitudinal MRI study of hippocampal volume in trauma survivors with PTSD. *The American journal of psychiatry*, *158*(8), 1248-51.

68. Lischke, A., Domin, M., Freyberger, H. J., Grabe, H. J., Mentel, R., Bernheim, D., & Lotze, M. (2017). Structural Alterations in the Corpus Callosum Are Associated with Suicidal Behavior in Women with Borderline Personality Disorder. *Frontiers in human neuroscience*, *11*, 196. doi:10.3389/fnhum.2017.00196.

69. Sheline Y. I. (2011). Depression and the hippocampus: cause or effect?. *Biological psychiatry*, *70*(4), 308-9.

70. Morey, R. A., Gold, A. L., LaBar, K. S., Beall, S. K., Brown, V. M., Haswell, C. C., Nasser, J. D., Wagner, H. R., McCarthy, G., Mid-Atlantic MIRECC Workgroup (2012). Amygdala volume changes in posttraumatic stress disorder in a large case-controlled veterans group. *Archives of general psychiatry*, *69*(11), 1169-78.

71. Lis, E., Greenfield, B., Henry, M., Guilé, J. M., & Dougherty, G. (2007). Neuro-imaging and genetics of borderline personality disorder: a review. *Journal of psychiatry & neuroscience : JPN*, *32*(3), 162-73.

72. Bluhm, R. L., Williamson, P. C., Osuch, E. A., Frewen, P. A., Stevens, T. K., Boksman, K., Neufeld, R. W., Théberge, J., … Lanius, R. A. (2009). Alterations in default network connectivity in posttraumatic stress disorder related to early-life trauma. *Journal of psychiatry & neuroscience : JPN, 34*(3), 187-94.

73. Broder E. (2005). The Neuroscience Of Psychotherapy: Building and Rebuilding the Human Brain. *The Canadian child and adolescent psychiatry review*, *14*(4), 121

74. Pretty, C., O'Leary, D. D., Cairney, J., & Wade, T. J. (2013). Adverse childhood experiences and the cardiovascular health of children: a cross-sectional study. *BMC pediatrics*, *13*, 208. doi:10.1186/1471-2431-13-208.

75. Resnick HS, e. (1989). Antisocial behavior and post-traumatic stress disorder in Vietnam veterans. – PubMed – NCBI. Retrieved from https://www.ncbi.nlm.nih.gov/pubmed/2613894.

76. Erikson, H.E. (1998). *Life Cycle Completed.* New York, United States of America: W.W Norton.

77. Shipherd, J., & Beck, J. (1999). The effects of suppressing trauma-related thoughts on women with rape-related posttraumatic stress disorder. *Behaviour Research And Therapy, 37*(2), 99-112. doi: 10.1016/s0005-7967(98)00136-3.

78. Brown, P. D (2016). *Attachment Disturbances in Adults: Treatment for Comprehensive Repair.* New York, US: W.W Norton & Co.

79. Bremner J. D. (2006). Traumatic stress: effects on the brain. *Dialogues in clinical neuroscience, 8*(4), 445–461.

80. Villarreal, G., Hamilton, D., Graham, D., Driscoll, I., Qualls, C., Petropoulos, H., & Brooks, W. (2004). Reduced area of the corpus callosum in posttraumatic stress disorder. *Psychiatry Research: Neuroimaging, 131(3),* 227-235. doi:10.1016/j.pscychresns.2004.05.002.

81. Khoury, L., Tang, Y. L., Bradley, B., Cubells, J. F., & Ressler, K. J. (2010). Substance use, childhood traumatic experience, and Posttraumatic Stress Disorder in an urban civilian population. *Depression and anxiety, 27*(12), 1077-86.

82. Winters, B. L., Gregoriou, G. C., Kissiwaa, S. A., Wells, O. A., Medagoda, D. I., Hermes, S. M., ... Bagley, E. E. (2017). Endogenous opioids regulate moment-to-moment neuronal communication and excitability. *Nature communications, 8,* 14611. doi:10.1038/ncomms14611.

83. Stanley, B., Sher, L., Wilson, S., Ekman, R., Huang, Y. Y., & Mann, J. J. (2009). Non-suicidal self-injurious behavior, endogenous opioids and monoamine neurotransmitters. *Journal of affective disorders, 124*(1-2), 134-40.

84. Bahk, Y. C., Jang, S. K., Choi, K. H., & Lee, S. H. (2016). The Relationship between Childhood Trauma and Suicidal Ideation: Role of Maltreatment and Potential Mediators. *Psychiatry investigation, 14*(1), 37-43.

85. Gupta, A., & Silman, A. J. (2004). Psychological stress and fibromyalgia: a review of the evidence suggesting a neuroendocrine link. *Arthritis research & therapy, 6*(3), 98-106.

86. Kendler, K., Karkowski, L., & Prescott, C. (2019). Causal Relationship Between Stressful Life Events and the Onset of Major Depression. Retrieved from https://ajp.psychiatryonline.org/doi/abs/10.1176/ajp.156.6.837.

87. Van Der Kolk, B. (2019). *The Neurobiology of Childhood Trauma and Abuse.* Retrieved

from http://www.traumacenter.org/products/pdf_files/neurobiology_c hildhood_trauma_abuse.pdf

88. Van Der Kolk, B. (2019). *The Neurobiology of Childhood Trauma and Abuse*. Retrieved from http://www.traumacenter.org/products/pdf_files/neurobiology_c hildhood_trauma_abuse.pdf

89. The role of childhood trauma in the neurobiology of mood and anxiety disorders: Preclinical and clinical studies. (2001). Retrieved from https://s3.amazonaws.com/academia.edu.documents.

90. Childhood trauma, psychosis and schizophrenia: a literature review with theoretical and clinical implications. (2005). Retrieved from http://psychrights.org/articles/actachildhoodtrauma2005.pdf.

91. Erikson, H.E. (1998). *Life Cycle Completed*. New York, United States of America: W.W Norton.

92. Broder E. (2005). The Neuroscience Of Psychotherapy: Building and Rebuilding the Human Brain. *The Canadian child and adolescent psychiatry review*, *14*(4), 121.

Chapter Six: Recognising and Changing Attachment Styles

93. Bowlby, J. (1997). *Attachment: Volume One of the Attachment and Loss Trilogy*. London, United Kingdom: Vintage Publishing.

94. Barnes, C. A. (1952). A statistical study of the Freudian theory of levels of psychosexual development. *Genetic Psychology Monographs, 45,* 105-174.

95. Suomi, S. J. (2008). Attachment in rhesus monkeys. In J. Cassidy & P. R. Shaver (Eds.), *Handbook of attachment: Theory, research, and clinical applications* (pp. 173-191). New York, NY, US: Guilford Press.

96. Brown, G., Mangelsdorf, S., & Neff, C. (2012). Father involvement, paternal sensitivity, and father−child attachment security in the first 3 years. *Journal Of Family Psychology, 26*(3), 421-430. doi:10.1037/a0027836.

97. Quinn, N. (2013). *Attachment Reconsidered: Cultural Perspectives on a Western Theory*. Basingstoke, United Kingdom: Palgrave MacMillan.

98. Barrett, L. (2002). *Human Evolutionary Psychology*. New Jersey, United States of America: Princeton University Press.

99. Barrett, L. (2002). *Human Evolutionary Psychology*. New Jersey, United States of America: Princeton University Press.

100. Sluckin, W. (1973). Imprinting and Early Learning. New York: Routledge, https://doi.org/10.4324/9780203788950.

101. Bowlby, J. (2006). *A Secure Base*. London, United Kingdom: Taylor & Francis Ltd.

102. Bowlby, J. (2006). *A Secure Base*. London, United Kingdom: Taylor & Francis Ltd.

103. Follan, M., & Minnis, H. (2010). Forty-four juvenile thieves revisited: from bowlby to reactive attachment disorder. *Child: Care, Health And Development*, *36*(5), 639-645. doi: 10.1111/j.1365-2214.2009.01048.x.

104. Mcleod, S. (2019). Mary Ainsworth | Attachment Styles | Simply Psychology. Retrieved from https://www.simplypsychology.org/mary-ainsworth.html.

105. Flaherty, S., & Sadler, L. (2011). A Review of Attachment Theory in the Context of Adolescent Parenting. *Journal Of Pediatric Health Care*, *25*(2), 114-121. doi: 10.1016/j.pedhc.2010.02.005.

106. Haft, W., & Slade, A. (1989). Affect Attunement and Maternal Attachment: A Pilot Study. *Infant Mental Health Journal*, *10*(3), 157-172. doi: 10.1002/1097-0355(198923)10:3<157::aid-imhj2280100304>3.0.co;2-3.

107. Crittenden, M.P.(2015). *Raising Parents: Attachment, Representation and Treatment*. London, United Kingdom: Taylor & Francis Ltd.

108. Ainsworth, M. (1979). Attachment as Related to Mother-Infant Interaction. *Advances In The Study Of Behavior*, 1-51. doi:10.1016/s0065-3454(08)60032-7.

109. Brown, D. (2016). *Attachment Disturbances in Adults: Treatment for Comprehensive Repair*. New York, United States of America: WW Norton & Company.

110. Brown, D. (2016). *Attachment Disturbances in Adults: Treatment for Comprehensive Repair*. New York, United States of America: WW Norton & Company.

111. Brown, D. (2016). *Attachment Disturbances in Adults: Treatment for Comprehensive Repair*. New York, United States of America: WW Norton & Company.

112. illemsen-Swinkels, S., Bakermans-Kranenburg, M., Buitelaar, J., Van IJzendoorn, M., & Van Engeland, H. (2000). Insecure and Disorganised Attachment in Children with a Pervasive Developmental Disorder: Relationship with Social Interaction and Heart Rate. *The Journal of Child Psychology and Psychiatry and Allied Disciplines, 41*(6), 759-767.

113. Howe, D. (2011). *Attachment Across the Lifecourse: A Brief Introduction.* England, United Kingdom: MacMillan Education UK.

114. Bretherton, I., & Munholland, K. A. (2008). Internal working models in attachment relationships: Elaborating a central construct in attachment theory. In J. Cassidy & P. R. Shaver (Eds.), *Handbook of attachment: Theory, research, and clinical applications*(pp. 102-127). New York, NY, US: Guilford Press.

115. Schindler, A., Thomasius, R., Sack, P., Gemeinhardt, B., KÜStner, U., & Eckert, J. (2005). Attachment and substance use disorders: A review of the literature and a study in drug dependent adolescents. *Attachment & Human Development, 7*(3), 207-228. doi: 10.1080/14616730500173918.

116. Willemsen-Swinkels, S., Bakermans-Kranenburg, M., Buitelaar, J., Van IJzendoorn, M., & Van Engeland, H. (2000). Insecure and Disorganised Attachment in Children with a Pervasive Developmental Disorder: Relationship with Social Interaction and Heart Rate. *The Journal of Child Psychology and Psychiatry and Allied Disciplines, 41*(6), 759-767.

Chapter Seven: The Importance of Safety

117. Van der Kolk, B. A. (2007). The Developmental Impact of Childhood Trauma. In L. J. Kirmayer, R. Lemelson, & M. Barad (Eds.), *Understanding trauma: Integrating biological, clinical, and cultural perspectives* (pp. 224-241). New York, NY, US: Cambridge University Press.

118. Cramer, H., Anheyer, D., Saha, F. J., & Dobos, G. (2018). Yoga for posttraumatic stress disorder – a systematic review and meta-analysis. *BMC psychiatry, 18*(1), 72. doi:10.1186/s12888-018-1650-x.

Chapter Eight: Connection with the Inner Child and Inner Self

119. Capacchione, L.(1991). *Recovery of Your Inner Child: The Highly Acclaimed Method for Liberating Your Inner Self*. London, United Kingdom: Simon & Schuster Ltd.

120. Capacchione, L.(1991). *Recovery of Your Inner Child: The Highly Acclaimed Method for Liberating Your Inner Self*. London, United Kingdom: Simon & Schuster Ltd.

121. Meadows, E. A., & Foa, E. B. (1998). Intrusion, arousal, and avoidance: Sexual trauma survivors. In V. M. Follette, J. I. Ruzek, & F. R. Abueg (Eds.), *Cognitive-behavioral therapies for trauma* (pp. 100-123). New York, NY, US: Guilford Press.

122. Brown, P. D (2016). *Attachment Disturbances in Adults: Treatment for Comprehensive Repair.* New York, US: W.W Norton & Co.

123. Agaibi, C. (2010). TRAUMA, PTSD, AND RESILIENCE: A Review of the Literature. Retrieved from http://psycnet.apa.org/record/1998-06729-004.

124. Kitayama, N., Brummer, M., Hertz, L., Quinn, S., Kim, Y., & Bremner, J. D. (2007). Morphologic alterations in the corpus callosum in abuse-related posttraumatic stress disorder: a preliminary study. *The Journal of nervous and mental disease, 195*(12), 1027-9.

125. Ogden, P. (2015). *Sensorimotor Psychotherapy: Interventions for Trauma and Attachment.* New York, United States of America: W.W. Norton & Company.

Chapter Ten: How to Recognise and Enjoy Emotions

126. Langner, C. A., Epel, E. S., Matthews, K. A., Moskowitz, J. T., & Adler, N. E. (2012). Social hierarchy and depression: the role of emotion suppression. *The Journal of psychology, 146*(4), 417-36.

127. Kreibig, S. (2010). Autonomic nervous system activity in emotion: A review. *Biological Psychology, 84*(3), 394-421. doi:10.1016/j.biopsycho.2010.03.010.

128. Adler, R., Rosen, B., & Silverstein, E. (1998). Empotions in Negotiation: How to Manage Fear and Anger. *Negotiation Journal, 14*(2), 161-179. doi: 10.1023/a:1024657321423.

129. Brown, P. D (2016). *Attachment Disturbances in Adults: Treatment for Comprehensive Repair.* New York, US: W.W Norton & Co.

130. Brown, P. D (2016). *Attachment Disturbances in Adults: Treatment for Comprehensive Re-*

pair. New York, US: W.W Norton & Co.

131. Brown, P. D (2016). *Attachment Disturbances in Adults: Treatment for Comprehensive Repair.* New York, US: W.W Norton & Co.

132. Bremner J. D. (2006). Traumatic stress: effects on the brain. *Dialogues in clinical neuroscience, 8*(4), 445-61.

133. McFarlane A. C. (2010). The long-term costs of traumatic stress: intertwined physical and psychological consequences. *World psychiatry: official journal of the World Psychiatric Association (WPA), 9*(1), 3-10.

134. Cole, P. M., Luby, J., & Sullivan, M. W. (2008). Emotions and the Development of Childhood Depression: Bridging the Gap. *Child development perspectives, 2*(3), 141-148.

Chapter Eleven: Transactional Analysis and Behaviours

135. Berne, E. (2015). *Transactional Analysis in Psychotherapy : A Systematic Individual and Social Psychiatry.* Martino Fine Books.

136. Stewart, I. (2012). *T A Today : A New Introduction to Transactional Analysis.* Leics, United Kingdom: Life space Publishing.

137. Berne, E. (2015). *Transactional Analysis in Psychotherapy : A Systematic Individual and Social Psychiatry.* Martino Fine Books.

138. Harris, T. (2011). *I am OK- You're OK.* New York, United States of America: HarperCollins Publishers Inc.

139. Baby Development: Your 10-Month-Old. (2019). Retrieved from https://www.webmd.com/parenting/baby/baby-development-10-month-old#1.

140. Harris, T. (2011). *I am OK- You're OK.* New York, United States of America: HarperCollins Publishers Inc.

141. Levine, P. (2018). *Peter Levine's Somatic Tools for Self Soothing.* Retrieved https://www.psychotherapynetworker.org/blog/details/358/video-peter-levines-somatic-tools-for-self-soothing.

Chapter Twelve: Learning to Love and Nurture Yourself

142. Brown, P. D (2016). *Attachment Disturbances in Adults: Treatment for Comprehensive Repair.* New York, US: W.W Norton & Co.

143. Pollard, J. K. (2002). *The Self Parenting Program: Core Guidelines for the Self Parenting Practitioner.* Malibu, CA, United States of America: Generic Human Studies Publishing.

144. Spratt, E. G., Friedenberg, S. L., Swenson, C. C., Larosa, A., De Bellis, M. D., Macias, M. M., Summer, A. P., Hulsey, T. C., Runyan, D. K., ... Brady, K. T. (2012). The Effects of Early Neglect on Cognitive, Language, and Behavioral Functioning in Childhood. *Psychology (Irvine, Calif.), 3*(2), 175-182.

145. Seabrook, E. M., Kern, M. L., & Rickard, N. S. (2016). Social Networking Sites, Depression, and Anxiety: A Systematic Review. *JMIR mental health, 3*(4), e50. doi:10.2196/mental.5842.

146. Twenge, J. M., Martin, G. N., & Campbell, W. K. (2018). Decreases in psychological well-being among American adolescents after 2012 and links to screen time during the rise of smartphone technology. *Emotion, 18*(6), 765-780.

147. Jelenchick, L., Eickhoff, J., & Moreno, M. (2013). 'Facebook Depression?' Social Networking Site Use and Depression in Older Adolescents. *Journal Of Adolescent Health, 52*(1), 128-130. doi:10.1016/j.jadohealth.2012.05.008.

Chapter Thirteen: Setting Boundaries

148. Broder E. (2008). Attachment from Infancy to Adulthood: The Major Longitudinal Studies. *Journal of the Canadian Academy of Child and Adolescent Psychiatry, 17*(3), 161.

149. Cloud, D. (2017). *Boundaries Updated and Expanded Edition: When to Say Yes, How to Say No To Take Control of Your Life.* Grand Rapids: Zondervan.

150. Blum, H. (2004). Separation-Individuation Theory and Attachment Theory. *Journal Of The American Psychoanalytic Association, 52*(2), 535-553. doi: 10.1177/00030651040520020501

151. Brown, D., Elliott, D., & Morgan-Johnson, P. (2016). *Attachment disturbances in adults.* United States of America: Norton.

152. Holmes, J., & Wilkie, J. (2014). *The search for the secure base* (1st ed.). London: Routledge.

153. Perry, B. (2002). Childhood Experience and the Expression of Genetic Potential: What Childhood Neglect Tells Us About Nature and Nurture. *Brain And Mind, 3*(79-100). Retrieved from https://s3.amazonaws.com/academia.edu.documents/33013470/mindbrain.pdf?

154. Patricia K. Kerig PhD (2005) Revisiting the Construct of Boundary Dissolution, Journal of Emotional Abuse, 5:2-3, 5-42, DOI: 10.1300/J135v05n02_02.

155. Steele, K., Van der Hart, O., & Boon, S. (2011). *Coping with Trauma-Related Dissociation: Skills Training for Patients and Therapists* (1st ed.). New York: WW Norton & Co.

156. Steele, K., Van der Hart, O., & Boon, S. (2011). *Coping with Trauma-Related Dissociation: Skills Training for Patients and Therapists* (1st ed.). New York: WW Norton & Co.

157. Friedman, J., & Boumil, M. (1995). *Betrayal of Trust: Sex and Power in Professional Relationships.* Westport: Praeger.

158. Cathryn Booth-Laforce, Wonjung Oh, Angel Hayoung Kim, Kenneth H. Rubin, Linda Rose-Krasnor & Kim Burgess (2006) Attachment, self-worth, and peer-group functioning in middle childhood,Attachment & Human Development, 8:4, 309-325, DOI: 10.1080/14616730601048209.

Chapter Fourteen: Overcoming the Impact of Powerlessness: How to Change Thought Patterns, and the Impact of Shame

159. Preidt, R. (2017). With Stress and Trauma Come Excess Weight in Women. Retrieved from https://www.webmd.com/diet/obesity/news/20171114/with-stress-and-trauma-come-excess-weight-in-women.

160. Moyer AE, e. (1994). Stress-induced cortisol response and fat distribution in women. – PubMed – NCBI. Retrieved from https://www.ncbi.nlm.nih.gov/pubmed/16353426

161. Stevanović, A., Frančišković, T., & Vermetten, E. (2016). Relationship of early-life trauma, war-related trauma, personality traits, and PTSD symptom severity: a retrospective study on female civilian victims of war. *European journal of psychotraumatology, 7*, 30964. doi:10.3402/ejpt.v7.30964.

162. Herman, J. (2015). Trauma and Recovery: The Aftermath of Violence- From Domestic Violence to Political Terror. New York, United States of America: Ingram Pub-

lisher Services.

163. Herman, J. (2015). Trauma and Recovery: The Aftermath of Violence- From Domestic Violence to Political Terror. New York, United States of America: Ingram Publisher Services.

164. Parisette-Sparks, A., Bufferd, S. J., & Klein, D. N. (2015). Parental Predictors of Children's Shame and Guilt at Age 6 in a Multimethod, Longitudinal Study. *Journal of clinical child and adolescent psychology : the official journal for the Society of Clinical Child and Adolescent Psychology, American Psychological Association, Division 53*, *46*(5), 721-731.

165. Dutton, D. (1999). Traumatic Origins of Intimate Rage. *Aggression And Violent Behavior*, *4*(4), 431-447. doi: 10.1016/s1359-1789(98)00027-5.

166. Grille, R. (2008). *Parenting for a Peaceful World.* Richmond, United Kingdom: CP Publishing.

Chapter Fifteen: Suggestions and Strategies for How to Keep Healing

167. Baumann, O., & Mattingley, J. (2012). Functional topography of primary emotion processing in the human cerebellum. *Neuroimage*, *61*(4), 805-811. doi:1016/j.neuroimage.2012.03.044

168. Patki, G., Li, L., Allam, F., Solanki, N., Dao, A., Alkadhi, K., & Salim, S. (2014). Moderate treadmill exercise rescues anxiety and depression-like behavior as well as memory impairment in a rat model of posttraumatic stress disorder. *Physiology & Behavior*, *130*, 47-53. doi: 10.1016/j.physbeh.2014.03.016

169. Johnson, M., Grossmann, T., & Kadosh, K. (2009). Mapping functional brain development: Building a social brain through interactive specialization. *Developmental Psychology*, *45*(1), 151-159. doi: 10.1037/a0014548

170. Follette, V., Palm, K., & Pearson, A. (2006). Mindfulness and Trauma: Implications for Treatment. *Journal Of Rational-Emotive & Cognitive-Behavior Therapy*, *24*(1), 45-61. doi: 10.1007/s10942-006-0025-2

171. Wong, J., & Brown, J. (2019). How Gratitude Changes You and Your Brain. Retrieved from https://greatergood.berkeley.edu/article/item/how_gratitude_changes_you_and_your_brain

172. Castillo, P. R., Mera, R. M., Fredrickson, P. A., Zambrano, M., Del Brutto, V. J., & Del Brutto, O. H. (2014). Psychological distress in patients with restless legs syndrome (Willis-Ekbom disease): a population-based door-to-door survey in rural Ecuador. *BMC research notes*, *7*, 911. doi:10.1186/1756-0500-7-911

173. R, V. (2019). The effect of meditation on psychological distress among Buddhist Monks and Nuns. – PubMed – NCBI. Retrieved from https://www.ncbi.nlm.nih.gov/pubmed/21391415

174. Black, D. (2013). *Good Boys, Bad Men: Confronting Antisocial Personality Disorder.* New York, United States of America: Oxford University Press.

175. Ryan, J., Chaudieu, I., Ancelin, M., & Saffery, R. (2016). Biological underpinnings of trauma and post-traumatic stress disorder: focusing on genetics and epigenetics. Retrieved from https://www.futuremedicine.com/doi/pdf/10.2217/epi-2016-0083.

176. Ryan, J., Chaudieu, I., Ancelin, M., & Saffery, R. (2016). Biological underpinnings of trauma and post-traumatic stress disorder: focusing on genetics and epigenetics. Retrieved from https://www.futuremedicine.com/doi/pdf/10.2217/epi-2016-0083.

177. Ryan, J., Chaudieu, I., Ancelin, M., & Saffery, R. (2016). Biological underpinnings of trauma and post-traumatic stress disorder: focusing on genetics and epigenetics. Retrieved from https://www.futuremedicine.com/doi/pdf/10.2217/epi-2016-0083.

178. Paterson, S. J., Heim, S., Friedman, J. T., Choudhury, N., & Benasich, A. A. (2006). Development of structure and function in the infant brain: implications for cognition, language and social behaviour. *Neuroscience and biobehavioral reviews*, *30*(8), 1087– 1105. doi:10.1016/j.neubiorev.2006.05.001

179. Wolynn, M. (2017). It Didn't Start with You: How Inherited Family Trauma Shapes Who We are and How to End the Cycle, New York, United States of America:Penguin Putnam Inc.

180. Zerucha, D., Denton, A., Cooley, M.D. (2003) 'The Beginnings of the Central Nervous System', in Your Body, How it Works, Human Development. USA: Chelsea Hill Publishing.

181. Berk, L. (2012). *Child Development.* United States of America: Pearson Education.

182. Han, S. (2018). Brain: Function and Anatomy of Parts, Diagram, Conditions, Health Tips. Retrieved from https://www.healthline.com/human-body-maps/brain#anatomy-and-function.

183. Han, S. (2018). Brain: Function and Anatomy of Parts, Diagram, Conditions, Health Tips. Retrieved from https://www.healthline.com/human-body-maps/brain#anatomy-and-function

184. Lagercrantz, H. (2016) 'The Stress of Being Born and First Breaths', in Infant Brain Development, USA: Springer International Publishing.

185. Bowlby, J., & Ainsworth, M. (1969) as citied in Brown (2016). Attachment Disturbances in Adults: Treatment for Comprehensive Repair. New York, US: W.W Norton & Co.

186. Zerucha, D., Denton, A., Cooley, M.D. (2003) 'The Beginnings of the Central Nervous System', in Your Body, How it Works, Human Development. USA: Chelsea Hill Publishing.

187. Brain Basics: The Life and Death of a Neuron | National Institute of Neurological Disorders and Stroke. (2019). Retrieved from https://www.ninds.nih.gov/Disorders/Patient-Caregiver-Education/Life-and-Death-Neuron

188. Hubel, D. H., & Wiesel, T. N. (1959). Receptive fields of single neurons in the cat's striate cortex. The Journal of physiology, 148(3), 574-91.

189. Broder E. (2005). The Neuroscience Of Psychotherapy: Building and Rebuilding the Human Brain. *The Canadian child and adolescent psychiatry review*, *14*(4), 121.

190. Castro, J. (2017). How Do Dolphins Sleep?. Retrieved from https://www.livescience.com/44822-how-do-dolphins-sleep.html.

191. Bremner J. D. (2006). Traumatic stress: effects on the brain. Dialogues in clinical neuroscience, 8(4), 445-61.

192. Schore, A. (2003). *Affect Dysregulation and Disorders of the Self.* New York: Norton.

193. Carter, R. (2015). The Brain Book: An Illustrated Guide to its Structure, Functions, and Disorders. London, United Kingdom: Dorling Kindersley Ltd.

194. Kitayama, N., Brummer, M., Hertz, L., Quinn, S., Kim, Y., & Bremner, J. D. (2007). Morphologic alterations in the corpus callosum in abuse-related posttraumatic stress disorder: a preliminary study. *The Journal of nervous and mental disease*, *195*(12), 1027–1029. doi:10.1097/NMD.0b013e31815c044f.

195. Schore, A. (2013). Affect Dysregulation and Disorders of the Self. New York: Norton Press.

196. Flinker, A., Korzeniewska, A., Shestyuk, A. Y., Franaszczuk, P. J., Dronkers, N. F., Knight, R. T., & Crone, N. E. (2015). Redefining the role of Broca's area in speech. Proceedings of the National Academy of Sciences of the United States of America, 112(9), 2871-5.

197. Broder E. (2005). The Neuroscience Of Psychotherapy: Building and Rebuilding the Human Brain. *The Canadian child and adolescent psychiatry review, 14*(4), 121.

198. Siegel, D. (2011). *Mindsight.* New York: Oneworld Publications.

199. Sheikhi, S., Saboory, E., & Farjah, G. (2018). Correlation of nerve fibers in corpus callosum and number of neurons in cerebral cortex: an innovative mathematical model. *International Journal Of Neuroscience, 128*(10), 995-1002. doi:10.1080/00207454.2018.1458725

200. Jackowski, A. P., Douglas-Palumberi, H., Jackowski, M., Win, L., Schultz, R. T., Staib, L. W., Krystal, J. H., … Kaufman, J. (2008). Corpus callosum in maltreated children with posttraumatic stress disorder: a diffusion tensor imaging study. Psychiatry research, 162(3), 256-61.

201. Ogden, P. (2015). Sensorimotor Psychotherapy: Interventions for Trauma and Attachment. New York, United States of America: W.W. Norton & Company.

202. Rothschild, B. (2011). The Body Remembers: The Psychophysiology of Trauma and Trauma Treatment. New York, United States: W.W. Norton and Company.

203. Elzinga, B. (2002). Are the neural substrates of memory the final common pathway in posttraumatic stress disorder(PTSD)?. *Journal Of Affective Disorders, 70*(1), 1-17. doi:10.1016/s0165-0327(01)00351-2.

204. Anand, K. S., & Dhikav, V. (2012). Hippocampus in health and disease: An overview. Annals of Indian Academy of Neurology, 15(4), 239-46.

205. Kim, E. J., Pellman, B., & Kim, J. J. (2015). Stress effects on the hippocampus: a critical review. Learning & memory (Cold Spring Harbor, N.Y.), 22(9), 411-6. doi:10.1101/lm.037291.114.

206. Elzinga, B. (2002). Are the neural substrates of memory the final common pathway in posttraumatic stress disorder (PTSD)?. *Journal Of Affective Disorders, 70*(1), 1-17. doi: 10.1016/s0165-0327(01)00351-2.

207. Vermetten, E., Schmahl, C., Lindner, S., Loewenstein, R. J., & Bremner, J. D.

(2006). Hippocampal and amygdalar volumes in dissociative identity disorder. The American journal of psychiatry, 163(4), 630-6.

208. Carter, R. (2015). The Brain Book: An Illustrated Guide to its Structure, Functions, and Disorders. London, United Kingdom: Dorling Kindersley Ltd.

209. Graham, A., Buss, C., Rasmussen, J., Rudolph, M., Demeter, D., & Gilmore, J. et al. (2016). Implications of newborn amygdala connectivity for fear and cognitive development at 6-months-of-age. Developmental Cognitive Neuroscience, 18, 12-25. doi:10.1016/j.dcn.2015.09.006.

210. Rich, A. M., Cho, Y. T., Tang, Y., Savic, A., Krystal, J. H., Wang, F., Xu, K., ... Anticevic, A. (2016). Amygdala volume is reduced in early course schizophrenia. Psychiatry research. Neuroimaging, 250, 50-60.

211. Levine, P. (1997). Waking the Tiger: Healing Trauma. United States of America: North Atlantic Books.

212. Cozolino, L. (2010). The Neuroscience of Psychotherapy: Healing the Social Brain. New York, United States of America: W.W. Norton and Company.

213. Cozolino, L. (2010). The Neuroscience of Psychotherapy: Healing the Social Brain. New York, United States of America: W.W. Norton and Company.

214. Glickstein, M., Strata, P., & Voogd, J. (2009). Cerebellum: history. Neuroscience, 162(3), 549-559. doi:10.1016/j.neuroscience.2009.02.054.

215. Carter, R. (2015). The Brain Book: An Illustrated Guide to its Structure, Functions, and Disorders. London, United Kingdom: Dorling Kindersley Ltd.

216. Cozolino, L. (2010). The Neuroscience of Psychotherapy: Healing the Social Brain. New York, United States of America: W.W. Norton and Company.

217. Van der Kolk, B. (2015). *The Body Keeps the Score*. UK: Penguin Books.

218. Cozolino, L. (2010). The Neuroscience of Psychotherapy: Healing the Social Brain. New York, United States of America: W.W. Norton and Company.

219. Kolk, B. (2015). The Body Keeps the Score. New York, United States of America: Penguin Books Ltd.

220. Ogden, P. (2015). Sensorimotor Psychotherapy: Interventions for Trauma and Attachment. New York, United States of America: W.W. Norton & Company.

221. Stevens, J. S., Reddy, R., Kim, Y. J., van Rooij, S., Ely, T. D., Hamann, S., Ressler, K. J., … Jovanovic, T. (2017). Episodic memory after trauma exposure: Medial temporal lobe function is positively related to re-experiencing and inversely related to negative affect symptoms. NeuroImage. Clinical, 17, 650-658. doi:10.1016/j.nicl.2017.11.016.

222. Stephens, M. A., & Wand, G. (2012). Stress and the HPA axis: role ofglucocorticoids in alcohol dependence. *Alcohol research : current reviews*, *34*(4), 468-83.

223. Ambade, V., Arora, M. M., Singh, P., Somani, B. L., & Basannar, D. (2011). Adrenaline, Noradrenaline and Dopamine Level Estimation in Depression : Does it Help?. *Medical journal, Armed Forces India*, *65*(3), 216–220. doi:10.1016/S0377-1237(09)80006-3.

224. Broder E. (2005). The Neuroscience Of Psychotherapy: Building and Rebuilding the Human Brain. *The Canadian child and adolescent psychiatry review*, *14*(4), 121.

225. Snyder, S. (2011). What Dopamine Does in the Brain. *Proceedings Of The National Academy Of Sciences*, *108*(47), 18869-18871. doi: 10.1073/pnas.1114346108.

226. Frazer, A., & Hensler, J. (2019). Serotonin Involvement in Physiological Function and Behavior. Retrieved from https://www.ncbi.nlm.nih.gov/books/NBK27940/.

227. Young S. N. (2007). How to increase serotonin in the human brain without drugs. *Journal of psychiatry & neuroscience : JPN*, *32*(6), 394-9.

228. Valentino, R., & Van Bockstaele, E. (2015). Endogenous opioids: The downside of opposing stress. *Neurobiology Of Stress*, *1*, 23-32. doi: 10.1016/j.ynstr.2014.09.006.

229. Yamaguchi, E., Siaulys, M., & Torres, M. (2016). Oxytocin in cesarean-sections. What's new?. *Brazilian Journal Of Anesthesiology (English Edition)*, *66*(4), 402-407. doi:10.1016/j.bjane.2014.11.015.

230. Magon, N., & Kalra, S. (2011). The orgasmic history of oxytocin: Love, lust, and labor. *Indian journal of endocrinology and metabolism*, *15 Suppl 3*(Suppl3), S156-61.

231. Jones, C., Barrera, I., Brothers, S., Ring, R., & Wahlestedt, C. (2017). Oxytocin and social functioning. *Dialogues in clinical neuroscience*, *19*(2), 193-201.

232. Guzmán, Y. F., Tronson, N. C., Sato, K., Mesic, I., Guedea, A. L., Nishimori, K., & Radulovic, J. (2013). Role of oxytocin receptors in modulation of fear by social memory. *Psychopharmacology*, *231*(10), 2097-105.

233. Guzmán, Y. F., Tronson, N. C., Sato, K., Mesic, I., Guedea, A. L., Nishimori, K., & Radulovic, J. (2013). Role of oxytocin receptors in modulation of fear by social memory.

Psychopharmacology, *231*(10), 2097-105.

234. Siegel, D. (2014). Pruning, Myelination, and the Remodelling Adolescent Brain. Retrieved https://www.drdansiegel.com/blog/2014/02/18/pruning-myelination-and-the-remodeling-adolescent-brain/

235. Siegel, D. (2012). *The Whole-Brain Child : 12 Revolutionary Strategies to Nurture Your Child's Developing Mind.* New York: Random House Inc.

236. Steinberg, L. (2011). *You and Your Adolescent.* New York: Simon & Schuster.

237. Sleep for Teenagers – National Sleep Foundation. (2019). Retrieved from https://www.sleepfoundation.org/articles/teens-and-sleep

Chapter Sixteen: The Heal For Life Healing Program

238. McCormack, L., & Katalinic, N. (2016). Learning to Heal from Those Who Know! The 'Lived' Experience of a Peer Support Program for Adult Survivors of Childhood. Trauma. *Journal Of Aggression, Maltreatment & Trauma*, *25*(10), 1021-1042. doi:10.1080/10926771.2016.1223247

239. Ullman, S., & Townsend, S. (2008). What is an empowerment approach to working with sexual assault survivors?. *Journal Of Community Psychology*, *36*(3), 299-312. doi: 10.1002/jcop.20198.

240. McCormack, L., & Katalinic, N. (2016). Learning to Heal from Those Who Know! The 'Lived' Experience of a Peer Support Program for Adult Survivors of Childhood. Trauma. *Journal Of Aggression, Maltreatment & Trauma*, *25*(10), 1021-1042. doi:10.1080/10926771.2016.1223247.

241. Edwards, C. (2009). Evaluation of the Effectiveness of the Heal for Life Healing Programme 2005-2009. Central Coast Research and Evaluation.

242. Sweeney, A., Filson, B., Kennedy, A., Collinson, L., & Gillard, S. (2018). A paradigm shift: relationships in trauma-informed mental health services. *BJPsych advances*, *24*(5), 319–333. doi:10.1192/bja.2018.29

Made in the USA
Coppell, TX
15 May 2021

55593505R00223